I0794629

The Black Pack

The Black Pack

Comedy, Race, and Resistance

ARTEL GREAT

Rutgers University Press

New Brunswick, Camden, and Newark, New Jersey

London and Oxford

Rutgers University Press is a department of Rutgers, The State University of New Jersey, one of the leading public research universities in the nation. By publishing worldwide, it furthers the University's mission of dedication to excellence in teaching, scholarship, research, and clinical care.

Library of Congress Cataloging-in-Publication Data

Names: Kayaru, Artel, 1981– author.
Title: The Black Pack : comedy, race, and resistance / Artel Great.
Description: New Brunswick : Rutgers University Press, 2025. | Includes bibliographical references and index.
Identifiers: LCCN 2024050546 | ISBN 9781978838130 (paperback) | ISBN 9781978838147 (hardcover) | ISBN 9781978838154 (epub) | ISBN 9781978838161 (pdf)
Subjects: LCSH: Murphy, Eddie, 1961– | Mooney, Paul, 1941–2021 | Townsend, Robert, 1957– | Wayans, Keenen Ivory. | Hall, Arsenio. | African American comedians. | African American wit and humor—History and criticism. | Black people—Race identity.
Classification: LCC PN1969.C65 K39 2025 | DDC 792.7602808996073—dc23/eng/20250206
LC record available at https://lccn.loc.gov/2024050546

A British Cataloging-in-Publication record for this book is available from the British Library.

rutgersuniversitypress.org

For my mother,
for always encouraging me
to shine my light

Contents

The Black Pack

Introduction

Black American Humor and Rituals of Resistance

"*Homey don't play that!*" "*Sexual Chocolate!*" "*Mo' money, mo' money!*" "*His momma name him Clay, I'm a call him Clay!*" Anyone with an eye for 1990s popular culture will instantly recognize these catchphrases and the Black cultural productions that propelled them into the American social imagination. The 1990s undeniably witnessed a fascinating and robust surge in Black visibility in Hollywood, marking a vibrant period for Black artists and audiences. An electric current coursed through the decade, pulsating with tacit energy fueled by the enthusiastic public reception of numerous studio-backed Black feature films, network television shows, and widely circulating made-for-TV movies. These projects not only showcased Black talent and themes, but when considered alongside the plethora of now-classic hip-hop albums, R&B records, and Black motion picture soundtracks released throughout the decade, one could argue that the era's cutting edge of mainstream culture was demonstrably shaped by Black artistic expression.

In the '90s, many of the most celebrated figures across America's top cultural categories were notably—Black. Toni Morrison famously won the Nobel Prize for Literature; Michael Jackson and Whitney Houston stood atop pop music's Mount Everest; August Wilson was the preeminent playwright of American theater; Michael Jordan and Bo Jackson dominated the sports arena; Spike Lee blew up with his Brooklyn-based cinema; the Huxtables were America's Black first family (decades before the Obamas); bell hooks, Henry Louis Gates Jr., and Cornel West emerged as leading public intellectuals; Hillman College was the top HBCU in the country; twenty-four-year-old John Singleton became the youngest Best Director nominee in the history of the Oscars; and Oprah Winfrey ruled the television airwaves as the undisputed queen of daytime talk shows—all while the pulsating bass lines of hip-hop music captured the world's attention. Among the brightest stars to achieve prominence during this exhilarating cultural milieu were the highly influential social humorists known as the "Black Pack."

The Black Pack was the name taken by a group of five comedians: Eddie Murphy (the superstar), Paul Mooney (the sensei), Robert Townsend (the Renaissance man), Keenen Ivory Wayans (the wild card), and Arsenio Hall (the hype man). Individually, these performers are recognized today as actors and pioneers of American humor. Yet few are aware of the history behind their groundbreaking collaborations as Hollywood's rebellious Black Pack—an elite comedic collective whose provocative material raised essential questions about the social power of art and humor. From 1987 to 1994, the Black Pack banded together and created twenty-four commercial media productions that subversively engaged humor and satire to champion Black lives. Their work promoted a resistant brand of comedy that, to varying degrees, poked holes in the nation's conventional racial and political narratives. In less than a decade, the Black Pack collaborated on some of the most hilarious, enduring, and profitable Black films and TV shows in Hollywood, including Keenen Ivory Wayans's *In Living Color* (1990–1994), Eddie Murphy's *Coming to America* (1988), and *The Arsenio Hall Show* (1989–1994). Each Black Pack production injected culturally specific comedic voices, perspectives, stories, and images into a predominately conservative white media landscape.

Growing up in Chicago, my family—parents, grandparents, aunts, uncles, cousins, and even neighbors—regularly congregated to immerse ourselves in the entertaining world crafted by the Black Pack. Throughout my childhood, we viewed Black Pack comedies at multiplexes, on rented Blockbuster (and sometimes bootlegged) VHS tapes, and on broadcast (and sometimes cable) television. The site of our collective screenings was typically my grandmother's house on the West Side of Chicago. Packed inside a small walk-in closet on the first floor was an unofficial and unassuming yet cherished and expansive videotape archive of Black movies and TV shows. Within that sacred space, my cousins and I spent so many weekends tirelessly watching countless VHS tapes created and cataloged there by my uncle. He claimed the archive, at one point, amassed a collection of over ten thousand videotapes. Each viewing was a revelation for me, each movie a thread in the fabric of my young cultural education. During these early formative years at my grandma's house, I had my inaugural encounters with seminal Black Pack films like *The Five Heartbeats* (1991) and *I'm Gonna Git You Sucka* (1988).

Coming to America was by far my favorite Black Pack comedy. My mother and I love that film. We were not casual viewers. Not at all. We were compulsive rewatchers. Superfans, repeatedly drawn back to the opulent majesty of Zamunda. Our obsession with multiple viewings of *Coming to America* was not only commonplace; it continued for years. In fact, while we watched the film, we did not just passively listen to the dialogue—we actively absorbed it. We gleefully recited the entire movie, along with the on-screen characters, echoing the film's dialogue in our living room. This, we conceived, was our playful competition, a metric for testing the depth of our cinematic passion. Whoever remembered the most lines from the movie won. The apex of fandom—in our shared universe built not just on enjoyment but on active memorization. At that point, I had no awareness of the broader implications of the film, the way it disrupted corporate power or resisted racist paradigms. For my mother and I, the allure of *Coming to America* and, indeed, all Black Pack comedies resided in the fact that they were just *funny*. The movies were, to us, simply embodiments of Black joy and laughter, and we were oblivious to the weight of their cultural and political meanings.

No one could have predicted that sneaking into the VHS archive at my grandma's house and watching those tapes over and over again would propel me on a nearly two-decade-long odyssey—an odyssey characterized by countless film screenings, meticulous research, archival visits, and the chronicling of historical data, ultimately culminating in this book dedicated to the Black Pack's humor, history, and cultural production. As a child, the enduring impact of these films was entirely obscure to me. I was clueless to the ways the Black Pack's influence resonated across Black communities nationwide. Reflecting on those times, I recall feeling an unarticulated sense of pride garnered from watching those old Black Pack videotapes. This undoubtedly stemmed from the manner in which the Black Pack's humor and moving imagery centered the Black world and challenged racial ideology. Of course, back then, this level of comprehension eluded my youthful grasp. Growing up, like so many Americans, we were afflicted with a dearth of media literacy.

That is, we were strictly media consumers, blissfully unaware of the complex issues and forces shaping the creation and consumption of commercial projects. My cousins and I did not possess the critical vocabulary associated with the study of cinema and media, a reality that hindered our ability to contextualize or even question the narratives and media imagery presented to us. In fact, no one in my immediate circle or seemingly across the broader fabric of our community held such intellectual tools. We simply reveled in the pure delight, connection, and sensational energy that pulsed through the screen with each viewing (or *rewatching*). Today, I understand that the pleasure my family and I derived from the Black Pack's project was intricately linked to the evocation of cultural solidarity their work engendered. Yet they were also edgy. Their comedy was intentionally transgressive and *politically Black*, which, of course, ruffled feathers in Hollywood.

Each member of the Black Pack began their professional careers performing as lowly stand-up comics, easily the most challenging gig in show business. Like dauntless gladiators, they clawed their way to the top of Hollywood's Mount Olympus by dishing out dangerous truths and cathartic laughter. What makes their body of work so compelling and impactful is their capacity to merge the irreverence of comedy with a politically Black social consciousness, attacking the underlying assumptions of race in America. They were confident and brash, connoisseurs of signifying or, perhaps more aptly, masters in the art of playing "the dozens." The dozens, of course, is an age-old Black expressive tradition that originated long ago in the shadows of street corners, taverns, and juke joints. The dozens also happens to be a verbal blood sport; whoever lands the wittiest, most comically vicious jabs wins:

Yo' momma so fat . . .
Yo' daddy so poor . . .
You so ugly . . .

And so on. Sometimes escalating into "fighting words" but always an artform. Before joining forces, each Black Pack member paid their dues separately on stage, making a name for themselves by lying and signifying, playing the dozens, and "killing" audiences at comedy clubs. For a stand-up comic, "to kill" is the pinnacle of onstage success. It is to have the audience in the palm of your hand—to be in the zone, the supreme state of comedic flow.

Stand-up comedy's roots are buried deep in the monologues of vaudeville performers of the late 1880s and early 1890s who portrayed clownish characters onstage; donned outlandish, eye-catching costumes; and used a variety of props as the focal point of their acts. Charley Case, a mulatto comic who passed as white, is thought to be the first performer to deliver a more laid-back vaudeville monologue. He stood in the center of the stage (at times in blackface) and talked directly to the audience. Rather than acting in the typical exaggerated style of the era, Case used low-key observational humor while speaking in a relaxed, conversational manner, which became the bedrock of the stand-up comedy format.[1]

The implementation of stand-up as a platform for social commentary, particularly within popular culture, has more recent origins, dating back to the mid-twentieth century. For instance, white comics like Mort Sahl, who wrote jokes for President John F. Kennedy and helped advance political satire with his early 1950s act; Irwin Corey, who used stand-up to cultivate a comedic persona as the double-talking leftist "professor"; the lesser-known Joe Ancis, who pioneered a neurotic cynical style; the "sick comics" like Mike Nichols and Elaine May; musical satirist Tom Lehrer; the controversial Lenny Bruce, who was well known for his integration of politics, free speech, and social satire; and, of course, the rabble-rousing George Carlin, whose "Seven Dirty Words" routine was central in the U.S. Supreme Court's landmark decision *Federal Communications Commission v. Pacifica Foundation, et al.*, which defined the power of the FCC to determine what material was considered acceptable for broadcasting over public airwaves. By the 1980s, the Black Pack were "killing" audiences on a regular basis, delivering carefully crafted onstage performances in the smoke-filled comedy clubs of New York, Chicago, and Los Angeles. Each member of the crew relentlessly ignited large crowds and "destroyed" countless microphones with jokes that ripped decorum to pieces.

The Black Pack's nickname itself draws attention to the group's oppositional stance. It was at a publicity event in August 1987, while promoting the release of his latest blockbuster film *Beverly Hills Cop II*, that Eddie Murphy made the public announcement.[2] "We have a group that I like to call the Black Pack. We basically hang out together, and bounce ideas off each other," Murphy explained before listing the group's members for reporters.[3] The Black Pack handle was coined by the outspoken social humorist Paul Mooney (the group's ideological guru). As the story goes, while Wayans, Townsend, Mooney, and other acquaintances hung out with Murphy in his plush hotel suite at L'Ermitage, Arsenio Hall made a case for unanimity among the comics, asking, "Why should we bicker when we would chisel a whole lot harder to success through unity?"

Another comedian quipped, "Yeah, nobody's gonna cast us in a John Hughes film." Then with his patented quick wit, Mooney retorted, "Nah, they got the Brat Pack. And we're the 'Black Pack,' homey."[4] With that, the crew's moniker was cemented—and they embraced their roles as Hollywood outsiders. They understood, after all, that Blackness intrinsically positions one as an outsider in America, teetering on the margins of society where the only certainty is *un*certainty.

The group's nickname is a cheeky allusion to the famous Hollywood cohorts, the ultracool "Rat Pack" of the 1960s (Frank Sinatra, Sammy Davis Jr., Dean Martin, etc.), known for their movies and Las Vegas nightclub performances, and the angsty "Brat Pack" of the 1980s (Molly Ringwald, Rob Lowe, Ally Sheedy, etc.), who appeared in a string of white coming-of-age films.[5] With their snarky sobriquet, the Black Pack thumbed their noses at the Hollywood establishment and savored their self-appointed roles as industry agitators. In less than a decade, they changed the face of American comedy and became A-list celebrities, partying at the hottest clubs in Los Angeles and New York City and dining in the finest restaurants in Beverly Hills and Manhattan. Murphy was the group's de facto leader. He was the gravitational force, the engine that drove the Black Pack movement, just as Sinatra was for the Rat Pack in Las Vegas. Murphy was comedy's first "rock star," and the Black Pack were his band of brothers. They had smash-hit movies, top-rated TV shows, and exciting HBO specials. They made millions, drove fancy cars, and had swanky pads. They set trends in comedy and fashion. They were fresh to def in leather pants or casket sharp in Armani suits, fedora hats or baseball caps, East Coast chic or West Coast cool. Pulling up to "Bubble Hill" or studio backlots in sleek limousines, they were Hollywood's Black comedic royalty.[6] When Arsenio Hall replaced Joan Rivers on Fox's late night talk show in 1987, the studio became an unofficial clubhouse for the Black Pack: they were always present, supporting one another, hanging out backstage, cracking jokes in the dressing rooms, or appearing as surprise guests on the show.[7]

Among the Black Pack's defining features were their tactical gambits that turned the alluring strangeness of Black American humor into a mainstream cultural product. Take Robert Townsend's satirical masterpiece *Hollywood Shuffle*, for example, which openly pillories the entertainment industry's stereotypic treatment of Black performers. In the movie, Townsend's character grapples with Hollywood's racist hiring and production practices and its penchant for casting Black actors in regressive roles as slaves, maids, and butlers. One incisive scene in the film hilariously

FIG. I.1. Paul Mooney as Jamal Harris, the NAACP president, in *Hollywood Shuffle*, 1987.

features Mooney portraying Jamal Harris, the president of the NAACP Hollywood branch. The scene marks one of the movie's many fever-dream sequences. Outside the home of Townsend's character, Bobby Taylor—an aspiring actor who "sells out" for Hollywood fame—the NAACP conducts a peaceful protest. Standing in front of the picket line, Mooney's character addresses a throng of reporters covering the event. He lays out the organization's agenda:

> *We feel that Black actors should not have to accept these stereotype roles such as crying slaves, tar babies, jungle bunnies. And I say that as long as Black actors play these roles, they'll never play the Rambos, until they stop playing the sambos.*

The Black Pack's project demonstrates the ways the group's discursive performances highlight what Hortense Spillers might describe as the distance between the "cultural vestibularity and the culture" of racial tropes in America.[8] One key feature of the Black Pack was their ability to seamlessly traverse multiple media platforms while communicating the radical pleasure of Black comedic frequencies. That is to say, they regularly appeared onstage, in films, and on television. They also seemed to possess a protean capacity to transition successfully to working behind the camera. Their efforts as multihyphenates—producers, consultants, writers, directors, actors—helped develop a space of agency for Black creatives, contributing to the mainstream acceptance of emerging Black talent previously overlooked or rejected by industry gatekeepers.

Growing up, I did not understand how Black Pack productions signaled new cultural and social horizons. I was far too young to interrogate how these brash comedians used humor to oppose toxic depictions of Black America. What I did understand, however, was the special way Black Pack movies and TV shows brought my community together and made people laugh—*hard*. Laugh so hard your face hurt. So hard it brought tears to your eyes. Deep belly laughs. *Hard*. I remember what a treat it was to witness so many smiling faces, laughing, huddled around my grandmother's television set, watching Black Pack comedies.

Before seriously studying the Black Pack's cultural practice as an adult, I had already established myself as a rising actor and stand-up comic in Chicago, regularly opening for prominent local comedians like Deon Cole (*blackish*), DeRay Davis (*Hip Hop Squares*), and Leon Rogers (WGCI radio). I later became the youngest sketch comic to perform on the main stage at the famous improv mecca, Chicago's Second City, the unofficial birthplace of *Saturday Night Live*. My first taste of Hollywood moviemaking came when I was cast in the dramatic high school flick *Light It Up* (1999), starring Usher Raymond and Forest Whitaker. Everything changed for me after I landed a supporting role in the smash-hit film *Save the Last Dance* (2001), which skyrocketed to become the number-one movie in America for two weeks in a row. And just like that, I couldn't walk through the mall anymore. It was quite a whirlwind experience. I moved to Los Angeles shortly thereafter, where I quickly landed my first starring role in a motion picture and won a Film Independent Spirit Award nomination. At that point, studio executives came calling, and movie roles began flowing my way. Yet the more success I experienced, the more I began to discern subtle, unspoken limitations that were in place for Black actors in Hollywood. Gradually, I observed that many of the roles being offered to Black performers were typically demeaning. The movie studios and television networks seemed strangely fascinated with Black actors playing coons, thugs, pimps, hoes, dope fiends, and so on. This observation was rather jarring to me as a young, serious-minded theater-trained artist from Chicago. The dominant industry appeared largely uninterested in sincere interior explorations of Black life. This realization did not sit well with me. Why was Hollywood so comfortable portraying Black people in such a manner? This was, after all, not how I viewed myself or the people thriving in my communities. So I decided to enroll at UCLA and learn everything I could about movies. I later graduated as the first Black valedictorian in the history of UCLA's School of Theater, Film, and Television.

I stumbled into researching the Black Pack in grad school, still at UCLA, following the release of *The Richard Pryor Show* DVD box set. After screening Pryor's series, I fell down a long and winding rabbit hole that led me to the Black Pack crew. I started rewatching their projects. The more I watched, the more I detected that these comedians were using the camouflage of comedy to expose and denounce racist discourses in Hollywood. The deeper I studied their humor, the more apparent it became: the Black Pack were playing an entirely different game from other comics. They were aspiring to achieve something more than just *jokes*. They were attempting to destabilize the rules of comedy by challenging racial politics from *within* a hostile commercial system. Take, for example, Eddie Murphy's hysterical and satiric "White like Me" mockumentary, filmed for his rare return as host of *Saturday Night Live*. The sketch unfolds as Murphy goes undercover in "whiteface" makeup to investigate the nation's racial issues. The sequence begins with Murphy staring into the camera, speaking directly to the audience:

> *A lot of people talk about racial prejudice. And some people go so far as to say that there are actually two Americas: one Black and one white. But talk is cheap. So I decided to look into the problem myself. Firsthand. To go underground and actually experience America—as a white man.*[9]

After undergoing a cosmetic transformation, Murphy emerges in full whiteface makeup as "Mr. White." While he navigates New York City as an undercover white man, Murphy has several jaw-dropping experiences. For instance, when he rides the city bus and the lone Black passenger exits, the public transit vehicle suddenly turns into an all-white cocktail party complete with music and free martinis. Perhaps most shockingly, Mr. White, while at a Manhattan bank, is rejected for a loan by a Black banker. However, when the branch manager, a white man, overhears their conversation in passing, he swiftly takes over the loan application process. When the Black banker walks away, the branch manager immediately gives Mr. White a substantial cash loan without credit, collateral, or any form of identification at all. This banking sequence is comically and intellectually sharp, lampooning the discriminatory lending practices and redlining policies that jeopardized and thwarted Black homeownership and social mobility for over one hundred years in America.[10] Throughout the nearly six-minute mockumentary, Murphy's clever racial satire exposes and critiques whiteness and the secret world of white privilege. He concludes,

> *So what did I learn from all of this? Well, I learned that we still have a very long way to go in this country before all men are truly equal. But I'll tell you something: I've got a lot of friends, and we've got a lot of makeup. So the next time you're hugging up with some really super groovy white guy, or even a great super keen white chick, don't be too sure. They might be Black.*

FIG. I.2. Eddie Murphy as Mr. White in "White like Me" on *Saturday Night Live*, 1984.

The comedic punch of "White like Me" obliterates counterfactual claims of Murphy as a vapid, apolitical Black celebrity squirming for crumbs at the Hollywood table. After nearly twenty years of deep research and study of the Black Pack's production of humor, it is blazingly apparent the group went out of their way to call attention to their inescapable Blackness—flipping the script on how Blackness was perceived in Hollywood and American society. This was, to say the least, a bold cultural move. By fastidiously moving between movies, stand-up, television, and back, the Black Pack's migratory comedic approach expanded their reach with audiences, enabling them to shrewdly smuggle subversive aesthetics, racial reversals, and pro-Black sensibilities onto Hollywood screens. The Black Pack's influence behind the scenes (led by Murphy's superstar power) also disrupted industry norms by ensuring the employment of qualified Black talent and technicians in what were typically white-held below-the-line production positions. In doing so, the group managed to activate a kind of creative "Blacktopia," or an unofficial communal space where unknown Black talent finally caught a break in the industry. Within this space, the Black Pack members supported each other artistically and were free to be outrageous and edgy yet commercially viable, bitingly satirical yet wholly entertaining.

The openly defiant critiques of the film industry embedded in the Black Pack's comedic material express new Black sensibilities—and a 1990s-style freshness that emphasized pro-Black points of view, upward mobility, and Black excellence as ways of opposing the insults of the century-plus onslaught of inglorious imagery in Hollywood. Their comedy explores the phenomenology of Blackness and poses the essential question "Who will survive in America?" an inquiry made famous by Gil Scott-Heron. The Black Pack's jokes are a social critique that turns anger into art, presenting an alluring comedic model now employed by some of today's top humorists. It is also true that the Black Pack films and TV shows flow easily with Terrence T. Tucker's notions of "comic rage" and Danielle Fuentes Morgan's ideas of "laughing to keep from dying." The group's cultural productions unmask anti-Black ideologies in Hollywood and reimagine the meaning of freedom and Black possibility in America. Ironically, by tackling racial politics under the cloak of comedy, the Black Pack was able to revise the terms of engagement in American humor and capture the country's imagination.

Yet the Black Pack's contributions to American comedy have not received serious treatment. Instead, their work has been largely overlooked and, at times, dismissed as kitsch, lowbrow, or vanity projects. Even in the era of their peak production, the Black Pack's comedic material was widely misunderstood by white critics, who were perhaps uncomfortable with the group's bold, in-your-face approach. For the first time, *The Black Pack: Comedy, Race, and Resistance* critically assesses the Black Pack cycle as a significant and underexplored body of work whose popular success ignited an increase in the production of Black-oriented movies and television shows in the 1990s. The group also launched a new wave of Black participation in key Hollywood filmmaking positions—a rare feat and unseen in the industry since the highly contested and controversial productions of the 1970s Blaxploitation moment.

The Black Pack: Comedy, Race, and Resistance provides the first comprehensive look at the Black Pack's comedic output and the social, historical, and political-economic context in which they achieved broad commercial success. Throughout U.S. history, laughter has, paradoxically, played an essential role in the saga of survival for Black Americans negotiating an unrelenting existential threat in a hostile racial environment. Humor and satire have long been powerful tools for Black writers, intellectuals, activists, and artists engaged in social critique. In discussing the importance of the Black Pack's impact on comedy and twentieth-century American film and television, I trace their oeuvre back to a long-standing heritage in Black American oral tradition that I call *Black resistance humor*—that is, a form of cultural expression that engages the subversive (sometimes confrontational) salty language of comedy, satire, parody, irony, and political humor as a means of giving voice to racial trauma, resisting corrupt authority, and promoting social justice and Black empowerment. Since the early nineteenth century, Black resistance humor has operated as a subterranean and indispensable vocabulary of Black social protest deployed to expose centuries-old racial hypocrisies in the American narrative. For generations, disaffected Black artists have practiced this form of cultural expression, from the folklore of Black tricksters in the antebellum period to the ironic fiction writings of William Wells Brown, Charles W. Chesnutt, and Langston Hughes. Historically, Black resistance humor has functioned to deconstruct and reconceptualize Blackness as a political signifier aimed at reorganizing the distribution of power in America. The stylistic dimensions of the Black Pack's production of culture expand the rituals of Black resistance humor as a crucial strategy, directly tackling cultural politics, racial truths, dogmas, righteous indignation, repressed anger, alternative histories, social dissent, and other issues and forces involving social power and identity in the United States. This comedic philosophy has also allowed its proponents to fly under the radar of authority by capitalizing on the politics of disguise afforded by burlesque humor.[11]

At the heart of Black resistance humor lies the history of the Black body in the West, a complicated history of survival in an utterly caustic and inhospitable terrain. The unimaginable horrors of the Middle Passage introduced countless souls to the holocaust of American enslavement, designed to erase African spiritual practices and initiate the denial of humanity, culture, and social memory. On a basic level, African peoples who were kidnapped and held hostage in the horrific world of U.S. slavery were fundamentally robbed of their subjecthood in the African context. They were subsequently transformed into the "objects" of Western oppression—no longer persons but instead objects or raw materials, if you will, who were victimized and exploited to build this nation's enormous wealth. The African peoples who found themselves so radically alienated physically, emotionally, politically, socially, and aesthetically from the context of their origin were trapped in, quite simply, a simultaneous world-ending and world-building process that forced into being a new hybrid identity formation in the West. Put another way, the African peoples who were mentally and physically tortured, raped, murdered, and held hostage under the grisly totalitarian regime of U.S. enslavement at a certain point ceased being Africans and, over time, transmogrified into *Black people*. For centuries, immeasurable amounts of energy and financial resources have been (and continue to be) invested in blocking Black progress (and political resistance) and the organization of independent Black institutions that openly demonstrate free and critical thinking.[12]

It should, then, come as no surprise that a deep-rooted distrust of the white establishment and its power structures developed among scores of Black Americans throughout history. The cruel madness of American enslavement and the institution of whiteness as an invisible political system of power, along with the seemingly ineffectual possibility of escape, demanded the development of inventive strategies for Black survival. The legal end of human chattel slavery in the United States, contrary to popular opinion, did not open the floodgates of full citizenship for Black Americans. Instead, the inequities of enslavement were rapidly followed up with scores of newfangled and treacherous tactics to foil, contain, and thwart Black progress: from grandfather clauses to Jim Crow laws, public lynchings to scientific racism and experimentation, overpolicing, ghettoization, urban renewal and public housing, the school-to-prison pipeline, the spurious war on drugs, and mass incarceration and the carceral state. Hence, the faces at the bottom of the well in American society remain disproportionately Black. In her book *In the Wake: On Blackness and Being*, Christina Sharpe suggests, "We are Black peoples in the wake with no state or nation to protect us, with no citizenship to be respected."[13] It is within this state of marginalization that the material, spiritual, aesthetic, political, and imagined identifications generated from shared Black transgenerational victories and traumas have led to distinct expressions that we now all understand and recognize to be *Black culture* (or Black American culture). That is to say, Black culture was born out of the need to rise, born out of legacies of great improvisation, born out of a life of constant collage. Although produced in the American crucible of inequality, Black people have somehow developed a remarkable capacity to make *something* out of *nothing*.

It is no wonder that, for many Enslaved Black Americans, the development of alternative strategies of resistance became necessary to prevent them from exhausting themselves toiling sunup to sundown, performing backbreaking labor on plantations. Alternative tactics included insurrection, running away / escaping, and perhaps the most common, the deliberate exhibition of behavior that was diametric to labor efficacy. This subtle act of Black protest (i.e., working slowly, "shuffling," being aloof, etc.) was hastily miscategorized as laziness rather than as a strategy of resistance to an inhumane system of white brutality. According to Mel Watkins, when many of the Enslaved "adopted subterfuge and the masking of real feelings as the central means of coping with slavery, African-Americans set in motion a social and psychological dynamic that has had far-reaching consequences. Most obviously, it established a split in their social behavior."[14] Indeed, among the Enslaved population, the performance of lethargy on southern plantations was a resistant expression of discontent, a way of demonstrating individual agency and pushing back against the miserable conditions they were forced to endure.

In some instances, as Darryl J. Littleton notes, many Enslaved Black tricksters "viewed their masters as self-important, pompous, and none-too-bright. Thus, [enslavement] humor centered on [Blacks] making fun of their captors without being detected."[15] In order to endure the horrors of their condition, Danielle Fuentes Morgan points out that "by purporting to be lazy, foolish or weak, not only did they foster a dynamic in which they reduce their own productivity (and the masters profit margin) but this subterfuge offered a degree of protection where the seemingly *unknowing* slave would not be viewed as a threat, even when they were."[16] Ironically, the misdirection, mimicry, and broken dialect of Enslaved Blacks frequently served as a source of amusement for whites. Watkins explains, "This *deliberate* linguistic misdirection allowed [the Enslaved] both to communicate surreptitiously with one another and, without detection, express humorously some of the pent-up outrage resulting from their treatment. . . . At the same time, maintaining the *appearance* of the naïve was crucial as a survival technique, providing the perfect guise for aggressive humor and wit."[17] The Black tricksters of the antebellum period were undoubtedly among the first wave of performers to experiment with and advance techniques of Black resistance humor as a special language—a language of wit and disguise that connected with the intrinsic rhythm and understandings of its audiences. It is instructive to note that Black resistance humor is not simply about getting laughs. Instead, there is *always* something at stake within the joke itself related to power and authority. For instance, something as seemingly innocuous as the recitation of "The Lord's Prayer" could also communicate a funny and coded message to other Black people: "Our Fader which art in heaben, white man owe me eleben and pay me seben, d'y kingdom come, d'y will be done, if I hadn't tuck dat I wouldn't git none."[18]

Some of the earliest recorded instances of nineteenth-century first-wave Black resistance humor are found in the richly ironic fiction of William Wells Brown, a towering literary figure and contemporary of the legendary writer, orator, and abolitionist Frederick Douglass. Brown was born into and later escaped from U.S. enslavement and became America's first Black novelist and playwright, publishing his book *Clotel* in 1853. Brown's stage play *The Escape, or A Leap for Freedom* (1858) uses complex irony to depict the horrors of enslavement. The play helped elevate Brown's stature in literary circles. In a one-man show, Brown performed the play himself, portraying each character and parodying what historian Glenda Carpio describes as "the stereotypes of race and gender produced by slavery—the wicked overseer, the tragic mulatta, the lascivious slave master, the heroic slave, the buffoonish 'coon'—in a hyperbolic mode that sabotaged their power. During his performances, Brown transformed into stereotypes across differences of race, gender, and class lines not only to lampoon racist ideologies but also to show the nonsensical nature of race and its identities."[19] In *The Conjure Woman* (1899), a work of short fiction by Charles W. Chesnutt, he uses a stark narrator to represent the scourge of American slavery, engaging humor to highlight the lack of dominion the Enslaved population possessed over their own physical bodies. Carpio argues that Chesnutt draws comedy out of dark situations, "showing how attempts to repossess the dispossessed body are almost always defeated by the institutionalized violence of slavery. Thus, laughter in his tales is often the sound of tragic recognition of dispossession."[20] Another early example of Black resistance humor in American literature is found in an 1855 enslavement narrative by Peter Randolph, *From Slave Cabin to Pulpit,* which describes the tales of Pompey, an Enslaved Black person, who employs deliberate linguistic misdirection to undermine plantation authority:

OVERSEER: Pompey, how do I look?
POMPEY: Oh, massa, mighty!
OVERSEER: What do you mean "mighty," Pompey?
POMPEY: Why, massa, you look noble.
OVERSEER: What do you mean "noble"?
POMPEY: Why, sar, you look just like one lion.
OVERSEER: Why, Pompey, where have you ever seen a lion?
POMPEY: I seen one down in yonder field the other day, massa.
OVERSEER: Pompey, you foolish fellow, that was a jackass.
POMPEY: Was it, massa? Well, you look just like him.[21]

Utilizing subterfuge, misdirection, and masking techniques, however, carried unintended consequences—specifically, the racial caricatures that were rapidly advanced in the wake. The "sambo" trope was among the first of many negative stereotypes to materialize in the American social imaginary. The circulation and promotion of the sambo trope led to dangerous and grotesque distortions paraded onstage in racist minstrel shows. By the early part of the nineteenth century, white minstrel shows had become the leading form of entertainment in both America and Europe. Edwin Forrest, Charles James Mathews, George Washington Dixon, and George Nichols were among the first white performers to apply burnt cork to their faces and appear on stage in "white blackface" before white audiences. While crude and outwardly demeaning, white blackface performances were oddly ironic and self-reflexive white impersonations of Black people. However, their imitations were unwittingly based on Black performances and behaviors that were secretly intended to mock whites.

When the presence of "Black blackface" minstrelsy sprang forth, Yuval Taylor and Jake Austen point out that some Black performers "alternately embraced, exploited, subverted, and turned stereotypes inside out, [and] quite often [became] tremendously successful with both Black and white audiences in the process."[22] The prime examples, of course, were the first Black stars of the Broadway theater scene, Bert Williams and George Walker, who pioneered the second wave of early Black resistance humor. Egbert Austin "Bert" Williams garnered an international reputation as the "first Black superstar." Williams and Walker owned the leading Black theater company of the era and helped popularize the "cakewalk" dance craze of the 1890s. Williams and Walker also used humor to "reinscribe" the late nineteenth-century "coon" minstrel trope. The comedy duo was always nattily clad, which visually opposed the "tattered and torn" Black caricatures so prevalent in American culture at the time. The performative dynamic between the two comics positioned Walker (who did not appear in blackface) as the sophisticated, articulate foil to the hapless Williams (who did perform in blackface). Williams and Walker's parody and subtle subversions appeared in their performances in stage plays like *Abyssinia* (1906) and *In Dahomey* (1903). In *Abyssinia*, which had a run on Broadway, Williams portrays the nouveau riche Jasmine Jenkins, who wins the lottery and invites his friend Rastus Johnson (Walker) and a group of friends to join him on a globetrotting tour. Williams and Walker use elusive vernacular tricks that carry double meanings throughout the play, creating what James C. Scott calls "hidden transcripts."[23] The duo's jokes held separate implications for Black and white audience members, raising the questions, Who is the butt of the joke, and who truly understands who the *real* butt of the joke is?

> WILLIAMS: What's the duty of a philoso—philoso—
> WALKER: Philosopher.
> WILLIAMS: What's his duty?
> WALKER: To look on the bright side of other people's troubles when you haven't any of your own.
> WILLIAMS: You're right, you're right.
> WALKER: Now we understand each other, I'll let you into a little secret.
> WILLIAMS: Before you tell me that secret, give me one of the crackers you've got in your pocket . . .
> WALKER: To pick up my narrative—
> WILLIAMS: If it don't make any difference to you, would you mind picking up a cracker at the same time?[24]

The repetition of the word *cracker* in this sequence provides humor to white audiences as an exaggerated expression of Jenkins's attempt to satiate his hunger. For Black audiences, on the other hand, the word "cracker" elicits a different source of laughter as a pejorative term for racist whites.[25] David Krasner points out that "Williams and Walker used language to parody racist representations in a manner that was original, neatly folding parody into the text without arousing undue attention. Credit must be given to their skill, which let them go undetected by [white] audiences."[26] Without question, Bert Williams suffered criticism for his use of blackface. He offers poignant insight into the psychological toll he paid for his social "doubleness" when he writes, "I shuffle onto the stage, not as myself, but as a lazy, slow-going negro. . . . The real Bert Williams is crouched deep down inside the coon who sings and tells stories."[27]

Subsequent Black comics like Mantan Moreland and Lincoln Perry (professionally known as Stepin Fetchit) were among Williams's admirers who achieved Hollywood fame in their own right by exploiting malapropisms and exaggerated performance styles. Unfortunately, their humor acquiesced to white producers' vulgar expectations, which championed anti-Black portrayals in an openly racist society. Although Moreland and Perry were financially rewarded for their caricatured performances, adapting to such debilitating conditions was damaging to the social psyche. As Ed Guerrero notes, the racial tropes promoted by comics like Moreland and Perry were "perpetually at war with the African American inner self and its historic, communal ideals: the freedom struggle, the quest for self-determination and self-presentation, dignity and collective vision of a liberated future."[28] Sadly, this tangled dichotomy of warring impulses continues to haunt Black comics today.

From the 1920s through the civil rights era, a third wave of Black resistance humor materialized in the literature of Harlem Renaissance authors like Zora Neale Hurston (*Their Eyes Were Watching God*), Rudolph Fisher (*The Walls of Jericho*), Wallace Thurman (*Infants of the Spring*), Langston Hughes (*The Ways of White Folks*), and Ralph Ellison (*The Invisible Man*). In the early 1940s, Hughes established himself as one of America's premier humorists by using satire and irony as a subversive form of protest in the creation of his literary figure Jesse B. Semple (later shortened to "Simple"), a ne'er-do-well Black everyman. Hughes's Simple character and his "Simple stories" became the source material for Hughes's weekly column in the prominent Black newspaper the *Chicago Defender*. In one such column, Hughes slyly employs the character to critique the nation's celebration of the centennial anniversary of the lawful end of U.S. slavery and the Civil War. Simple muses,

> This here Centennial of the Civil War and the stuff white folks is intending to celebrate in honor of the North and South and they are going to put on parades and meetings and battles and things like they were a hundred years ago. One way of making people remember what the Civil War were all about might be to bring slavery back for a month or two—only this time reverse it. Make white folks the slaves and me the master. I would like to own some of them white Semples on my grandma's side which were the ones, I understand, that gave me my name. [. . .] Maybe I could work out of them some of the money they owed my grand folks and never paid. [. . .] From dawn till after dusk I would find something for them to do and come end of the week, not pay a cent. That would be a real good way, I figure, to celebrate this Centennial. Make it real, not just play-acting—and bring slavery home to its own doorstep. One hundred years, it is time to turn the tables.[29]

Simple's commentary and Harlem exploits were often deceptively unassuming yet revealed the issues and forces facing Black Americans. Similarly, Ellison's protest novel, *Invisible Man*, uses irony and humor to articulate a sense of fury aimed at white oppression of Black Americans. Teeming, rage-laden humor festers in the psyche of the book's unnamed protagonist. Terrence Tucker argues that *Invisible Man* is a crucial example of Black literature that demonstrates that "humor can succeed as a method of resistance."[30] The novel would become Ellison's singular masterpiece, an American classic.

The suggestive and irreverent comedy of vaudeville and chitlin' circuit holdovers like Moms Mabley and the blue chicanery of Redd Foxx were also important to the advancement of the third wave of Black resistance humor. The rebellious monologues and stand-up comedy routines of Jackie "Moms" Mabley are rooted in a cultural familiarity with Black folk traditions that ingratiated her queer and defiant humor with Black audiences. Mabley adopted an immersive character affectionately referred to as "Moms" as her onstage persona. Her wide, toothless grin; floppy shoes; ornate and tattered gingham housecoats; and quirky hats composed her trademark costume. Her ironic "down-home" ethnic performance style also connected Mabley's comedic rhythms with resistant elements that challenged issues of sexual representation and gender politics while also highlighting the racial restrictions of Black life in both urban and rural environments. On stage, she quipped,

> *Now they want me to go to New Orleans. . . . It'll be Old Orleans 'fore I get down there. The Greyhound ain't goin' take me down there and the bloodhounds run me back, I'll tell you that.*[31]

Mabley's contemporary, Redd Foxx is best known for his starring role on the NBC sitcom *Sanford and Son* (1972–1977). He rose to prominence in the 1940s and 1950s along with Mabley, performing stand-up in Black-owned clubs across the country. His jokes were edgy, scatological, and scathingly funny. Foxx released nearly fifty comedy albums, yet his oppositional humor was relegated to underground nightclubs and largely ignored in the mainstream for the majority of his career.

A fourth wave of Black resistance humor emerged in the 1960s, led by comedian Dick Gregory's blistering critiques of the ancient network of American racism. The sardonic wit of Nipsey Russell and Godfrey Cambridge's social satire that highlighted the absurdities of white bigotry were also instrumental in this fourth wave. Russell was a sharp satirist and one of the first Black comics to perform before predominantly white audiences. He adopted a cool, intellectual comedic persona to tackle pressing topics like integration and racial politics. On the other hand, Cambridge was primarily a film actor, starring in Ossie Davis's directorial debut, the crime comedy *Cotton Comes to Harlem* (1970). It was his virtuoso performance in Melvin Van Peebles's *Watermelon Man* (1970) that helped transform the film from an insipid caricature comedy into a boisterous, politically charged satire.[32]

The film notably features Cambridge in cinema's first on-screen appearance of Black "whiteface" makeup and performance. It was Gregory, however, who stood as the paramount Black satirist of the 1960s. He took an assertive approach to challenge America's neurotic racial anxieties. Gregory's stand-up comedy serves as a direct social critique. Foxx recognized that "while other comedians had broken new ground for the Black humorist . . . Dick Gregory did far more than all the other[s] put together. He led Black comedians out of the stereotyped rut whites had forced him into for so long by almost literally biting the white hands that were feeding him."[33] After paying his dues in small nightclubs across the country, in 1961, publishing mogul Hugh Hefner hired Gregory to perform at the all-white Playboy Club in Chicago. Gregory's appearance at the club proved to be the turning point in his career:

> *Good evening ladies and gentlemen. I understand there are a good many Southerners in the room tonight. I know the South very well. I spent twenty years there one night. . . . I'm really for Abraham Lincoln. If it hadn't been for Abe, I'd still be on the open market. . . . You know the definition of a Southern moderate. That's a cat that'll lynch you from a low tree. . . . You gotta say this for whites, their self-confidence knows no bounds. Who else could go to a small island in the South Pacific, where there's no crime, poverty, unemployment, war, or worry and call it a primitive society.*[34]

At the height of his professional popularity, Gregory became increasingly devoted to political activism and frequently canceled his comedy shows to participate in civil rights protest rallies and marches. Unfortunately, his decision had heavy consequences and resulted in Gregory ultimately being ostracized in Hollywood.

Radical comics Richard Pryor and Paul Mooney ushered in the fifth wave of Black resistance humor in the 1970s, and both were key figures in the development of the Black Pack movement. Mooney operated as Pryor's comedy cowriter. Together, they helped advance a new Black comedic identity. Pryor soared into the stratosphere of a cultural icon, and Mooney helped shape Pryor's jokes with a penchant for racial critique. In fact, Mooney is responsible for writing jokes for some of Pryor's most famous routines. Together, the duo broke new ground in American humor, using street language and profanity to address the nation's searing racial temperature and political unrest—topics that were altogether foreign in mainstream film and television. Pryor was the Black Pack's comedic father figure, while Mooney served as the group's ideological architect.

Throughout the 1980s and '90s, the Black Pack utilized the rituals of Black resistance humor as their weapon of engagement in America's culture wars. In order to comprehend the full spectrum of meanings embedded in their production of culture, we must consider the social constructions of manhood and masculinity in America. The Black Pack's humor, in many ways, is aimed at a recuperation of Black masculinity linked to the efforts of the civil rights movement, particularly protests like the "I Am a Man" campaigns. These activist demonstrations attempted to liberate the Black male body from a demeaning social order that forced Black men to step down from sidewalks when whites approached. The "I Am a Man" campaigns were also aimed at ending the racial violence endured by Black communities facing an American apartheid system that sanctioned the lynching of Black men without due process under the law. The intensity of this condition was described, although with stereotypic underpinnings, by Norman Mailer, who points out, "Any [Black man] who wishes to live must live with danger from his first day, and no experience can ever be casual to him, no [Black man] can saunter down a street with any real certainty that violence will not visit him on his walk. [He] has the simplest of alternatives: live a life of constant humility or ever-threatening danger."[35] The issues and dilemmas of Black masculinity, largely unchanged by the passage of time, are further complicated by racial pathologies that remain pervasive in the motion picture industry. The cultural critic bell hooks argues that "representations that socialize Black males to see themselves as always lacking, as always subordinated to more powerful white males whose approval they need to survive, matter in white patriarchy. Since competition between males is sanctioned within male-dominated society, from the standpoint of white patriarchy, Black masculinity must be kept in check. Black males must be made subordinate in as many cultural arenas as possible."[36]

A radical vision of Black masculinity arose from the social turbulence of the 1960s, particularly within the Black Power movement and its aesthetic branch, the Black Arts movement. Leaders like human rights advocate Malcolm X, charismatic Chicago Black Panther Party leader Fred Hampton, and fiery poet/author Amiri Baraka are but a few examples of men who embodied a refusal to conform to the dominant culture's obsequious constructions of Black manhood during the 1960s. The influence of such radical thinkers inspired many Black youths to seek a decolonized critical consciousness. This type of political education and community organizing was actively repressed by the establishment.[37] Thus, due to their refusal to conform, many radical-thinking Black male leaders of the 1960s and '70s were methodically murdered or unjustly imprisoned by the system.

By the 1980s, notions of Black masculinity remained in flux. The Reagan administration's application of racist social policies and the emphasis on a "greed is good" moral and financial imperative further marginalized many poor and working-class Blacks into deeper states of underdevelopment. The arrival of the Black Pack signaled, on the one hand, a renewed assertion of Black masculinity that marked itself as pro-Black, heterosexual, and socially engaged, and on the other hand, the group was also driven by the acquisition of fame and financial freedom. The Black Pack's exertions of social and political agency as comic artists involve a stark recognition of the racial terrors faced by Black people in America. The group furthered a tradition that Brandon J. Manning might describe as "Black men engaging in a public meaning-making process that foregrounds Black masculine emotionality and interiority while simultaneously inviting white consumption and misunderstanding."[38] Their approach to addressing racial issues shifted away from the prophetic traditions of Black leaders in the civil rights and Black Power movements—a period when leadership success or failure was not contingent on financial imperatives, the size of one's bank account, or the amount of "followers" one gains on social media. For this reason, the collective strivings for Black political freedom and self-determination that were central to American social progress would, by the end of the 1990s, become largely supplanted by an overwhelming drive to accumulate capital. Luxury cars, designer fashion, Air Jordan sneakers, and other flashy consumer goods became the hallmarks of success. The Black Pack represents a fascinating bridge connecting these two seemingly disparate worlds in the postsoul period. Although they aggressively pursued a free-market agenda that challenged racism in the Hollywood system, the Black Pack contemporaneously ensured that the system rewarded them financially. Call it a win-win: get rich and die *laughing*. Likewise, their close-knit interconnectedness provided a foundation of camaraderie between Black men, publicly promoting principles of intraracial brotherhood, an image rarely depicted in the dominant media.

The Black body remains a clear and present threat in the white imagination. The persistent state-sanctioned killings of unarmed Black women and men are damning manifestations of the worst expression of America's racialized violence against Black citizens. Each victim a reluctant martyr: frozen in the national imagination as an involuntary symbol of Black pain.[39] Twisted distortions of the "criminal Black male" have, of course, been woefully carved into our nation's social psyche through the medium of cinema, dating as far back as the racist depictions in early silent-era films like Thomas

Edison's *Ten Pickaninnies* (1904), Edgar Lewis's *The Nigger* (1914), and most infamously, D. W. Griffith's *The Birth of a Nation* (1915). Such early motion pictures crystallized perfidious myths of Black social deviance and racial inferiority that subsequently spawned countless reincarnations in Hollywood's catalog of virulent Black screen images. Sadly, the film industry continues to sanction and celebrate visual metaphors that, quite simply, replicate demeaning attitudes and behaviors toward Black women and men. This persistent racial "othering" often overdetermines the politics of identity for Black Americans, how we relate to ourselves and others, and how we tend to be perceived in the broader society.

In discussing such cascading catastrophes, this book analyzes a vital chapter in American history, when the Black Pack's provocative humor became all the rage in popular culture. Their success enabled the group to use the Hollywood machine to lampoon the industry's authority and empower Black creatives and audiences by confronting issues of race and Black cultural politics through film and television. A key factor during the Black Pack's ascendance was their capacity to engender a sense of cultural solidarity within Black communities. They enthralled audiences with an array of stand-up comedy performances, studio-financed feature films, broadcast television shows, cable network programs, home video rentals, music videos, music albums, and comedy records that seemed to permeate daily life in many Black communities. Their comedic material deftly manages to articulate what Tina Campt describes as "the visual frequency of a Black gaze" directly to Black audiences on a vernacular level while captivating broader national audiences by bringing the margins into the mainstream.[40] Pitted against the conservative political backdrop of the Reagan and Bush administrations in the 1980s and 1990s, the Black Pack's ideological battles against institutional authority helped redefine the lines of cultural influence in Hollywood. And underneath the glossy patina of commercial entertainment, the Black Pack's humor, with its satire and ironic racial critiques, exploded into popular culture with a rapturous social velocity.

The conceptual framework of Black resistance humor, so crucial for Black cultural expression throughout American history, is evident in the manner in which each Black Pack member uses comedy to cast a harsh light of reality on the darkness of American racial delusions. Their comedic efforts brought boldness and cool logic to the most crucial questions of race in this country. For instance, when Arsenio Hall was interviewed by *Vanity Fair* magazine about his original stint as guest replacement host on the Fox network's late night program *The Late Show*, he described his hiring as follows: "The first time, I got [the job was] because Frank Zappa canceled. I joked that Rupert Murdoch called 1-800-CAUCASIAN and no one answered. So, they had to give me a shot."[41] Not long after, he signed a deal to create *The Arsenio Hall Show*, which skyrocketed to the number-one spot in the late night television ratings by providing a nightly forum for the cool and edgy expression and celebration of Black cultural figures, underground Black music artists, and the audacious hip-hop artifacts that reflected the emerging culture.

Although the Black Pack's work disrupts traditional racial hierarchies by centralizing Black themes and characters, there are instances when the representation of gender and queer identities conform to dominant notions of masculinity and patriarchal power. *Eddie Murphy: Raw* (1987) and *In Living Color*'s "Men On" characters are two such examples. Murphy's *Raw* oozes with an inflated assertion of macho vigor and lamentably presents a rearguard notion of women as sexual objects. Likewise, the appraisals of Black queer identity on Keenen Ivory Wayans's *In Living Color* are rooted in antiquated stereotypes and amount to little more than over-the-top caricatures. Murphy and Wayans received considerable public backlash for these regressive portrayals. With his final Black Pack film, *Boomerang*, Murphy strives for a modicum of atonement, attempting to offer more nuanced and empowering portrayals of Black women and intersectionality in America. Notwithstanding glaring deficiencies regarding gender and sexuality, or perhaps in the face of them, the Black Pack demonstrates their vision of Black masculinity and cultural solidarity as a logical extension of post–civil rights movement efforts.

By the late 1980s, the Black Pack spearheaded the arrival of a sixth wave of Black resistance humor, which also featured comedians like Whoopi Goldberg, Spike Lee, Robin Harris, and Tim Reid. Their body of work engages Black resistance humor in a variety of modes, including double meanings, satire, social inversions, and other subaltern critiques. Historically, critical writings in the study of humor have laid out four broad categories in which a situation, person, action, or phrase is understood to be "funny." These categories of humor include superiority comedy (sarcasm, put-downs, satire), incongruity comedy (sight gags, puns, malapropisms), arousal comedy (slapstick, sexual references), and social currency comedy (parody, play, joking to fit in).[42] Likewise, Mikhail Bakhtin's theory of the carnivalesque illustrates a mode of humor that liberates, subverts, reverses, or destabilizes power structures through transgressive acts, offering a helpful framework through which the Black Pack's cultural work may be critically reassessed.[43] Robert Stam points to the effectiveness of Bakhtin's literary ideas applied to media culture, arguing that historically marginalized groups around the world often use comedy against the grain of the dominant society.[44] This line of thinking reveals how the Black Pack's humor shifts the notion of who can be the butt of jokes in Hollywood and, to some extent, disarms white audiences, making them laugh at their own racism. My contextualization of the historical factors surrounding the formation of the Black Pack and the creation, circulation, and consumption of their work provides new interpretive readings and critical insights. I also discuss how they extend the heritage of Black resistance humor by utilizing irreverence and street parlance to speak to Black audiences in a coded language that often required viewers to be savvy enough to get their jokes.

Exploring the rhetoric of Black vernacular traditions is, no doubt, critical to examining the Black Pack's comedic material. One such tradition, Houston Baker argues, is blues music, a genre indicative of an unfolding "racial epic" in which Black Americans find voice and connection to their ancestral roots. In considering the Black Pack, there is an interesting correlation between the oppositional nature of their comedy and the cultural function of the blues. This instinct is also described in the blues criticism articulated by Amiri Baraka's concept of "the changing same" and Henry Louis Gates Jr.'s notion of the blues and "signifying" as primary metaphors for Black oral traditions.[45] Like blues music, the Black Pack's humor is preoccupied with discovering, articulating, and carving out its own place in society.[46] This may also be true, perhaps, to a certain degree, of all Black music: gospel, jazz, hip-hop, and so on. The Black Pack's cultural output at once embodies the mastery of the formal elements of comedy while simultaneously engaging in the deformation of that mastery by injecting their jokes with the trickery and double meanings central to the strategies of Black resistance humor.[47]

Full of ambivalences and contradictions, the Black Pack productions explore substantive issues of race, visibility, power, and class in the United States while cleverly shifting media platforms. This discursive process of convergence and overlap reveals what Stuart Hall calls "the mark of difference inside forms of popular culture."[48] This book also chronicles a confluence of social, political, economic, and technological factors—namely, the impact of government regulations and the rise of VCRs and home entertainment on the proliferation of Black expressive culture in the 1980s and '90s. The Black Pack's network and cable television interventions greatly benefited from newly established FCC regulations like the Prime-Time Access Rule (PTAR), the Financial Interest and Syndication Rules (Fin-Syn), and the 1984 Cable Act, which generated a lucrative business environment for independent television producers. The PTAR and Fin-Syn regulations directly "forbade the national networks from owning or profiting from the shows they broadcast." Later, "the 1984 Cable Act paved the way for several competing cable channels to challenge the traditional network broadcasters—ABC, CBS, and NBC."[49] These regulatory policies aided in the growth of several media corporations with financial interests in gaining Black viewership, including Home Box Office (HBO), Black Entertainment Television (BET), and the Fox Broadcasting Company. In addition, newly available consumer products such as VCRs and home entertainment systems generated an entirely different domestic viewing phenomenon. These technologies deepened the Black Pack's social influence. It allowed their work to reach a critical mass, permeating the daily lives of Black audiences through processes of repeated home viewings, personal collecting, repurposing, and community recirculation—similar to the unofficial VHS archive in the first-floor closet at my grandma's house in Chicago.

Embedded in the Black Pack's humor is a head-on collision with the politics of crossing over. Traditionally, Black comics have been required to conform to the performance of racial caricatures in order to "cross over" in Hollywood. Adherence to the constraints of racial difference often dictates Black performers' ability to gain mainstream acceptance and reach popular audiences. As Ellis Cashmore rightly puts it, "Black people [are] admitted into the mainstream entertainment industry on the condition that they conform to one of the traditional stereotypes."[50] Usually, Black performers "who challenged [those stereotypes] were denied, while those who played the game enjoyed a modicum of success."[51] For Black comics, the subtext of crossing over implies the presence of an often-illegible Blackness that is only rendered legible in the dominant culture once it has "crossed over" rivers of systemic racism and institutional inequality. Richard Dyer defines "a crossover star [as] one who appeals to more than one culture; one who, though rooted in a particular tradition with a particular audience, somehow manages to appeal, and sell, beyond the confines of that audience."[52] For Black American comedians, crossing over has often required an adherence to a strict set of "white codes" regarding Black expressivity that demand "acceptable" performances that maintain the status quo of racial hierarchies. The popularity of the Black Pack's resistant brand of comedy is even more meaningful, however, as a key reversal in the customary obligations of the politics of crossing over and its complicated history.

Chapter 1 of this publication delves into the critical genealogy of the Black Pack, illustrating the collective's ancestral connection to the comedic legacy of Paul Mooney and Richard Pryor. I foreground Mooney and Pryor's groundbreaking, albeit brief, stint on NBC with the sketch comedy series *The Richard Pryor Show*, which premiered in 1977. This television program establishes the ideological template later adopted and expanded by the Black Pack. Special attention in chapter 1 is given to examining and historicizing the gospel of comedy according to Mooney, who preached that the best jokes are about "trouble." I detail Mooney's in-your-face style with its acerbic analysis of a white America preoccupied with race and his indelible influence on the evolution of Pryor's comedic legacy and the development of the Black Pack crew.

Chapter 2 probes the economic forces behind Eddie Murphy's meteoric rise to the zenith of the Hollywood industry in the 1980s. The early part of the decade saw Murphy evolve from a bit player on *Saturday Night Live* to the show's main attraction and seamlessly transition into a wildly successful movie star by adroitly situating his streetwise vernacular style within an all-white cinematic milieu in flicks like *48 Hrs.* and *Trading Places*. By 1987, Murphy's films had grossed nearly $1 billion for Paramount Pictures, which he leveraged to spearhead the Black Pack movement. Chapter 2 explores the production, circulation, and consumption of Murphy's Black Pack films, including *Eddie Murphy: Raw*, *Coming to America*, *Harlem Nights*, and *Boomerang*. This period marks a 180-degree shift in Murphy's cinematic focus toward developing and producing a series of movies that center Black themes, characters, and points of view for the enjoyment of Black audiences.

Chapter 3 looks at Robert Townsend's masterpiece *Hollywood Shuffle*, which critiques the industry's discriminatory practices and becomes the Black Pack urtext. Cowritten by Keenen Ivory Wayans, the film also features a cameo from Paul Mooney and an illuminating spoof of Eddie Murphy's game-changing impact on the industry. This chapter examines vital industrial shifts like the development of ancillary markets and the rise of home entertainment technology and its effect on the proliferation of Black Pack productions. I also detail how *Hollywood Shuffle*'s commercial success catalyzed the Black Pack's formation and created a ripple effect that launched careers and significant cultural works like *Eddie Murphy: Raw*, *The Five Heartbeats* (both directed by Townsend), and Wayans's explosive sketch comedy series *In Living Color*. With *Hollywood Shuffle*'s popularity, more Black Pack members were welcomed into the industry as directors, writers, and producers and developed lucrative relationships with Hollywood studios.

Chapter 4 takes a case study approach to exploring the two major Black Pack television productions, *The Arsenio Hall Show* and *In Living Color*.

Hall's syndicated program toppled the legendary *The Tonight Show Starring Johnny Carson*. Hall's series ran 1,248 episodes and disrupted traditional patterns of late night viewership. In addition, *The Arsenio Hall Show* provided a nightly forum for the expression of edgy Black American humor, music, fashion, politics, and culture. Not to mention then presidential candidate Bill Clinton's appearance on the program, sporting dark sunglasses and playing tenor saxophone—a watershed moment in American popular culture and presidential politics. This chapter details how *In Living Color*'s groundbreaking use of irony, parody, and racial satire aided the newly established Fox Broadcasting Company in solidifying itself as the fourth major television network. The series breathed new life into the dying sketch comedy genre by satirizing racial issues, celebrities, and popular events. Chapter 4 also explores how both *The Arsenio Hall Show* and *In Living Color* skyrocketed in popularity by activating a new visual language imbued with a rebellious streetwise energy and the aesthetics of hip-hop music, fashion, and culture that pushed back against the practice of restricting politically Black artistic expression on broadcast networks.

Lastly, the coda accounts for the industrial conditions that shaped the end of the Black Pack cycle and the group's lasting influence on new generations of American comedians. I consider Black histories and Black futures, offering a collection of "future-forward" insights that explore the state of Black resistance humor and its continued resonance with popular audiences. I consider the work of modern social comedians like Chris Rock, Wanda Sykes, Dave Chappelle, Katt Williams, and Michael Che alongside the work of writer/producer Kenya Barris, Amanda Seales, Jerrod Carmichael, and Donald Glover as prominent descendants of the Black Pack's comedic legacy. I also provide a critique of the Black Pack's current endeavors and offer an assessment of race, resistance, and Black American humor in a contemporary cultural landscape.

In yet another paranoid and virulent social and political climate, Black Americans once again find themselves pushing back against noxious anti-Black agendas and the devastatingly lethal virus of American racism. The nation is breaking open. Again. This time it is the coldest winter of our discontent in the twilight of late America. And it is now, perhaps as it has been forever, boundlessly exhausting to be Black in this country and always already required to navigate a willfully hostile world far too eager to make deadly assumptions regarding one's will to live or merely be in the world. Such assumptions, as it were, have not, of course, been produced by Black people. These contradictions represent perhaps the greatest national failures that have putrefied the very roots of the American system of reality—for far too long. Still, Black Americans continue to rise, to resist, to subvert, to rebel. In booms, in busts, in movements, in peaks, in cycles, in vogue, in vain.[53] Ironically, and perhaps predictably, the outcry for social justice in the early part of the twenty-first century has generated an energetic burst of interest in Black cinema and visual culture, and the role of Black American comedy and satire has been elevated to a vanguard level of cultural relevancy.

Today, the cutting edge of Black American humor is imbued with a renewed sense of social urgency and critiques, signaling, perhaps, a return to an era in our culture when comedians like the Black Pack emerged as Hollywood rebels and as symbols of resilience in a racially and politically charged nation. Just as skillful as they are at playing the dozens, the Black Pack are equally proficient at "playing the fool." That is, however, not to be confused with being *foolish*. Quite the contrary, the Black Pack uses comedy to make fools of "the wise." Their "playing the fool" in fact represents a paradox: the irony of their humor, though categorized as purportedly vapid and foolish by some, also reveals the Black Pack as beholders of wisdom, illuminating social ills with an ease that evades the powers that be. They are clever fools—wise fools, full of wisdom and fortitude, calling attention to the austere and malignant scourge of whiteness and systemic racism that floats like a corpse in the waters of American life, boldly urging white folks to wake up because—the jokes on *you*. From the jump, the Black Pack encouraged Black artists to raise their voices in both comedy and culture, and now their work has inspired new generations. And this time, they're coming for forty acres—and a *movie*.

1

Planet Provocative

Paul Mooney, *The Richard Pryor Show*, and Revolutionary Laughter

With his typical brilliance and acute vision, James Baldwin homed in on the dilemma of race in the United States when he declared during a 1961 radio interview, "All you are ever told in this country about being Black is that it is a terrible, terrible thing to be. Now, in order to survive this, you have to really dig down into yourself and recreate yourself, really, according to no image which yet exists in America. You have to impose, in fact—this may sound very strange—you have to *decide* who you are, and force the world to deal with you, not with its *idea* of you."[1] Baldwin's insights articulate the complex issues and challenges bound up in the formation of Black American identity and serve as an essential framework for digesting the main ingredients that compose Paul Mooney's special recipe for radical comedy, which includes a heavy serving of razor-sharp political edge and an unyielding social force that confronts the suffocating weight of the American racial condition. Mooney once fittingly described his comedy as a nuclear bomb: "It just blows up and flattens everybody."[2] He approached Black resistance humor with an explosive intensity that laid waste to pretense. His comedy forces us to wrestle with the pernicious racial ghosts that define our nation's past, haunt our present, and threaten to engulf our future. Mooney's relative obscurity (if one can call legendary cult status obscure) is a consequence of his unflinching comedic approach. For years, his career was actively suppressed in Hollywood. Yet he rose above the din to become your favorite comedian's *favorite* comedian. Mooney's take on humor far surpasses mere one-liners and punchlines; his acerbic barbs represent a form of cultural criticism, brazenly dismantling, brick by brick, the lies underpinning the very idea of the American dream:

> *Thank God, Paul Revere was white, because if he was Black, they'd have shot his ass. "He done stole that horse, let's kill him! Kill him!" And who do they say sewed the flag, what's her name? Betsy Ross? Now come on—they had slaves back then. Betsy Ross was asleep at six. You know some big Black mama was up all night sewing that damn flag! "Honey, oh, Lawd, have mercy, I'm just up so late sewing this flag, I'm seeing stars!" And she's thinking about the stripes on her back, from the whip. So, there we get it, the stars and stripes. But as soon as the white men got there, the white lady Betsy Ross jumped up [talking about,] "See what I did?"*[3]

The element of danger that crackles through Mooney's warhead comedic style is precisely what attracted Richard Pryor. Despite Pryor's established Hollywood success, he was captivated by Mooney's fearless defiance in the face of the white gaze. This quality set Mooney apart from every Black comic on the scene. At the time, Pryor's relationship with Hollywood mirrored the precarious dance of America's relationship with Black people—a twisted tango of love and loathing.

Pryor's career in Hollywood embodied the profound contradictions Black artists often face in the film and television industry. On the one hand, Pryor reveled in the glittering mirage of stardom: money, fame, power, sex (and not in that order)—a seductive cocktail not easily refused. But on the other hand, beneath the allure lurked a viper's nest—that is, the spiritual and psychic snares of the Hollywood industry and the enervating ways it seeks to control and censor Black creative expression. This tension echoes America's troubling and dichotomous embrace of Black culture, a love affair tainted by the nation's abhorrent devaluation of Black lives. Or, perhaps better stated, America loves Black culture but menaces Black people. Pryor's artistic frustration stemmed from this dichotomy. In the 1960s, he was a man torn apart, driven by internal conflict. During these early years, "Hollywood [was] telling [Pryor], you can have everything you want, but we have to put you through a deflavorizer first," Mooney asserted. "He [wanted] to find a way out of the box that white people want[ed] to keep him in."[4] Mooney and Pryor were intent on raiding the fortress of Hollywood to rewrite the rules of engagement on their own terms, for better or worse. Their tight-knit partnership offered a pathway toward conquering the industry while remaining true to their daring comedic vision.

Pryor and Mooney met at a house party on Sunset Boulevard in 1968. It was impossible to predict that their serendipitous run-in would alter the contours of American humor, primarily because the two comics were not immediately compatible. Their first encounter unfolded when Pryor, out of the blue, approached Mooney (a complete stranger), extending a bawdy invitation to a sex party, presumably reflecting the 1960s free-love ethos. Mooney politely demurred, taken aback by Pryor's childlike candor. Time, however, would weave a different narrative. Gradually, a friendship developed between the two men, and a unique comedic affiliation blossomed into a "shadow partnership." Pryor, the charismatic front man, served as the public face of their alliance, while Mooney was the unseen yet essential ghostwriter. Together, their unruly comedy sowed the seeds that spawned the Black Pack movement two decades later.

By the late 1960s, Pryor had already performed on *The Ed Sullivan Show*—the pinnacle for stand-up comics of the era. Despite his success, Pryor struggled to find his authentic comedic voice. He was well aware that his stand-up routines were not true to his real-life experiences nor to his rather seedy childhood growing up in an Illinois brothel. Instead, Pryor's comedy conformed to the sanitized, nonthreatening, colorless formula the white-dominated industry deemed acceptable for Black performers. It was Mooney who unlocked the idea of "revolutionary laughter" in Pryor's consciousness or, as Danielle Fuentes Morgan posits, the type of "laughter that itself inhabits a tricky space of simultaneous delight and sorrow to inspire justice."[5] Mooney exposed Pryor to the essential connections between three distinct Black American traditions: the blues, jazz, and comedy—each improvisational, fluid, and resistant. These traditions are also historically interconnected to shifting formations of Black identity and the ever-evolving dimensions of Blackness in American culture. At the height of the Black Power movement, Mooney was attuned to the palpable and rebellious social energies of the times, which saw Black Americans openly demanding freedom and justice. Repeatedly, he explained to Pryor, "The only way to do something more substantial on-stage . . . is to discuss one of the defining features of the American experience: race."[6] For Mooney, to ignore the politics of difference in America was to disregard the nation's most pressing social issue. Publicly tackling racial politics head-on with unfiltered truth was Mooney's most disruptive and enduring innovation in American comedy.

In order to truly grasp the history, social horizon, and cultural moves of the Black Pack, we must first consider the vital influence of Mooney and Pryor on the evolution of the Black Pack's comedy. While Pryor was not a member of the Black Pack, he did star in one Black Pack film, the Eddie Murphy–directed period piece *Harlem Nights* (1989), which underscores the interconnectedness of the group's comedic philosophy. Conversely, Mooney was, in fact, a pivotal member of the Black Pack and a cornerstone in the development of their resistant ideology. Before aligning with them, Mooney spent years working as a stand-up comic and as a writing partner for Pryor. Together, Mooney and Pryor fostered the advancement of Pryor's now-iconic brand of renegade humor, which influenced every comedic generation that followed. Pryor's legendary comedy albums became blueprints for countless aspiring comedians, irrespective of race. Moreover, the Black Pack's production of culture traces back to a lineage of radical humor pioneered by Mooney and Pryor, particularly their work on NBC's *The Richard Pryor Show* (1977). Their collaboration on this short-lived sketch comedy series outlined a brand of racial satire that paved the way for the Black Pack's lucrative deprovincialization of Hollywood discourses in the 1980s and 1990s.

The Richard Pryor Show premiered on September 13, 1977, representing a critical moment in American television. Produced by Burt Sugarman Productions, *The Richard Pryor Show* introduced the world to several soon-to-be comedic stars. The program also served as an arena for the collision of racially and politically charged satire, starkly contrasting with the prevailing conservative discourses that dictated prime-time television. Nostalgic white sitcoms like *Happy Days* (1974–1984) ruled the Nielsen ratings, forming the bedrock of television's prime-time shows. This dominance was further cemented by the FCC's newly established "Family Viewing Hour" policy, instituted in 1975, which mandated that networks reserve their daily 8 p.m. to 9 p.m. time slot for "family-friendly programming."[7] However, Mooney and Pryor's edgy and often controversial sketch series was rooted in a stinging analysis of America's racial politics, diametrically opposed to the very notion of "family friendly," ultimately making it a subversive counterpoint to every program in prime-time. While Mooney and Pryor's provocative style played well in nightclubs across the country and on comedy albums, their transition to network television proved tumultuous. The 1970s television landscape was largely devoid of racial confrontation from comedic voices that championed a distinctly Black perspective. For the most part, audiences were accustomed to folksy Midwestern-style comedy, exemplified by all-white sitcoms like *Laverne & Shirley* (1976–1983). The arrival of Pryor's brash persona and that of gadfly Mooney, who were dedicated to ushering in a new Black comic identity, proved jarring for NBC censors and network executives. In their sketch series, Pryor was the unquestioned superstar, and Mooney was the architect behind his brilliance, crafting Pryor's jokes with a signature penchant for incisive racial commentary.

In 1977, Pryor's stand-up performances were all the rage in American comedy. Renowned for his trailblazing integration of street language and profanity into his routines, Pryor hilariously confronted topics such as race, class, police brutality, politics, and sexuality. With *The Richard Pryor Show*, he and Mooney seized the opportunity to elevate these crucial issues and give voice to the challenges confronting Black American communities. Emerging during the socially turbulent post-Nixon era, their sketch series became a fierce battleground—a clash of ideologies between network executives and the duo over creative control and the appropriateness of the show's comedic material. In that respect, the television careers of Mooney and Pryor signal a crucial expansion in the tradition of Black resistance humor as they tossed grenades of insurgent wit into their sketch program to confront the absurdity of racism in the fight for social justice. They were catalysts for the infiltration of private Black cultural critiques of the dominant power structure into public discourse, effectively rupturing the boundaries that long confined such musings to the margins of American society.

Throughout the 1960s, Black American humor was shaped by two towering figures: Bill Cosby and Dick Gregory.[8] Cosby, with his easy charm, gained crossover success on television, while Gregory, a social agitator, flirted with mainstream acceptance but was primarily relegated to performing on the nightclub circuit. Like Mooney and Pryor, Gregory's humor was a weapon honed on the whetstone of racial critique. His comedic material addressed Black American social conditions during the civil rights era with a blend of cool wit and urbane confidence that challenged and disarmed audiences:

> *Don't get me wrong, I wouldn't mind paying my taxes if I knew it was going to a friendly country. . . . I hate to see any baseball player having trouble, because that's*

> *a great sport for my people. That is the only sport in the world where a [Black man] can shake a stick at a white man and won't start no riot.*[9]

Gregory's defiance, of course, extended beyond pithy gibes. He was highly engaged as a political activist, famously running for U.S. president as a write-in candidate for the Peace and Freedom Party at the height of his popularity in 1968. Conversely, Cosby's comedic trajectory aligned with the American establishment's embrace of integration and assimilation. He shattered barriers for Black advancement on network television by focusing on "universal" themes of family, marriage, and childhood. The careers of Cosby and film star Sidney Poitier represent a noticeable parallel; that is, both achieved commercial success in their respective mediums by fashioning performances of Blackness that did not appear to threaten the dominant order.

Cosby and Poitier achieved remarkable commercial success within the Hollywood machine by adopting a strategy of ideological conformity. Poitier, the premier Black actor in American cinema, became the first Black performer to win an Academy Award for Best Actor as the servile handyman Homer Smith in *Lilies of the Field* (1963). Cosby, on the other hand, was the first Black actor to star in a TV drama, playing Rhodes scholar secret agent Alexander Scott on the NBC series *I Spy* (1965–1968), a character that adhered to a nonthreatening archetype. For his performance, Cosby became the first Black actor to win an Emmy Award for a Leading Role in a Dramatic Series, clinching the trophy in three consecutive years. Poitier's and Cosby's ascent in show business was contingent on representing a palatable image of Blackness for a white audience eager to believe in racial progress, however illusory.

The contrasting comedic styles of Gregory and Cosby represent a longstanding tension within Black American thought and activism. This binary can be traced throughout the twentieth century, from the Pan-Africanist ideology of Marcus Garvey juxtaposed with W. E. B. Du Bois's emphasis on education to the Black self-reliance advocated by Malcolm X compared to Dr. Martin Luther King Jr.'s early vision of racial harmony and the beloved community. Within Hollywood's economy of unequal power dynamics, Poitier's and Cosby's elevation in show business was contingent on their strict adherence to screen performances that, for the most part, played by established rules—never questioning authority or appearing to rock the boat. They were the "right men" for their era, akin to Fritz Pollard and Jackie Robinson, who were similarly designated to break the color barriers of white racial repression of Black talent in the National Football League and Major League Baseball, respectively.

Cosby's dominance as the preeminent Black comedian of the 1960s significantly influenced Pryor's initial forays into stand-up. Seeking to replicate Cosby's success, Pryor meticulously crafted a persona emulating Cosby's "safe" comedic style. In his autobiography, *Pryor Convictions, and Other Life Sentences*, Pryor acknowledges his deliberate imitation, writing, "I decided that's who I was going to be from then on. Bill Cosby. [I became] Richard Cosby."[10] For a period, his strategy yielded considerable rewards. Pryor ascended from a rough-and-tumble brothel in Peoria, Illinois, to the national scene, landing multiple appearances on *The Ed Sullivan Show* and *The Tonight Show Starring Johnny Carson*. By 1967, Pryor was commanding an impressive fee of $3,000 per week to perform two shows a night at the Aladdin Hotel in Las Vegas. While undeniably lucrative, Pryor's days of mimicking Cosby were numbered. After several weeks of performing at the Aladdin, Pryor developed an overwhelming sense of artistic frustration, yearning for a more authentic expression, which culminated in a now-legendary public "meltdown." While performing, Pryor abruptly stormed off the stage midroutine, leaving the audience bewildered.[11] He left the hotel and returned to Los Angeles. Upon the urging of his manager, Pryor reluctantly returned to Las Vegas to fulfill his contractual obligations.

On October 2, 1967, while back on stage at the Aladdin, Pryor's artistic exasperation reached a breaking point. He abandoned his carefully curated "safe" Cosby-esque persona, unleashing a torrent of obscenities at the audience that the *Hollywood Reporter* later deemed sufficient to "blister the ears off a longshoreman."[12] Later, in his rebuttal to the *Los Angeles Times*, Pryor articulated his profound sense of creative indignation: "I was doing material that wasn't funny to me. I saw how I was going to end up. I was false. I was plastic."[13] Expounding further to *Rolling Stone* magazine, he described the stifling conformity of his Aladdin routine: "The life I was leading [in Vegas] wasn't me. I was a robot. 'Beep. Good evening ladies and gentleman, welcome to the Sands Hotel. Maids here are funny. Beep' . . . I didn't feel good."[14] The second Las Vegas incident, characterized by the hotel management as another "meltdown," resulted in Pryor's dismissal from the gig. The moment marked a significant turning point in the evolution of his comedic voice. In his memoir, Pryor describes the experience, writing, "[I was] having an epiphany. I knew my days of pretending to be as slick and colorless as Cosby were numbered. There was a world of junkies and winos, pool hustlers and prostitutes, women and family screaming inside my head, trying to be heard."[15] These restless voices bubbling in Pryor's psyche yearned for expression. With Mooney's encouragement, Pryor began to experiment onstage, integrating personal stories and distinct cultural accents into a new and rebellious comedic persona. As Terrence Tucker points out, Pryor's "contribution came in the transformation of despair and self-destruction into comic observations on the human condition . . . [and] his inclusion of a broad range of emotions that move his comic routines beyond entertainment."[16] Indeed, Pryor's brilliance resides in his ability to translate human emotion into commentaries on the human condition.

Black-Man and Robin

Paul Mooney's radical comedic frequencies turbocharged the groundwork laid by Dick Gregory, with whom he shared a sartorial flair and a commitment to social commentary. But Mooney's rapier jokes were even more contentious, pushing boundaries with an insurgent voice that relentlessly engaged the satirical treatment of race as the driving force of his creative strategy. Mooney's humor, whether delivered on stage or penned in television writers' rooms, vilified and poked holes in the racist practices and idealized facade of America. Perhaps his most enduring work came behind the scenes, crafting material for comedic giants like Richard Pryor, Redd Foxx, Dave Chappelle, and Black Pack member Keenen Ivory Wayans on the hit series *In Living Color* (1990–1994). Mooney's comedic style is singular and complex. He routinely incorporated U.S. history into his material to debunk racist ideologies, exposing "how racial conflict, and the obsessive ways that it colonizes American minds, can divest *everyone*, albeit at different registers, of a sense of reality."[17] At its core, Mooney's humor aims to reestablish a sense of reality—from a Black perspective. His mordant take on race often provoked discomfort among white audiences. Walkouts during his stand-up performances were not uncommon, and in many instances, he courted them:

> *White folks get tight-faced and nervous when I start making fun of [them]. When I imitate middle-class white speech, I see a flicker of unease cross [their] faces. . . . Then, when I go into ghetto riff, the smiles return. They're fine as long as I am making fun of the same kind of people they make fun of, chinks, spics and [Blacks]. But as soon as I start talking about them, I can clear a room.*[18]

Mooney's jokes elicit a form of revolutionary laughter, tapping into complex rhythms that underscore a reclamation of cultural power from the grip of white authority. His comedy resonates with a deep understanding of Black experiences, fostering a sense of solidarity and empowerment through shared cultural references and historical contexts. His ideological stance was, of course, a volatile artistic gambit that inevitably operated as a barrier to broader mainstream recognition of his talent.

Mooney's comedic journey lacked the early flash of Pryor's beginnings. Television appearances and lucrative Las Vegas residencies were not a part of his trajectory. In 1963, he left the chocolate streets of Oakland for the harsh realities of Hollywood, where dreams often flounder. He quickly secured a spot in the West Coast branch of the famed Second City improv group. Upon discovering that the troupe's performances were unpaid, Mooney opted to leave and, rather unconventionally, joined a one-ring circus. For over a year, he toured as the ringmaster while juggling odd jobs to make ends meet. It was not until a fateful encounter with a skinny, frenetic comic named Richard Pryor that new artistic possibilities blossomed.

Following their initial meeting in 1968, Mooney persistently argued that their comedic work could have utility in Black communities. He contended that most Black comedians (including Pryor) "have a *double consciousness* . . . they have one self for the master and one self that's 'just between us . . .' If they want to gain a wide cross-over audience, Black comics [have] to be careful what they say. But that's not me. I don't have double consciousness. I am who I am. I'm the first comic to bring a 'just between us' Black voice to the stage."[19] Pryor, one year removed from his Aladdin Hotel meltdown/epiphany, respected Mooney's rebellious spirit. "Thing about you, Mooney," Pryor explained, "you don't give a shit. You ain't scared of white people."[20] Mooney's unflinching honesty was precisely what Pryor desired to integrate into his own performances. So he brought Mooney on board as his new "shadow partner" and cowriter. They began performing at the top white-owned clubs on the Sunset Strip, including the Whiskey a Go Go in West Hollywood, the Troubadour, and Joan Rivers's Ye Little Club in Beverly Hills.

Mooney's and Pryor's comedic partnership weaponized Black resistance humor to remove the veil that designates whiteness as invisible. Richard Dyer argues, "As long as race is something only applied to non-white peoples, as long as white people are not racially seen and named, they/we function as a human norm. Other people are raced, we are just people. There is no more powerful position than that of being 'just' human. The claim to power is the claim to speak for the commonality of humanity."[21] When applying this interpretive frame, one realizes that Mooney's take-no-prisoners comedic bravura is preoccupied with dislodging whiteness from its position of cultural, political, and moral authority. Pryor's and Mooney's radical comedy attacks oppressive hierarchies that overdetermine Black life in terms of social mobility, the legal system, economic opportunities, and political representation. In addition to making their rounds in Hollywood's hottest comedy clubs, Mooney and Pryor extended their comedic riffs at Black-owned nightclubs in the Crenshaw District of Los Angeles. The duo implicitly recognized that the social order that distinguished the coarseness of Crenshaw from the glitz of Sunset Boulevard was a result of racist Jim Crow strategies. By establishing their presence in both settings, they disrupted stand-up comedy's status quo. Their talent even attracted white celebrities like Steve McQueen and Marlon Brando, who occasionally ventured across the racial divide, south of the 10 freeway, into "the hood" to witness the duo's acts firsthand.

Beyond the predominantly white comedy circuit, Black nightclubs offered a vital creative space for Mooney and Pryor. Venues like Redd Foxx's Jazz Go-Go and Maverick's Flat on Crenshaw operated as Black communal spaces, providing an insulated environment where Pryor and Mooney could experiment and hone their defiant comedic voices.[22] As James C. Scott astutely observes, "Neither everyday forms of resistance nor the occasional insurrection can be understood without reference to the sequestered social sites at which such resistance can be nurtured and given meaning."[23] Black comedy clubs mirrored the creative ferment of jazz clubs during the bebop era of the 1940s. Just as Miles Davis, Max Roach, and Thelonious Monk sharpened their musical chops through nightly jam sessions at Harlem hotspots like Minton's Playhouse, Mooney and Pryor used Black nightclubs to rehearse and harmonize their transgressive comedic chords, aligning their humor with the broader Black cultural ethos.

These venues, as Lisa Kennedy notes, embodied the concept of "the Black familiar," fostering a unique social atmosphere.[24] Spaces like Maverick's Flat presented the energy and freedom for experimentation. In these communal spaces, Pryor and Mooney could push boundaries and test out new material that deliberately disrupted comedy's "formal conventions [in order] to describe their own experience and position in a way that *might* let their intention be received by the audience."[25] Despite the era's practice of de facto and de jure segregation that confined many Black Americans to disadvantaged urban ghettos, Black communal spaces like Jazz Go-Go offered a sanctuary, a sense of cultural cohesion, and a space of self-affirmation.

Navigating Hollywood and Black Power

The 1968 assassination of Dr. Martin Luther King Jr., the foremost leader of the civil rights movement, unleashed a torrent of fierce uprisings across the country, a stark manifestation of simmering rage. Three years prior, the assassination of human rights advocate Malcolm X spurred the formation of the Black Panther Party for Self-Defense, whose members swiftly became prime targets of government repression. By the spring of 1968, with the two most prominent Black leaders of the era publicly slain, the flames of indignation cast a long shadow over the nation. King's death, in particular, left many Americans disaffected. The great tragedy of the moment was perhaps best captured in the poignant words of James Baldwin, who remarked in a radio interview that to be Black "in this country and to be relatively conscious is to be in a state of rage almost all of the time."[26] Within this cauldron of discontent, a revolutionary impulse surged in Black communities, underscoring an indispensable urgency for the establishment of independent Black cultural and political institutions that emphasized solidarity and pride. This spirit formed the bedrock of the youth-led revolutionary imperatives of activists engaged in the Black Power and Black Arts movements.

The rise of the Black Power movement coincided with a period of professional strain for Richard Pryor. The social pressure and anxieties of navigating the predominantly white entertainment industry weighed heavily on him. Despite financial success, Pryor felt stifled by the industry's rigid demands. The appeal of the rising Black social energy loomed ominously over his psyche. Between sips from a bottle of Courvoisier, Pryor candidly confessed to Paul Mooney, "I'm in a meeting down in motherfucking Hollywood, Mr. Mooney, and I ain't kidding, all I see is [devils], horns, and tails! Really! All these folks around me got cloven feet and forked tongues!"[27] Under the rubric of suspicion and the establishment's smothering gaze, Pryor felt creatively asphyxiated. He admitted, "Mooney, I'm losing my motherfucking mind. I'm going crazy. This city is driving me nuts."[28] Pryor's confessions reveal the internal conflict of his attempts to reconcile the revolutionary spirit of the times with the demands of comedic performance and the artifice and allure of Tinseltown. As Mooney observed, "What Richard wants [at the time] is what I want, what everyone in the world wants. To be accepted, to be loved for who we are, not for some playacting phony version of ourselves."[29] Seeking relief, Mooney proposed a solution: a move from Los Angeles to the more progressive Bay Area of Northern California. He believed a change of scenery would offer them a necessary detox from the social, artistic, and spiritual traps they faced in Hollywood.

In the Bay Area, Pryor found himself ensconced in a tiny apartment in Berkeley, fully immersed in its politically charged environment. Here, he was exposed to the radical teachings of Malcolm X and Huey P. Newton and the creative and intellectual energies of figures like Angela Davis, Amiri Baraka, Claude Brown, and other prominent leaders of the Black Power / Black Arts movement. This rich milieu of Black radical thought was light-years removed from the superficialities of Hollywood and significantly nurtured the evolution of Pryor's rising social consciousness. By the 1970s, income inequality saw a dramatic expansion between Black and white families. As Robin D. G. Kelley notes, during this period, "30.6 percent of Black families earned income below the official poverty line, compared with 8.7 percent of white families."[30] This bleak economic reality vividly illustrates a grim portrait of a dualistic America—one Black, one white. Black musicians across genres—from the soulful soundscapes of Marvin Gaye's protest songs "What's Going On" and "Inner City Blues" to Curtis Mayfield's funk and gospel-infused anthems "People Get Ready" and "If There Is a Hell Below"—gave voice to the vexed conditions facing Black communities with rhythms that resonated with the spirit of resistance and redemption. In the intensity of this political atmosphere, Pryor and Mooney honed a firebrand comedic style, increasingly infusing their material with pressing social issues. They focused their comedic efforts on removing the masks of double consciousness often adorned by Black comedians. This act of "unmasking" sought to not only reconfigure how Blackness was defined within the American narrative but also lay bare the irrationality of systemic racism while simultaneously celebrating the richness and complexity of Black culture in a way that resonated with audiences.

In the Black-owned clubs of Oakland, Mooney and Pryor further escalated their comedic experiments, incorporating profanity and Black vernacular street language into their performances, reflecting the cultural and linguistic nuances of their audience. By absorbing the era's rising social energy, the duo tapped into what Terrence Tucker describes as "comic rage," or "an African American cultural expression that utilizes oral tradition to simultaneously convey humor and militancy . . . to reveal hypocrisies in the construction of American identity, history, and culture."[31] Fuentes Morgan offers a similar perspective, arguing, "Laughing to keep from dying is the survival tactic that operates in two registers—the ability to inspire laughter in those who would cause harm becomes a form of protection in the plausible deniability of *just jokes*; the necessity of inspiring knowing in-group laughter opens up Black interior space that wards off psychic, or even physical, death."[32] From this view, Pryor and Mooney, consumed by the swirling dynamics of political demonstrations, social protests, and Black unrest, sought to entertain and educate, inspiring revolutionary laughter (to keep from dying) with resistant humor as their sword and shield in the fight for justice and equality.

The Bay Area offered a welcome change for both comedians. For Pryor, it was a fresh environment, while for Mooney, having grown up in Oakland and attended high school with Huey Newton, it was a return to source. This familiarity provided a warm sense of community, with frequent visits to Mooney's grandmother's home, where she showered them with heaping servings of delectable soul food delights. For a year, Pryor sequestered himself in a modest studio apartment, studying the speeches of Malcolm X and honing his comedic craft. Mooney, meanwhile, traveled back and forth to Los Angeles, continuing to perform on the Sunset Strip and Jazz Go-Go in the Crenshaw District. His stand-up routines began to defy "the language of the oppressor and instead create[d] a new language in a search for a just articulation of a nuanced selfhood."[33] The more Mooney studied history and culture, the more he incorporated irreverent jabs into his material:

> *Don't let Chinese people fool you—they didn't invent rice. Rice didn't come from China, it came from Africa, like a lot of shit, we invented a lot of shit, okay? The piano. The English found the piano in the middle of the jungle and brought it back to England. They put white keys on it, fucked it up, ruined it.*[34]

Similarly, Pryor's growing social awareness and his dive into Black studies infused his comedic artistry with the dynamic forces of Black literature, music, and cultural politics. His intellectual awakening led him to abandon the traditional decorum of stand-up. In fact, it was onstage at a Berkeley nightclub where Pryor, for the first time, provocatively dropped comedy's atomic bomb, the use of the N-word. This act signaled a radical shift in the landscape of comedic performance, reflecting the complexities of racial identity and resistance:

> *Cops put a hurting on yo' ass, man. They really degrade you. White folks don't believe that shit. They don't believe cops degrade you—[*white voice imitation*]—"Oh come on. Those beatings? Those people are resisting arrest. I'm tired of this*

> *harassment of police officers." . . . White folks get a ticket, they pull over like—"Gee officer, what can I do for you? Glad to be of help." Nigger got to be coming at it a whole different way. Talking about—[* loud and slow Black voice*]—"I am reaching . . . into my pocket . . . for my . . . license. Because I . . . don't wanna be . . . no motherfuckin' accident!"*[35]

It is essential to recognize that Pryor's invocation of the N-word here does not target any individual, nor does it function as a racial epithet. Rather, he employs the term in a complex and critically reflective manner to rebuke the failures of America and confront the falsehoods inherent in its avowed principles of equality and its indifferent stance toward the inequities one faces in the Black world. Pryor's strategic use of language, then, serves not merely as a censure but as an indicting force against system-wide injustices and the moral failings of a racially divided society.

It is also true that Lenny Bruce, a pioneering white comedian, had already opened up comedy's Pandora's box onstage, using profanity to punch up his jokes that reflected an antiestablishment ethos. Bruce caught flack for his saucy one-liners directed at public figures like Eleanor Roosevelt and a recently widowed Jacqueline Kennedy. Pryor and Mooney often bristled at the frequent and, in their view, simplistic comparisons drawn by critics between their comedic output and Bruce's work. As Scott Saul rightly explains, "Lenny Bruce used obscenities to spike his social commentary. . . . For Richard, obscenities were not usually leveraged for an explicit point; they were just an indispensable part of the way he expressed himself. . . . Bruce was a satirist who made points; Pryor was a searcher who explored."[36] Bruce was undeniably a vanguard of free speech and provocative language onstage. However, Pryor and Mooney were orchestrating a social comedy that was altogether distinct. They forged a performance style that employed tricksterism, satire, vernacular street language, and Black parlance to diagnose the pandemic of American racism. Their stint in the Bay Area was a sabbatical from the toxic madness of Hollywood. It provided them with the crucial time and space of detachment the duo needed to refine a comedic philosophy that blended pathos with politics, creating their own contribution to the rituals of Black resistance humor. In 1972, Pryor ended his Berkeley sojourn and rejoined Mooney in Los Angeles with a mission to use the social velocity of radical comedy to shake up the American entertainment industry.[37]

Return of the Repressed

Richard Pryor's reemergence in Hollywood coincided with a landmark development in Black television. Producers Norman Lear and Bud Yorkin had recently cast comedian Redd Foxx in the American adaptation of the working-class British program *Steptoe and Son* (1962–1974). NBC's new sitcom, *Sanford and Son* (1972–1977), offered a rare glimpse into Black life on a major network.[38] Foxx, who rose to prominence in the 1950s with his stand-up performances on the nightclub circuit, was particularly noted for his ribald humor. Throughout his illustrious career, he released fifty comedy albums, selling over fifteen million copies, earning him the nickname "King of the Party Records." *Sanford and Son* spins the tale of Foxx as Fred Sanford, an elderly salvage dealer who makes a living selling "junk" with his adult son Lamont (Demond Wilson) in the Watts area of Los Angeles. Fred Sanford, in his management of a business centered around what others deem "junk," highlights an interesting correlation akin to what Rogèrio Sganzerla describes as the "aesthetics of garbage." This concept counters the dominant society's pristine discourses by celebrating the creative potential found in the discarded and overlooked.[39] Sanford assumes the role of a cunning jester who uses every available opportunity to condemn American hypocrisy and "stick it to the man."

Behind the scenes, Foxx was vocal and adamant about his preference for a robust Black presence in the show's writer's room. As the star, he petitioned NBC executives to hire Mooney and Pryor as staff writers on the series. Despite their lack of television writing credits, they landed the gig. Given Pryor's pre-Berkeley cynicism about entrenched industry racism, one might assume they would have anticipated the challenges they faced within the confines of network television production. However, the reality proved more daunting.

Bolstered by the public backing of producers Lear, Yorkin, *and* Foxx, Mooney and Pryor entered the writer's room with a sense of assurance. But their optimism quickly faded. Some NBC executives viewed the duo's inclusion on the series as a token gesture. This tension manifested not only in pushback against their creative ideas but in the general sense of alienation they endured among the predominantly white writing team. Mooney, in particular, faced criticism from the show's white writers, who regularly undermined and rebuffed his creative ideas.[40] His scripts for *Sanford and Son* were often dismissed or labeled as "too angry."[41] Yet James Cone offers a different perspective, suggesting that "anger and humor are like the left and right arm. They complement each other. Anger empowers the poor to declare their uncompromising opposition to oppression, and humor prevents them from being consumed by their fury."[42] Mooney and Pryor's repertoire embraces anger, rooted in the rituals of Black resistance humor, a deliberately radical tradition aimed at a reclamation of selfhood, a defiant shout for recognition in the face of erasure. Their script ideas for *Sanford and Son* channel the unrest in the Black world, crushed under the weight of the American racial condition. Mooney and Pryor's intent to incite revolutionary laughter on the show would not be fully realized; however, their work on the sitcom foreshadowed the development of a resistant comedic style—one that would be perfected decades later by the Black Pack.

Although Mooney and Pryor were longtime friends of Foxx, the star of the series, the duo's experiences as writers on the program accentuate the limitations placed on Black storytelling and the obstinate racial barriers within the industry's power hierarchy. Still, the duo persisted, eventually cowriting two memorable episodes for *Sanford and Son*'s season two: "The Dowry," which aired September 29, 1972, and "Sanford and Son and Sister Makes Three," which followed on December 1, 1972. Shortly after completing the second episode, Pryor resigned from the series. Mooney later followed suit, although Foxx would bring him back to pen one final episode for season three: "Fred Sanford, Legal Eagle," which aired January 11, 1974.[43] In Mooney's swan song, he spins a hilarious narrative where Fred's son, Lamont, grapples with frustration after receiving an unjust traffic citation from a white police officer. Throughout the episode, Mooney adeptly navigates the fraught terrain of racial politics and the historical trauma surrounding Black encounters with law enforcement. The dialogue in the episode demonstrates Mooney's provocative comedic approach:

> FRED (TO LAMONT): If you had the green light, you can't get a ticket.
> LAMONT: You can if the light is green and you're Black and the cop is white.
> FRED: You got to fight it.
> LAMONT: Don't be ridiculous. You can't fight a traffic ticket.
> FRED: I'm not ridiculous, you are. You get a ticket from a white cop in a blue uniform in a Black neighborhood. It makes you so mad that you're seeing red. But you ain't going to fight it because you're too yellow. Now what are you? A man or a box of crayons?[44]

In this sequence, Mooney provides a lens to examine racial profiling during police encounters and the ever-present anxiety such moments conjure in the Black social psyche. Fred's admonition of Lamont reveals a contradiction understood by many Black citizens, a truth one might discuss behind closed doors in the privacy of Black communities. Yet Mooney makes the conversation public, bringing it to the forefront of the episode. He evokes revolutionary laughter by compelling audiences to confront the legitimacy of racialized policing practices.

After leaving *Sanford and Son*, Pryor's career gained momentum in Hollywood. His comedic voice was now thoroughly radicalized, having undergone a yearlong transformation. He toured extensively and released a series of critically acclaimed stand-up albums. A significant breakthrough arrived with his casting as "Piano Man" in the motion picture *Lady Sings the Blues* (1972). Starring Diana Ross as the troubled chanteuse Billie Holiday, the film garnered five Academy Award nominations, and Pryor's nuanced performance was met with praise. He further showcased his versatility by winning an Emmy Award as a writer for his work on the three-episode CBS comedy special *Lily* (1973) and delivering a notable performance as "Slim" in the Blaxploitation film *The Mack* (1973). Pryor capped off a remarkable year by hosting the Golden Globe–nominated concert film *Wattstax* (1973). Filmed at the Los Angeles Memorial Coliseum, the documentary offers an inside perspective on the collaborative effort between Stax Records and organizers of the Watts Summer Festival, commemorating the anniversary of the Watts Rebellion of 1965. Juxtaposed against the psychedelic atmosphere of the Woodstock music festival, *Wattstax* marked a decidedly soulful counterpoint, celebrating Black power. Al Bell, the president of Stax Records, spearheaded the festival as a benefit concert designed to celebrate and empower Black communities through music and solidarity. The concert featured iconic performances from recording artists like Isaac Hayes, the Staple Singers, and the Bar-Kays, while speeches like Jesse Jackson's stirring invocation of "I Am Somebody" served as a rallying cry for Black pride and unity. Throughout the *Wattstax* film, Pryor's on-screen commentary is both hilarious and incisive, drawing attention to American social issues such as the crippling epidemic of police violence plaguing Black communities:

> *California is a weird state. They have laws for pedestrians, but they don't have laws for people at night when cops accidentally shoot people. They accidentally shoot more niggas out here than anywhere in the world! Every night we pick up the paper—a nigga accidentally shot in the ass! How do you accidentally shoot a nigga six times in the chest?* [white voice imitation] *"Well, my gun just fell and went crazy."*[45]

Pryor's well-placed barbs land perfectly like stiff jabs of social criticism. He evokes revolutionary laughter by eviscerating the enduring racial biases embedded in American policing practices, a critique that, unfortunately, remains painfully relevant today. The film, with its focus on Black music, social justice, and resilience, bears a thematic resemblance to the Academy Award–winning *Summer of Soul* (2021), a documentary highlighting rediscovered footage of the Harlem Cultural Festival in 1969. The success of *Wattstax* underscored the economic potential of Black entertainment and its capacity to challenge and reshape cultural narratives.

In 1974, Pryor cowrote the screenplay for the western satire *Blazing Saddles* with Mel Brooks and gave a humorous cameo as "Sharp Eye Washington" in the caper comedy *Uptown Saturday Night*, opposite Sidney Poitier and Bill Cosby. Pryor's stand-up career also flourished, with his comedy albums selling millions of units, earning him three Grammy Award wins between 1975 and 1977. While he was publicly hailed as a comedic genius, behind the curtain, Paul Mooney continued to play a significant role in shaping Pryor's material. Reflecting on their partnership, Mooney wrote, "I think: this thing we have, this Batman-and-Robin thing, can somehow turn into something that means money and good times for both of us. I toss Richard lines. He puts them out to the audience. The audience flings money at him. Richard throws money at me."[46] It was a match made in comedy heaven. Pryor's and Mooney's symbiotic collaboration mirrored the partnership between jazz legends Duke Ellington and Billy Strayhorn. Their musical partnership spanned nearly three decades, with Ellington calling Strayhorn "my right arm, my left arm, all the eyes in the back of my head, my brainwaves in his head, and his in mine."[47] However, Ellington was the person who received much of the public acclaim, while Strayhorn's role remained largely unrecognized. Comparably, Mooney's contribution to Pryor's comedy act was also essentially unacknowledged in the public eye, despite its undeniable significance.

Fascination and Terror on NBC

The 1970s ushered in a period of noteworthy success for the NBC network with a lineup of popular programs including the police procedural drama *Adam-12* (1968–1975), the variety show *Rowan & Martin's Laugh-In* (1967–1973), and *The Flip Wilson Show* (1970–1974), which became television's first successful Black sketch comedy series. Clerow "Flip" Wilson Jr., the affable star of the program, gained a crossover popularity with his nonthreatening, jocular charm. During its first seasons, *The Flip Wilson Show* was the second most-watched television series in America.[48] However, Wilson's sketches often leaned heavily on rearguard "ethnic humor," marked by exaggerated antics and racial tropes that Donald Bogle describes as "a collection of repackaged stereotypes that belonged to another era."[49] Wilson's comedy does not engage the incisive edge characteristic of Black resistance humor that calls into question the nation's prevailing power dynamics. Instead, the show's comedy navigated racial politics with a degree of ambiguity, a predictable move that has historically served as the driving force in a Black comedian's ability to garner mainstream success.[50]

Following the cancellation of *The Flip Wilson Show* after four seasons, NBC's prime-time ratings spiraled into a precipitous decline.[51] By the mid-1970s, under the leadership of newly appointed president Herb Schlosser, the network endeavored to capture the attention of younger viewers by rolling out a slew of made-for-TV movies, miniseries, and specials. In earlier decades, as William Boddy points out, "NBC executive Pat Weaver had emphasized specials as an exclusive television form and as a signature aesthetic at NBC [and] specials became a weapon used to wrest control of programming away from single-advertiser sponsorship."[52] However, Schlosser's attempts to revive this industrial model faltered in his bid to engage the network's coveted eighteen- to thirty-four-year-old demographic, resulting in economic struggles for NBC and a frantic search for new programming solutions.[53] Many of the new series launched in 1975 were swiftly canceled in the face of established competition. The network's lone survivor of the 1975 season was the fledgling late night sketch comedy program *NBC's Saturday Night* (later renamed *Saturday Night Live*).[54] When Lorne Michaels, the show's creator, recognized the buzz around Richard Pryor's comedy, he approached him with an offer to guest host an episode. Pryor, however, hit Michaels with a long list of demands, chief among them the appointment of Paul Mooney as his personal comedy writer. Michaels, keenly aware of what Pryor's involvement would mean for the show's ratings, flew Mooney to Miami for an interview with NBC executives. After subjecting Mooney to hours of questions, NBC reluctantly acceded to Pryor's terms and agreed to hire Mooney. However, during the weeklong production process, Pryor was quite vocal about his discontent with Mooney's treatment during negotiations.[55] Despite the rift, the network launched a robust marketing campaign, heralding Pryor, America's preeminent comedian, as the guest host of *NBC's Saturday Night*, generating considerable anticipation and excitement around the struggling program.

The Pryor and Mooney episode aired on December 13, 1975, featuring the soulful singer and poet Gil Scott-Heron as the musical guest, whom Pryor personally requested appear on the show. Pryor's stint as host marks a watershed moment in television history. The episode's most iconic segment, the "Word Association" sketch penned by Mooney, stands as a landmark in American comedy. The sketch offers a hilarious and politically Black critique of the nation's racial pathology. In this breakout scene, Chevy Chase, a white *SNL* cast member, assumes the role of a human resources worker conducting an interview with Pryor for a position as a janitor. The meeting takes a sharp turn when the interviewer initiates a word association exercise to gauge the applicant's psychological fitness for the custodial role. Through Mooney's astute writing and Pryor's masterful performance, the sketch unfolds as a potent demonstration of their radical comedic ethos:

CHASE: White.
PRYOR: Black.
CHASE: Bean.
PRYOR: Pod.
CHASE: Negro.
PRYOR: Whitey.
CHASE: Tar baby.
PRYOR [*miffed*]: What did you say?
CHASE: Tar baby.
PRYOR: Ofay.
CHASE: Colored.
PRYOR [*bringing it*]: Redneck!
CHASE: Jungle bunny.
PRYOR: Peckerwood!
CHASE: Burrhead!
PRYOR: Cracker!
CHASE: Spearchucker.
PRYOR: White trash!
CHASE: Jungle bunny!
PRYOR: Honky!
CHASE: Spade!
PRYOR: Honky! Honky!
CHASE: Nigger.
PRYOR: Dead honky![56]

FIG. 1.1. Chevy Chase and Richard Pryor in "Word Association," *Saturday Night Live*, 1975.

With Pryor's performative prowess and Mooney's politically Black writing skills, they challenged NBC censors and audiences to confront the pervasive racial anxieties entrenched in the American workplace. Mooney and Pryor's razor-sharp comedic edge destabilizes the racial status quo, using humor as an instrument to express the stifling frustrations faced by many Black Americans subjected to racist microaggressions in the workplace. Pryor's stellar act as guest host of *NBC's Saturday Night* played a pivotal role in elevating the show to its status as a cultural phenomenon.

Behind the scenes, the production process was the source of a weeklong tension between Pryor, Mooney, and the network. Pryor's well-documented mercurial language and behavior left NBC apprehensive about potential repercussions with advertisers if he were to improvise or deviate from the script during the live broadcast. So the network opted to prerecord the episode to mitigate the risk. Upon learning the decision, Pryor threatened to abandon the show unless it aired live, as was customary for previous guest hosts, including the outspoken white comic George Carlin. Following heated debates between Mooney, Pryor, and NBC executives, the network relented and agreed to broadcast the episode live. Nonetheless, shortly after the program aired, Michaels informed Pryor and Mooney that network brass forced him to incorporate a five-second delay on the show—marking the first tape-delayed broadcast in U.S. television history. Despite this censorship and NBC's apparent duplicity, the episode achieved what Michaels and the network had hoped: it was a ratings coup.

Over the ensuing months, Pryor enjoyed a string of impressive film roles. Fresh off his inaugural Grammy win for Best Comedy Album, Pryor starred in three movies that resonated deeply with audiences and cemented his status as a cultural icon. First, *Bingo Long and the Traveling All-Star Kings* (1976) was a commercial hit produced by Berry Gordy's Motown Productions for Universal Pictures. This all-Black sports comedy was inspired by the history of Negro League baseball and featured Pryor alongside luminaries like James Earl Jones and Billy Dee Williams. Despite a $9 million budget, the film grossed an impressive $33 million at the box office. Pryor's success continued with the interracial buddy comedy *Silver Streak* (1976), costarring Gene Wilder. The 20th Century Fox production proved even more popular, exceeding $51 million in box office revenue. The film's positive reception led to a series of collaborations between Pryor and Wilder: *Stir Crazy* (1980), *See No Evil, Hear No Evil* (1989), and *Another You* (1991). Finally, Pryor showcased his comedic chops with a memorable cameo as "Daddy Rich," a slick, money-hungry televangelist who thrives at the intersection of half preacher and half pimp in the disco soul slacker film *Car Wash* (1976). These back-to-back successes left an indelible mark on audiences and secured Pryor's position at the forefront of American popular culture.[57] Less than a decade removed from his self-imposed exile in Berkeley, Pryor achieved his ambition: he was undeniably America's top comedian. *Time* magazine declared him the "new Black superstar."[58] Hollywood further validated his A-list status with an invitation to cohost the forty-ninth Academy Awards ceremony along with film icons Jane Fonda, Ellen Burstyn, and Warren Beatty.

The Oscar ceremony aired on March 28, 1977, and Pryor's performance was well received. Although his opening monologue was considerably mild, he subtly landed a few resistant jabs at the establishment: "I am here tonight to explain why Black people will never be nominated for anything. This show is going out to 75 million people. None of them are Black. We don't even know how to vote. There's 3,349 people in the voting thing and only two Black people—Sidney Poitier and Harry Belafonte."[59] Here, Pryor calls out the persistent issue of racial exclusion at the Oscars, a long-standing concern that continues to trouble the Academy today. His commentary, delivered in a year with no Black nominees, served as a pointed reminder of the institution's historical shortcomings in recognizing Black performers. Pryor's subtle barbs were a precursor to Eddie Murphy's public expression of a similar critique delivered at the Oscar ceremony eleven years later. This enduring argument continues to spark ongoing discussions about racial disparity in the Academy, exemplified by the viral hashtag #OscarsSoWhite.

The Rise and Fall of *The Richard Pryor Show*

As NBC's ratings continued to wane, the network once again sought to capitalize on Pryor's popularity by offering him his own television series. He declined the offer, still harboring resentment after the network censored his episode of *Saturday Night Live*. Undeterred by his initial refusal, NBC persisted. After extended negotiations, the parties reached an agreement for Pryor to host one comedy special for the network. The deal included language stipulating that Pryor would retain creative control over the program's content. The resulting production became *The Richard Pryor Special?* The episode was cowritten with Mooney, who was excited by the opportunity.

Airing on May 5, 1977, the special showcased Pryor's comedic brilliance but also set a new standard, establishing a resistant ideological blueprint for Black sketch comedy. The program blended insightful politically Black satire with short dramatic vignettes and captivating musical performances, offering a multifaceted exploration of Black culture. This combination made Mooney and Pryor's special not only funny but simultaneously thoughtful and provocative. The inclusion of special guest appearances further elevated the appeal of the special. For instance, *Saturday Night Live* star John Belushi's presence on the special provided a bridge between Pryor's comedic voice and the "not ready for prime-time players," while activist-poet Maya Angelou enriched the program's artistic tapestry with a captivating dramatic sequence that offered a nuanced look at the interiority of Black working-class women. The program also featured a musical rendering of Stevie Wonder's insightful tune "Black Man," a song with lyrics that celebrate the often-overlooked contributions of Black people in America, further enunciating the special's overarching message of unity and Black pride.

The Richard Pryor Special? was a ratings smash, fueling NBC's desire for a new weekly series. Thus, the network reignited its quest for Pryor. He turned down their offers, leery of the high-stress demands that accompany producing, writing, and starring in a weekly television program. But the more Pryor refused, the more aggressively NBC pursued, culminating in the network hiring an airplane to fly over his San Fernando Valley home with a floating banner that read, "Surrender, Richard," a vivid symbol of their determination.[60] When NBC offered Pryor a mind-numbing $2 million for ten episodes, the parties began negotiations. Pryor's team demanded two key stipulations: the comedian would retain creative control over the show's content, and the program would air in the coveted 9 p.m. timeslot in all major markets. The network agreed and finalized the deal. Mooney and Pryor began crafting *The Richard Pryor Show*, approaching the new series as their opportunity to champion a culturally affirming, politically Black artistic agenda. Mooney, in addition to his roles as writer and actor, assumed the role of casting director, demonstrating his keen eye for comedic talent. He scouted comics at the Laugh Factory, the Improv, and the Comedy Store, ultimately yielding a stellar lineup of future stars, including Robin Williams, Marsha Warfield, Tim Reid, John Witherspoon, Sandra Bernhard, Glenn Turman, and Brad Garrett. The anticipation surrounding the series was palpable. An *Ebony* magazine article captured the buzz, declaring it was "in many ways, the highlight of the new television season, the *pièce de résistance* among the mediocre, look-alike situation comedies and variety shows in the 1977–1978 line up. It [meant] that, for at least one hour a week television would not be tapioca pudding, for the mere thought of *The Richard Pryor Show* on NBC-TV prompted excitement."[61] Mooney and Pryor's vision for the series was simple: combine provocative comedy with the hippest musical performances and artistic interludes, creating space to elevate Black voices and perspectives within the televisual landscape.

The trouble between Pryor and NBC began with a breach of contract. In a unilateral move, the network, without advanced notice, rescheduled *The Richard Pryor Show* to broadcast at 7 p.m., violating their agreed-upon 9 p.m. airtime. This move thrust the series into competition during television's legally mandated "family viewing hour." The network's actions were a ploy aimed at leveraging Pryor's superstar status to counterprogram and challenge the dominance of hit ABC sitcoms *Happy Days* and *Laverne & Shirley*. However, the earlier time slot necessitated that Pryor and Mooney dilute the show's vision for edgy comedic material to comply with stricter regulatory guidelines that governed prime-time broadcasts. NBC executives hoped that scheduling Pryor earlier would siphon younger viewers away from ABC. But their power play backfired and spectacularly undermined *The Richard Pryor Show*'s prospects for success before it aired a single episode.

More tension arose after filming the pilot. When NBC censors reviewed the episode, they deemed Pryor's one-minute opening monologue unsuitable to air during the family viewing hour. The segment unfolds with a close-up of Pryor's face, addressing the studio audience, defiantly insisting that he refuses to compromise his artistic integrity to placate television executives. As the camera widens to a full-body shot, Pryor appears onstage, bare-chested, completely nude, and ostensibly castrated. This provocative special-effects gag was a politically charged commentary on the industry's repression of Black voices, conjuring unsettling imagery reminiscent of Billie Holiday's "strange fruit" and the mutilation of Black male bodies under the specter of white terrorism. When NBC demanded Pryor reshoot the opening, he staunchly refused. Thus, instead of airing the original opening monologue, the network opted to broadcast one minute of "dead air" before transitioning to the show's opening title sequence.

The fallout from the monologue controversy led to several NBC affiliates in Michigan, North Carolina, Massachusetts, and Pennsylvania pulling the show from their lineups. Pryor was infuriated by both the scheduling change and artistic censorship. He threatened to withdraw from the show altogether. As news spread, the network attempted to do damage control and released a public statement, downplaying the conflict and portraying Pryor favorably. The network asserted, "NBC Broadcast Standards made the judgment that one sketch was inappropriate, and a brief edit was made. We think the program is terrific and that Richard Pryor is one of America's most innovative and talented performers."[62] Nevertheless, Pryor, feeling betrayed, demanded a renegotiated contract. Under the reworked deal, he reduced his commitment to "four episodes instead of ten, with Pryor holding the option to do more [episodes] if he wished, plus two or three specials a year."[63] Although they agreed to these concessions, NBC's heavy-handed tactics ultimately locked *The Richard Pryor Show* in a ratings deathmatch with *Laverne & Shirley* and *Happy Days*, the two highest-rated sitcoms on television. Under the weight of these constraints, Pryor's series struggled to find its audience.

Despite facing persistent battles with NBC censors, Mooney and Pryor remained steadfast in their determination to push the boundaries of comedic expression; they had an axe to grind. Among Mooney's most bitingly satirical sketches were "40th President" and "Egypt 1909," both of which highlight Mooney's prowess for writing radical humor that cuts to the core of social issues. In "40th President," Pryor plays the newly elected first Black U.S. president, a role he envisioned three decades before the arrival of Barack Obama. Although the concept of a Black president was a particularly outlandish notion in the conservative period of the Nixon era, the idea had previously been artistically explored across various genres, including the short musical comedy *Rufus Jones for President* (1933), featuring Ethel Waters and a seven-year-old Sammy Davis Jr. In addition, *Babes on Broadway* (1943), which included Judy Garland's racist blackface minstrel performance, and literary works like Irving Wallace's *The Man* (1964) and Philip K. Dick's science-fiction novel *The Crack in Space* (1966) each engage the trope of the first Black president.

In Mooney's jocular sketch, Pryor assumes the role of president and navigates a news conference, slyly code-switching as he fields questions from the press corp. He acknowledges a reporter from *Ebony* magazine (Tim Reid), who greets the president with the Arabic salutation "Assalamualaikum, my brother," a nod to Malcolm X and the Nation of Islam. Pryor coolly responds, "Wa Alaikum as-salaam." When another reporter (Marsha Warfield) identifies herself as a journalist for *Jet* magazine, Pryor salutes her respectfully. She inquires,

> REPORTER: On your list of candidates for director of the FBI, are you including the name of Huey Newton?
>
> PRESIDENT: Yes, I figure that Huey Newton is best qualified. He knows the ins-and-outs of the FBI if anybody knows. I believe he would be an excellent director.[64]

Mooney's writing in this segment expresses insurgent undertones. The president's endorsement of Newton's candidacy demonstrates a decidedly oppositional Black political consciousness, a knowing wink to Black audiences familiar with the FBI's nefarious tactics and the clandestine COINTELPRO operations that targeted progressive Black leadership and systematically destroyed the Black Panther Party for Self-Defense. In her insightful book *Laughing Mad*, Bambi Haggins argues that "the significance of the [Newton] reference was quite possibly lost on a mainstream audience, who knew Newton only from either the anti-Panther rhetoric in mainstream media or the revolutionary prowess that had inspired the 'Free Huey' campaign in the late sixties."[65] Mooney and Pryor use the sketch to employ the satirization of race, symbolically reversing the dynamics of power, revealing subtle nuances of the Black world that lie "behind the public face of stereotype and limited imagination."[66] The writing and performance in this sketch smuggle in a critique of American social realities, offering subversive pleasure for Black viewers.

In "Egypt 1909," Mooney and Pryor achieve perhaps the most pointed and irreverently funny sketch of the series. Through deep referential ironies, the sketch spins an ironic retelling of human history, disrupting narratives of white superiority. The scene opens with Robin Williams, Pryor, and a team of white archaeologists who have just discovered an ancient Egyptian pyramid. Inside the pyramid's tomb, Pryor serendipitously stumbles upon the "Book of Life." As he begins to read the book's contents aloud, its revelations prove quite remarkable:

> PRYOR: In the beginning, when man arrived on Earth, the Black gods did leave the spacecraft, and they walked and they named the beasts of the sea and the animals of the land, and man in his Blackness did walk the earth. They discovered medicine, and they discovered time.... These were all Black people! Wait a minute, there ain't nothing in here about whitey—this is ours, jack! Wait 'til the brothers hear this! I'm gonna get this book outta here, baby! We can change the history. Civilization will be changed.[67]

With the true (Black) origins of ancient civilization threatened to be exposed, the white archaeological team deliberately abandons Pryor. They lock him inside the tomb along with the "Book of Life" and summon bulldozers to the site to destroy the evidence, laughing to themselves, "There's nothing to see here." What Mooney and Pryor demonstrate in this sketch is a radical counternarrative to dominant historical assumptions regarding the origin of civilization, deconstructing the illusions of whiteness. The "Book of Life" details the ancient Black civilizations that inhabited the earth and the existence of Black thinkers who invented the sciences and used advanced technologies millennia before the advent of Western imperialism. Pryor's assertive portrayal and Mooney's incisive script align with an engagement of Afrofuturism, a literary, cultural, and aesthetic tradition that combines science-fiction, magic realism, and Afro-centered ideologies. Afrofuturism also interrogates and reconfigures past events as a rejection of dominant narratives and values while pointing toward a liberated Black futurity.

The Afrofuturist impulses of "Egypt 1909" express a transgressive politics against the grain of Western society's racially biased history, providing audiences with a resistant Black origin story. By employing irony and parody, the sketch elicits revolutionary laughter rooted in the experience and social formations of the viewer. Mooney and Pryor use Black resistance humor to express anger with the nightmare realities of Black social circumstances. "Egypt 1909" questions white hegemony, dismantling assumptions of racial superiority while highlighting the historical erasure of Black innovation and achievement. Their comedic subversion empowers Black viewers by reclaiming a hidden past and exposing the mechanisms that perpetuate the idea of normative whiteness. Mooney and Pryor's radical retelling of history, while a major thorn in the side of the network, set forth the stylistic and ideological blueprint that was integral to the future success of the Black Pack.

Through their exercise of creative control over the show's comedic material, Mooney and Pryor persistently reimagined dominant narratives. However, a significant ideological disconnect persisted between the two comedians and NBC executives. The network served a function beyond mere profit generation and audience engagement; it also served as the cultural authority charged with preserving and maintaining the prevailing social order. But Mooney and Pryor's provocative use of politically Black satire ran counter to the network's vision. The comedic duo encouraged active, critical engagement and challenged audiences to confront the American racial realities often obscured in popular culture. NBC's bottom-line pursuit of control, predictability, and established formulas ultimately thwarted its own interests in making *The Richard Pryor Show* a breakout success. While seeking to capitalize on Pryor's brand-name popularity, the network desired to temper the show's political edge, aiming for a more sanitized comedic

FIG. 1.2. Richard Pryor and Robin Williams (right) in "Egypt 1909," *The Richard Pryor Show*, 1977.

approach that was "safe" like Flip Wilson. This incongruity encapsulated the program's ideological battleground between commercial imperatives and cultural disruption.

The aura of fascination and terror that initially attracted NBC to Pryor—his outrageous talent and rebellious comedy—became the very obstacle preventing their successful collaboration. The network, reliant on high ratings for advertising revenue, sought to exert aggressive control over *The Richard Pryor Show*'s production of humor. Mooney and Pryor, on the other hand, envisioned the series as a platform to promote Black solidarity and cultural critique. Their aim was to infuse mainstream television with an oppositional Black vocality. But *The Richard Pryor Show* ultimately fell victim to Hollywood's propensity for neutralizing dissenting voices. Despite the critical acclaim of *The Richard Pryor Special?* and considerable media buzz, *The Richard Pryor Show* consistently underperformed in the ratings.

The program's failure, however, is largely attributed to the network's unilateral scheduling changes, which consigned the series to a doomed timeslot, pitted against formidable top-rated sitcoms. In essence, NBC's realization that Mooney and Pryor's entropic comedy was not "safe" sealed the fate of the television venture. *The Richard Pryor Show* ended after airing only four episodes. Mooney and Pryor's work on the program, despite its woefully short run, was widely influential, particularly for their satirical treatment of race that was "sometimes ironic, evasive, and oblique, sometimes playful and purely entertaining, and sometimes aggressively militant."[68] In the end, the network paid Pryor his full $2 million salary to walk away from the program. He later offered candid insights in an exclusive interview with *Ebony* magazine, shedding light on the show's behind-the-scenes dynamics and the challenges he encountered:

> The problem with the censors is they don't want people to communicate. I think it's on purpose and very political. . . . I think after [NBC] got me they didn't want me when they realized I wasn't going for that okie doke pressure thing. They wanted . . . the same old stuff. I said "No, I don't work that way." [The comedy] should be from my point of view of Black awareness and where I come from and what I see. They couldn't see that. One week of truth on TV could just straighten out everything. One hundred and twenty-seven million people watch television every night; that's why they use it to sell stuff. They've misused it a long time so now it's just a business, that's all. They're not going to write shows about how to revolutionize America. The top-rated shows are for retarded people.[69]

And so it goes: within the panoptical chambers of network television, predictably, voices as bold and rebellious as Pryor's and Mooney's proved incompatible with the paranoid era of post-Watergate America.

The Emergence of the Black Pack

Following the cancellation of *The Richard Pryor Show*, Paul Mooney landed supporting roles in two feature films. He portrayed Inspector Caine in the Richard Pryor vehicle *Which Way Is Up?* (1977) and the legendary crooner Sam Cooke in the music-driven biopic *The Buddy Holly Story* (1978). The following year, Mooney and Pryor struck gold again with the resounding success of the stand-up film *Richard Pryor: Live in Concert* (1979), which emerged as the most profitable film in the country, raking in $15.8 million on a budget of $300,000.[70] The duo's collaborative efforts continued with two additional stand-up concert films, *Richard Pryor: Live on the Sunset Strip* (1982) and *Richard Pryor: Here and Now* (1983). After Pryor's highly publicized near-death experience when he lit himself on fire during a 1980 drug-fueled frenzy, Mooney played a pivotal role in persuading him to repair his public image.

When Pryor reemerged from this devastating tragedy, the duo collaborated on the short-lived children's series *Pryor's Place* (1984–1985), for which Mooney served as a writer. The Saturday-morning program, set in an inner city environment, featured Pryor interacting with a cast of children and puppet characters that mirrored the format of established shows like *Sesame Street* (1970–). Mooney and Pryor's last significant collaboration came on Pryor's lone directorial effort, *Jo-Jo Dancer, Your Life Is Calling* (1986). This semiautobiographical film, based on Pryor's near-death experience, was cowritten by Mooney, Pryor, and Rocco Urbisci. The movie was produced as part of a massive four-picture $40 million deal with Columbia Pictures under Pryor's newly formed production company, Indigo Films. However, by the mid-1980s, Pryor was unfortunately diagnosed with multiple sclerosis. Although he kept his condition private, the disease took a heavy toll. At the same time, the industry was undergoing rapid transformations, witnessing the emergence of a new crop of young, scrappy comedians influenced by Pryor's and Mooney's illustrious artistic output.

Leading the charge was comic phenom Eddie Murphy, fresh off a string of smash-hit movies. However, Mooney and Murphy, both future leaders of the Black Pack, were not immediately compatible. Murphy, prior to his rise to fame, had encountered Mooney on the New York comedy scene and harbored resentment toward him. He later confessed, "I used to hate [Paul Mooney]. I was always seeing [him] with stars, and I got mad."[71] Another early encounter between them, on the set of Pryor's film *Brewster's Millions* (1985), was fraught with tension. Mooney confronted Murphy about the young comic allegedly appropriating elements of Mooney's stand-up routine—a major faux pas in the comedy world.[72] Pryor intervened, facilitating dialogue between the two comics and helping them foster mutual respect. Ironically, Mooney later mediated a similar conflict between Murphy and a rising comedian, Keenen Ivory Wayans, a future member of the Black Pack. Murphy threatened legal action against Wayans, who contemplated a countersuit. Recognizing the harmful implications of their discord, Mooney intervened, admonishing them, "Don't do it. It's Black-on-Black crime, brothers. Black people fighting, you know white people love the shit out of that."[73] Mooney later facilitated a reconciliation between Wayans and Murphy, who ultimately became close friends and collaborators.

In a bold cultural move, Murphy hired Mooney as the opening act for his 1987 comedy tour, *Eddie Murphy: Raw*. His strategy was a departure from convention, as opening acts were typically reserved for musical performances, which underscores Murphy's respect for Mooney's humor. Comedian Dave Chappelle later reflected on the significance of this decision, stating, "The *Eddie Murphy: Raw* tour in the 1980s was the hottest ticket in town. When fans came in wanting to see Eddie Murphy, for the first half of the show, they got Paul Mooney."[74] Murphy explained the strategic value of his choice: "When you have Paul Mooney in front of you, you have to be on the top of your game when you come out to perform."[75] The social energy generated by Murphy, Mooney, Wayans, and other emerging Black comics began reverberating in Hollywood. In March 1987, Robert Townsend and Keenen Ivory Wayans struck cinematic gold with the breakout film *Hollywood Shuffle*, a satirical critique of the entertainment industry's racist representational politics. The film stars Townsend and Wayans, who cowrote the screenplay, and features a hilarious cameo from Mooney as the president of the NAACP's Hollywood branch. That summer the release of *Beverly Hills Cop II* (1987) further solidified Murphy as a massive box office draw. For his upcoming concert film, *Eddie Murphy: Raw*, Murphy hired Townsend to direct the project and Wayans to cowrite the movie's opening sketch, cementing their spirit of creative collaboration.

Boosted by Murphy's megawatt star power, the Black Pack made its grand entrance onto the cultural stage. At a publicity event, Murphy announced the formation of his comic band of brothers, playfully dubbed "the Black Pack" by Mooney, who emerged as the crew's ideological architect. The group, comprising Murphy, Mooney, Townsend, Wayans, and Arsenio Hall, united with shared culturally rebellious comedic sensibilities. Through spirited brainstorming sessions and collaborative efforts, their artistic output captivated the nation. The Black Pack's cultural productions, infused with social commentary and an unapologetically political edge, achieved a level of mainstream success that had eluded Pryor and Mooney a decade earlier. The high-powered seven-year peak of the Black Pack cycle was marked by a sophisticated engagement with the rituals of Black resistance humor, defiantly confronting Hollywood's historical parade of caricatured comic "darkies" on-screen.

Following Wayans's directing debut, *I'm Gonna Git You Sucka* (1988), he created *In Living Color* for the nascent Fox Broadcasting Company. He quickly enlisted Mooney's talents as a writer for the series. Mooney's arrival sent ripples of anticipation and trepidation through the Fox network. As original cast member T'Keyah "Crystal" Keymàh recalls, "When word got out that Paul Mooney was coming to the show, there was a panic among the white writers."[76] But Wayans understood the experience and immense value that Mooney would add to the series. Mooney spent three seasons writing for *In Living Color*, injecting the poetics of Black resistance humor into his sketches. He created a host of iconic characters, among them the anti-Black brothers "Tom and Tom," portrayed by Keenen Ivory Wayans and his brother Damon, as well as the confrontational, militant jester "Homey D. Clown."[77] The "Tom and Tom" characters were phenotypically Black yet ideologically aligned with whiteness, serving as a satirical critique of the ways systemic oppression has been internalized and perpetuated by some Black Americans.

Mooney's provocative creation, the truculent Homey D. Clown (portrayed by Damon Wayans), rose as a standout character on *In Living Color*, capturing the audience's imagination and becoming a cultural phenomenon. Homey satirized the quaint middle-class archetype of the cheerful, friendly clown. In an era dominated by the pervasive McDonald's fast-food chain with its famous "Happy Meals" for children, Homey stood in stark contrast to the restaurant's wholesome mascot clown Ronald McDonald. Homey was the *anti*–Ronald McDonald. His acerbic jokes shattered the veneer of childhood innocence with a no-holds-barred commentary on America's anti-Black ideologies. With Mooney's incisive wit, Homey fearlessly mocked the establishment, condemning attempts to constrain Black Americans and perpetuate systemic injustices or, as Homey put it, "to hold me down and structure the society so Homey ends up in jail."[78] Mooney's combative clown also launched the defiant catchphrase "Homey don't play that" into the lexicon of 1990s popular culture. Even Pryor was a fan of *In Living Color*. He and Mooney occasionally viewed the program together at Pryor's home, basking in the fruits of their labor. Reflecting on one such instance, Mooney wrote in his memoir *Black Is the New White*, "It feels as though our pigeons are coming home to roost. The momentum we started on *The Richard Pryor Show* is playing out with Eddie Murphy, the Wayanses, and other comics."[79] Pryor agreed—their labor had not been in vain. Their collective efforts and comedic legacy continued to reverberate, shaping the landscape of American humor.

FIG. 1.3. Paul Mooney's Homey D. Clown (Damon Wayans), *In Living Color*, 1990.

In the spring of 1992, a wave of intense social unrest swept the nation in the wake of the acquittal of four white Los Angeles Police Department officers who viciously assaulted Rodney King, an unarmed Black motorist. This brazen act of police violence, captured on videotape for the world to see, ignited a firestorm of outrage when the not-guilty verdict was announced. The incontrovertible visual evidence apparently was insufficient to secure justice for Mr. King and, by extension, Black America. Once again, the nation was confronted by the harrowing reality of entrenched racist systems, which ravage and dehumanize Black lives. The following year, Mooney released his very first solo comedy album, aptly titled *Race* (1993). On the album, Mooney unleashes new fiery comedic material, fearlessly attacking the pernicious racial ghosts and social maladies infecting the country:

> *Because I'm recording, I want to say some good things about white people. Because sometimes white people freak out when they see me—[*white voice imitation*]—"He hates us! He doesn't like us!" I don't hate you—I hate your parents for having you.*[80]

With uncompromising wit and atomic humor, Mooney rips decorum to shreds and challenges the invisible structures of whiteness and systemic racism that contain and suppress Black cultural and political agency:

> *I always thought of Frankenstein's monster as a Black man. All the white people are always chasing him. "Get him! Get him!" That crowd of cracker-ass villagers with torches is a lynch mob. The monster runs exactly like the caricature of a Black man running from a mob, wild-eyed, grunting like an animal. . . . The villagers are terrified of him, just like crackers are terrified of the Black man. . . . And when they catch him, he whups the villagers' ass, just like a Black man.*[81]

Mooney's rhetorical strategy eschews the limitations of respectability politics and creates "new realms in which social justice might be enacted by disrupting social expectations and demonstrating the connection between laughter and ethical beliefs."[82] The *Race* album makes whiteness visible, using comedy as a bulwark against the moral chaos that lurks beneath the surface of American society, culminating in Mooney's first solo Grammy nomination.

As the new millennium approached, Mooney's influence expanded with supporting roles in the stoner film *Half Baked* (1998), the Blaxploitation parody *Undercover Brother* (2000), and Spike Lee's trenchant examination of race and neominstrelsy, *Bamboozled* (2000). As Ed Guerrero argues, Mooney's performance in *Bamboozled* "suggests in the broader project of neo-minstrelsy, type, and stereotype are fluid, often interchangeable representations that can assume many masks, poses, and layered expressions in consumer culture."[83] By 2003, Dave Chappelle secured a production deal on the Comedy Central cable network to create a new sketch series, *Chappelle's Show*. One of Chappelle's first orders of business was to hire Mooney as both a writer and an actor. However, before committing to the project, Mooney established his unequivocal parameters, stating, "I've been in this business too long. I can't get into another bullshit situation where I have producers and executives picking apart my shit."[84] Chappelle reassured Mooney that his creative autonomy would be protected, and Mooney joined the project, bringing his combustible flare to a new generation of millennial viewers.

FIG. 1.4. Paul Mooney as Negrodamus, *Chappelle's Show*, 2004.

FIG. 1.5. "Mooney on Movies," *Chappelle's Show*, 2004.

Their collaboration resulted in yet another direct descendant of Pryor's and Mooney's visionary work on *The Richard Pryor Show*.

Chappelle's Show garnered a significant following; however, it proved to be a double-edged sword. The series courted controversy with its deployment of racial epithets and its hyperbolic and at times evasive and ambivalent treatment of American politics, race, and popular culture. Mooney's writing and performances, however, accounted for several breakthrough moments on the show, with sidesplitting appearances in sketches such as "Ask a Black Dude" and "Mooney on Movies." He also lent his talent to a socially inverted satire of the white apothecary Nostradamus, best known for his doomsday prophecies. In this sketch, Mooney portrays "Negrodamus," who fielded questions from the audience and responded with a wry and subversive twist:

> AUDIENCE MEMBER: Negrodamus, why is President Bush so sure Iraq has weapons of mass destruction?
> NEGRODAMUS: Because he has the receipt.
> AUDIENCE MEMBER: Negrodamus, why do white people love Wayne Brady?
> NEGRODAMUS: Because Wayne Brady makes Bryant Gumbel look like Malcolm X.[85]

Throughout his tenure on the show, Mooney's rebellious approach confronts racial essentialism and amplifies repressed facets of the Black social psyche, transforming anxieties into thought-provoking comedic expression. His work on the series underlines the absurdity of race in America and ironically propelled Mooney to the high point of his public acclaim in a decades-long career. However, the show's success was ephemeral. Chappelle abruptly resigned from the wildly popular series following an epiphanic moment on stage that echoed Pryor's harrowing experience at the Aladdin Hotel in Las Vegas four decades earlier.

During the cultural upheaval of the 1970s, amid widespread challenges to institutional authority, Mooney and Pryor wielded their comedic voices to confront Black representational politics head-on. Serving as the visionary architects behind *The Richard Pryor Show*, they laid the groundwork for a new wave of socially engaged comedy embodied and expanded by the Black Pack. Unsurprisingly, given the surplus repression in Hollywood, their politically Black social satire ignited a Homeric power struggle with NBC network executives, who struggled to contain the comics' resistant voices within the confines of mainstream television. Yet Mooney and Pryor used their platform as a battleground to thumb their nose at the industry's racist archive. Their comedic arsenal was rich with subversive techniques, employing parody and racial reversals among their tools of disruption. Through these rhetorical strategies, they sought to unravel the complexities embedded in American life and highlight the "tension that opens up a hidden interior into kaleidoscopic Blackness, those multifaceted, private recesses of Black identity and selfhood that are often unknown to or overlooked by those who would simplify Blackness to render it consumable and commodifiable."[86] At its core, *The Richard Pryor Show* espouses a comedic ideology grounded in social criticism that ridicules the political dynamics of power in a post–civil rights America.

Mooney's substantial and enduring body of work spans over five decades, shaping the contours of modern comedy. His profound impact on the career trajectories and success of performers like Pryor, the Black Pack, and Chappelle undeniably secures his place in the pantheon of the most influential comedians in American history. In his memoir, Mooney poignantly reflected on his often-overlooked contributions to the comedy world, writing, "I'm unheard-of by white people. I'm stealth for white people. I'm silent to white people. After a half-century doing comedy, I'm some sort of secret. I'm known for being unknown. Or maybe I'm unknowable. Or maybe some people just don't want to know me."[87] Or perhaps Mooney was "too *Black* for Hollywood." His blistering wit pilloried conventional boundaries. If he is, in fact, unknown as he suggests, his artistic output most certainly is not. Mooney's unapologetically Black social commentary expands the rituals of Black resistance humor, which demonstrably hindered his crossover appeal. His relentless comedic jabs pummeled whiteness and the Hollywood mechanisms that pressure Black performers to reproduce racial caricatures in exchange for money, fame, and mainstream acceptance.

For Mooney and Pryor, their evocations of revolutionary laughter offered the possibility of reclaiming Black interiority, selfhood, and agency in the face of the inescapable gargoyles of American racism. In a manner reminiscent of Dick Gregory before them, Pryor and Mooney sidestepped the debilitating double consciousness adopted by so many Black comedians. Mooney and Pryor refused to "wear the mask that grins and lies," said best by the poet Paul Laurence Dunbar.[88] The duo's contributions to nurturing the development of the Black Pack are both undeniable and immeasurable. Pryor was their hero, a revered comedic idol, the *true* "king of comedy." For Mooney, he stood as a towering figure: "Richard Pryor is the funniest man America has ever seen. (Mark Twain is runner-up. Richard is *Dark* Twain.)"[89] Mooney's and Pryor's efforts as trailblazing humorists, writers, and comedic strategists drafted the ideological blueprint that informs the Black Pack's cultural moves that exploded in the 1980s and '90s. Their inventive and visionary contributions inspired successive generations of American comics, positioning humor as a transformative language that cannot be taught, a language of energy and observation—lost and found in timeless moments, on countless stages, in front of ever-changing crowds. One might compare Mooney and Pryor to extraterrestrial voyagers, venturing into an uncharted comedic galaxy and paving the way for others to follow. They were, after all, the first Black American comedians to arrive on Planet Provocative.

2

Black Star Power

The Economics of Eddie Murphy and the Rise of the Black Pack

When describing the absurdity of navigating the racial condition facing Black people in America, the acclaimed novelist Ralph Ellison prudently observed, "Knowing the reality of a society that had the power to treat you as though you were actually inferior, but knowing within yourself that you were not, you were thrown into a position in which you were either going to develop a sense of humor or . . . die of frustration, of a sense of the irrational."[1] Ellison's words capture the necessity of comedy as a tool for survival that undergirds Black cultural expression—a dynamic no one mastered with more ease and moxie than Eddie Murphy. Rarely does an individual achieve superstardom with the alacrity that marks Murphy's rise in Hollywood. A significant contributor to his meteoric ascension to "Mr. Box Office" in the 1980s was his impeccable ability to seamlessly inject streetwise Black vernacular expressions into an idyllic white milieu. His early Hollywood success is tied to what film historian Ed Guerrero describes as the containment of the Black cinematic presence within the "protective custody" of a white male authority figure, maintaining the dominant industry's expectations regarding "acceptable" performances of Blackness.[2] Murphy's early career was, in fact, built on a string of successful interracial buddy films. Historically, the buddy film genre focuses on two white men with contrasting personalities and backgrounds who are forced to coexist and develop mutual respect. Take Neil Simon's *The Odd Couple* (1968), for example. The interracial buddy film, on the other hand, expands these tenets by demonstrating the potential for male bonding across racial divides.

The interracial buddy setup, with its deep roots in American literature, traces back to seminal works like Daniel Defoe's *Robinson Crusoe* (1719) and Mark Twain's *Adventures of Huckleberry Finn* (1884). Sidney Poitier and Tony Curtis, shackled together in Stanley Kramer's social problem film *The Defiant Ones* (1958), crystallized the motifs of the interracial buddy genre on Hollywood celluloid. The format further expanded and gained widespread appeal through the comedic pairings of Richard Pryor and Gene Wilder in *Silver Streak* (1976) and Sylvester Stallone and Carl Weathers in the boxing classic *Rocky* (1976). Fast-forward to the early 1980s and Eddie Murphy, armed with magnetic charisma, revitalized the interracial buddy genre with a string of action comedies—*48 Hrs.* (1982), *Trading Places* (1983), and *Beverly Hills Cop* (1984). These films were critically acclaimed and commercially explosive, shattering box office records. Murphy's first three movies, to the studio's delight, each debuted at number one. His rise to stardom, culminating in his designation as arguably the decade's top box office draw, mirrored the groundbreaking success of Sidney Poitier in the late 1960s. Poitier's unprecedented string of hits—*To Sir, with Love* (1967), *In the Heat of the Night* (1967), and *Guess Who's Coming to Dinner* (1967)—garnered praise and snagged the coveted number-one spot at the box office. This level of success was an Olympian feat, not simply for a Black actor, but for any performer in Hollywood. In comparison, Murphy's first five films yielded a staggering financial return of nearly $1 billion in revenue for Paramount Pictures, solidifying his status as a commercial powerhouse.[3] By 1987, having changed the face of Hollywood comedy, Murphy reached a critical juncture in his career, curiously deciding to move away from performing in predominately white-themed films to spearhead a new movement toward Black comedic modernity.

Set against a rising tide of discontent at the onset of the Reagan era, the stand-up-comic-turned-auteur Robert Townsend struck a cultural nerve and scored a sleeper hit with his independent film *Hollywood Shuffle* (1987). This irreverently hilarious satirical work laid bare the racist limitations placed on Black performers and the discriminatory practices endemic to the entertainment industry. Townsend includes a rather amusing sequence in the movie that deftly satirizes the massive impact of Murphy's success on Black actors. Murphy had become such a star that every studio in Hollywood was now searching for an Eddie Murphy "type" to profit from their own cash cow. For Townsend, it was important for Murphy to have an opportunity to watch the film. So he set up a private screening for Murphy, who instantly connected with Townsend's comedic sensibility. Soon Murphy, with his industry clout decisively intact, began aligning himself with an aspirational and subversive enterprise. He joined forces with Townsend and a cadre of rising comedic artists and developed an informal collective they called the Black Pack, aimed at undermining Hollywood's restrictive hold over the regimentation of Black voices. Leveraging his newfound cultural power and influence behind the scenes, Murphy consolidated the Black Pack (four of his close friends) in an attempt to forge a pioneering Black creative practice. This ambitious project sought to circumvent Hollywood's containment strategies, allowing Black artists to tell their own stories in their own way. The group consisted of Paul Mooney, the acerbic wit; Eddie Murphy, the superstar; Arsenio Hall, the hype man; Keenen Ivory Wayans, the wild card; and Robert Townsend, the Renaissance man. The cultural productions born from Murphy's Black Pack cycle depict the world from distinctly Black points of view, what Tina Campt describes as "a Black gaze." For Campt, a Black gaze represents a radical shift, transforming the "optics of 'looking at' to the politics of looking *with, through, and alongside another*. It is a gaze that requires effort and exertion."[4] Murphy's Black Pack films are imbued with this fresh cultural specificity, working as a politicization of the personal by addressing the aesthetic concerns of underserved Black audiences.

It was at a press conference for *Beverly Hills Cop II* that the crew's official christening occurred. Their elder statesman, the radical comedian Paul Mooney, coined the Black Pack moniker, which served as an irreverent and racially charged riposte to two prominent Hollywood groups. One was the "Rat Pack," a 1960s Las Vegas fixture known for their music, films, nightclub performances, and boozy hijinks—comprising Frank Sinatra, Dean Martin, and their lone Black "sidekick," Sammy Davis Jr.[5] The other was the "Brat Pack," a group of young white actors—Molly Ringwald, Rob Lowe, Ally Sheedy, Emilio Estevez, and others—who dominated the teen coming-of-age genre in the 1980s.[6] The Black Pack, by contrast, represented a potent force for comedic art and political agency, a collective determined to disrupt the racial gatekeeping that permeated Hollywood.

The Black Pack collaborated on writing, directing, producing, performing, and developing commercial film and television projects that blended humor with social criticism. Their comedic alchemy resulted in a provocative assault on America's racial condition, delivered through a range of over twenty politically Black film and television productions released within a single decade. Historian David Krasner's concept of "reinscription" proves particularly useful when analyzing the Black Pack's comedic strategy. Krasner posits that reinscription is a cultural tactic whereby marginalized groups can resist dominant media narratives and reclaim their image by subverting and redefining the racial caricatures manufactured in the monstrous interiors of the white imagination.[7] In the case of the Black Pack, their ideologically sharp techniques of reinscription echo the long tradition of Black resistance humor—that is, humor that dismantles reductive portrayals, carving out space for the complexities of individual and collective Black identities in America. The Black Pack's oeuvre articulates a core mission: to interrupt the white-controlled apparatus that confined Black voices and images on screen and recode social meanings of Blackness in a broader cultural context. Murphy's Black Pack films use humor as a subtle and practical yet politically charged weapon. His strategic deployment of social comedy triggered a redistribution of power from inside the behemoth structures of Hollywood film and television. Operating from within the belly of the beast, the Black Pack used laughter as a Trojan horse, smuggling resistant Black vocality into mainstream entertainment, challenging and reshaping the dominant narratives around Black identity and agency.

Eddie Murphy's Black Pack pictures, however, stand as a curious lacuna within critical discourse. And yet it is rare for such a coherent and self-contained collection of cultural material to offer itself for analysis. Produced between the late 1980s and into the '90s, Murphy's Black Pack cycle provides a rich tapestry of comedic material, including *Eddie Murphy: Raw* (1987), the HBO special *Uptown Comedy Express* (1987), *Coming to America* (1988), *Harlem Nights* (1989), and *Boomerang* (1992). With each venture, Murphy exercises his Hollywood clout by creating works that focus on Black themes and characters. These films starkly contrast with the cinematic conventions that propelled his rise to fame in white action comedies. During this period, his projects reveal a politically Black vocality that defies essentialist concepts of film Blackness, using the artifice of burlesque comedy and satire as a form of cultural protest.[8] Murphy's engagement with the traditions of Black resistance humor seeks social "justice in the subversion itself rather than in placing a didactic message as the immediate and sole purpose" of the work.[9]

The result is a collection of films that mark a consequential yet critically neglected interruption of the industry's normative dimensions of power. These movies cultivate a fresh vision of Black alterity, grapple with class struggle, and offer oppositional renderings of historical events launched from within the heart of the Hollywood industrial complex.

History rarely presents us with examples of commercially successful and resistant Black creative voices. For that matter, the Hollywood culture industry has a poor track record when it comes to nurturing culturally affirming Black movies, let alone fostering productions that celebrate Black culture on its own terms. My critical assessment of Murphy's Black Pack films eschews simplistic interpretations and easy readings, instead seeking to illuminate the rebellious spirit, the subtle strokes of racial satire, and the enduring power that have garnered these projects' long-standing resonance. While my discussion of Murphy demonstrates critical touchstones of the Black Pack movement, not every film evaluated here may seem immediately satirical or resistant in a conventional sense. Yet a crucial aspect of my argument lies in understanding the way these texts advance oppositional humor through their "wry engagement with the ridiculousness of racial assumptions and their awareness that these assumptions work to stifle the selfhood of the racialized."[10] My analysis of Murphy's Black Pack cycle reveals a fascinating paradox. While undeniably enmeshed within the Hollywood machine, Murphy's films engage in a Rancièrian "redistribution of the sensible."[11] Each movie articulates a counterdialogue with the industry itself. In doing so, Murphy's comedic discourse empowers Black creators and audiences alike, fostering a renewed sense of cultural agency while offering a corrective to the catastrophic effects of Hollywood inequality.

The Comedy Wunderkind

By age nineteen, Eddie Murphy was a comedic supernova and already a household name. His star-making arrival on *Saturday Night Live* from 1980 to 1984 single-handedly revived the series from its ratings doldrums.[12] Murphy's emergence on the national stage paralleled, perhaps bizarrely so, the political ascension of Ronald Reagan—the former B-movie actor and governor of California—who clinched the U.S. presidency in 1980 by capturing 51.6 percent of the popular vote when only 54 percent of eligible voters participated in the electoral process. Disillusionment with Jimmy Carter and a simmering white blowback against the social strides made by Black

Americans during the civil rights era spurred a dramatic shift in national sentiment. Reconciliatory government policies aimed at alleviating system-wide racism gave way to a focus on a sanitized, idealized vision of America that centered the perceived moral deficiencies of Black citizens. This manufactured narrative conveniently obscured the genuine social and economic anxieties gnawing at the white middle class.[13] Reagan's climb to power served as a rallying cry for conservative forces, igniting a renewed culture war that targeted the social and political gains of Black Americans. The era's divisive rhetoric weakened the fabric of American society, severing the threads of empathy and shared purpose that once bound us together. The nation, it seemed, had become increasingly tolerant of anti-Black rhetoric and populist resentment, echoing the divisive politics espoused by figures like Richard Nixon and George Wallace. This conservative movement became known as "Reaganism," which Robert Dallek defines as a "return to old-fashioned Republicanism—large tax cuts for the rich, less government help for the poor, weaker enforcement of civil rights, fewer controls on industry, less protection for the environment, and emotional rhetoric on the virtues of hard work, family, religion, individualism, and patriotism."[14] Reaganism was a masterfully crafted exercise in symbolic politics designed to appease the anxieties of wealthy and middle-class whites gripped by fears of economic stagnation, financial insecurity, and a resurfacing of the social turbulence that roiled the 1960s.

Cloaked in the rhetoric of traditional American values, a virulent rearticulation of anti-Black stereotypes began dominating public discourse in the 1980s. This conservative-driven white backlash, as Glenda Carpio points out, often bore very real consequences as the inequitable "differences in wages, access to healthcare, housing, family income, and more [were] constantly attributed to the cultural and individual failures of African Americans."[15] This political shift unleashed a swell of antigovernment, antitax, and antiwelfare policies that also proved to be, by and large, anti-Black. By the second term of the Reagan administration, as historian Robin D. G. Kelley notes, "about one out of every three African Americans, most of whom were women and children live[d] below the poverty line."[16] The era's partisan lexicon further exacerbated American racial pathologies by emphasizing visual metaphors of Black inferiority tethered to what Christina Sharpe describes as "living in the wake" of enslavement. Sharpe argues, "Living in the wake means living in and with terror in that in much of what passes for public discourse *about* terror we, Black people, become the *carriers* of terror, terror's embodiment, and not the primary objects of terror's multiple enactments; the grounds of terror's possibility globally."[17] By the 1980s, living in the wake had conjured relentless anti-Black depictions and visual symbols of the "welfare queen," the "career criminal," and the "deadbeat dad [which] became synonymous with Black femininity and Black masculinity" in the national imagination.[18] The era was also marked by distressing media images of "crack babies" and crime waves broadcast on nightly news programs, coupled with the spurious "war on drugs" in U.S. inner cities. This campaign turned out to be, more pointedly, a war on Black America under the guise of drug and crime prevention, effectively reshaping the social landscape and devastating Black communities in ways that have left many struggling to recover.

The relentless barrage of media images of violence, birthed from the insidious arrival of crack cocaine, incited a moral panic, a national nightmare weaponized to shape public discourse around the war on drugs and bogus claims of Blacks as "superpredators" who were genetically predisposed to violence.[19] Yet in the shadows, high-ranking government officials, intoxicated by a sense of impunity, had orchestrated the illegal sale of military-grade weaponry to Iran to finance the Contras, a rebel army in Nicaragua. The cost of this Faustian bargain, courtesy of the Contras, was a state-sponsored deluge of raw cocaine deposited in the United States, igniting the explosive crack epidemic that decimated many Black communities. Soon draconian drug laws materialized, aptly described by Michelle Alexander as the "New Jim Crow," resulting in harsh mandatory minimum sentences for crack cocaine offenses.[20] Such overly punitive measures launched a ferocious surge in the U.S. prison population, disproportionately impacting Black citizens. The systemic condition of mass incarceration has sadly become a cornerstone of American social reality that continues to cast its long shadow.

The ascent of Eddie Murphy and, by extension, the broader cultural phenomenon of the Black Pack cannot escape the context of social and political mayhem from which it emerged. Within this environment, as Saidiya Hartman observes, the liberatory narratives of the civil rights and Black Power movements, respectively, "had ceased to be a blueprint for the future, the decisive break the revolutionaries had hoped to institute between the past and the present failed. The old forms of tyranny, which they had endeavored to defeat, were resuscitated and the despots live long and vigorous lives."[21] The consequences of this grim and exigent context necessitated new articulations of cultural defiance and resilience. In the face of an inherently corrupt political apparatus, comedians like Murphy and the Black Pack were compelled to forge innovative strategies to express opposition. Disguise, both literal and metaphoric, became a potent tool in their cultural battle.

By 1980, *Saturday Night Live* had lost the hip edginess that initially captivated a generation of disillusioned youth a decade earlier. Murphy arrived on the show soon after the departure of its creator, Lorne Michaels. Murphy stepped into this vacuum, a whirlwind of brash audacity. His comic arsenal consisted of crafting outlandish characters: the gruff Mr. Robinson, a parody of the genteel children's puppeteer on *Mister Rogers' Neighborhood* (1968–2001); Little Richard Simmons, a striking fusion of the rock 'n' roll legend and the fitness guru; and an inebriated Gumby, a stark counterpoint to the Claymation character's cheerful innocence. Murphy also gained recognition for his flawless impersonations of Black cultural figures like James Brown, Stevie Wonder, Bill Cosby, and Muhammad Ali. His prolific performances invigorated *Saturday Night Live* and reestablished the program as a viable series for NBC. The show's weekly broadcasts became unmissable events, drawing audiences across racial and social divides. It comes as no surprise that Murphy's talent was swiftly drafted into the big leagues of Hollywood film production. His comic prowess allowed him to graduate from a "not ready for prime-time player" to a bona fide movie star. Murphy starred in consecutive blockbuster films while still a cast member on *SNL*. One can argue that he transitioned to film stardom more successfully than any of the show's famous alumni, becoming known as comedy's first "rock star." After his string of widely profitable interracial buddy films, Murphy stood alone as Paramount Pictures' "billion-dollar baby" with a remarkable Midas touch. However, his cinematic positioning as a fast-talking street hustler upheld the maintenance of Hollywood's master narrative regarding Black bodies on screen. His first five films sustained the industry's prevailing archetype of the nonthreatening Black subordinate, tailor-made for white consumption. These roles, while commercially successful, offered little progress. Many Black audiences, however, found solace in these characters, even if they were confined to certain ideological limitations.

Within the matrix of Hollywood cultural production, before the crystallization of hip-hop as a commercial juggernaut that launched a global cornucopia for white corporations and Black consumer markets, and well before the archetype of the "hip-hop mogul," Eddie Murphy parlayed his celebrity across multiple media platforms. His burgeoning career as a music recording artist is a key example of his rising cultural influence. He marketed his highly recognizable entertainment brand in a way that displayed a protean capacity for self-promotion. His debut album, *How Could It Be*, was released

FIG. 2.1. Eddie Murphy and Rick James in the "Party All the Time" music video, 1985.

on Columbia Records in 1985 and peaked at number seventeen on the R&B charts and twenty-six on the coveted Billboard Top 200. The driving force behind the record's traction was the single "Party All the Time," a collaboration with the funk maestro Rick James, whose indelible imprint on the funk genre had been firmly established with his song "Super Freak," which spent three weeks at number one on the Billboard charts in 1981. Decades later, Murphy's brother, Charlie, made a name for himself, depicting the relationship between his brother Eddie and the notoriously hard-partying James on the sketch series *Chappelle's Show* (2003–2006). The outlandishly funny sketches with Dave Chappelle as Rick James catapulted the catchphrase "I'm Rick James, bitch," into American popular culture. Murphy's "Party All the Time" music video enjoyed heavy rotation on BET and MTV, propelling the song to number two on Billboard's Hot 100. This dual cable network exposure highlights Murphy's tremendous crossover appeal in the 1980s.

Although Murphy's music career is much maligned, he released two more albums during the Black Pack period: *So Happy* (1989) and *Love's Alright* (1993). *So Happy* found Murphy collaborating with Nile Rodgers, the sonic architect behind chart-topping hits for Diana Ross, David Bowie, and Madonna. Larry Blackmon, lead vocalist of the funk band Cameo, also lent his prowess to the record. The album achieved modest success, peaking at number twenty-two on the R&B charts, spawning the jocular tune "Put Your Mouth on Me," which peaked at number two on the Hot 100 singles. *Love's Alright*, Murphy's last album of the Black Pack era, was released on the iconic Motown record label. Despite the debut single "Whatzupwitu" featuring the marquee presence of the "King of Pop," Michael Jackson, the album was a critical and commercial flop. The single's accompanying music video, a visual spectacle pioneering the use of computer-generated imagery and special effects, stood as a testament to the era's technological advancements, yet the record fell flat. Murphy and Jackson had previously joined forces on Jackson's multiplatinum opus *Dangerous* (1991). Jackson featured Murphy in his epic nine-minute music video / short film for the hit single "Remember the Time." The video, directed by John Singleton—fresh off an Oscar nomination for his 1991 debut feature *Boyz n the Hood*—premiered simultaneously on Fox, MTV, and BET. At age twenty-four, Singleton was the youngest Academy Award nominee for Best Director and a hot commodity in Hollywood. The music video was also notable for its advanced use of visual and special effects seamlessly interwoven with elaborate costuming and dance choreography. The lavish production, set against the backdrop of ancient Egypt, boasted a stellar cast: Murphy as the king, the statuesque Somalian supermodel Iman as the queen, basketball legend Earvin "Magic" Johnson as the bailiff, and Michael Jackson as an enigmatic wizard.

FIG. 2.2. Eddie Murphy and Iman as king and queen in the "Remember the Time" music video, 1992.

Murphy's ability to migrate across multiple media platforms (film, music, broadcast television, cable, VHS, and DVD) illustrates a pioneering business model later expanded and maximized by the hip-hop moguls who followed. This business strategy allowed Murphy to create cross-platform synergy and develop deeper levels of brand awareness and consumption that permeated the everyday lives of his audience. In that sense, Murphy laid the groundwork for other Black artists to capitalize on a critical mass of public recognition that allowed them to gain corporate investment and increase financial productivity. His strategy was perfected and brought to a logical extension during the era of immense liquidity in the bull markets of the late 1990s and early 2000s. O'Shea "Ice Cube" Jackson, Shawn "Jay-Z" Carter, and Curtis "50-Cent" Jackson are examples of hip-hop artists who were able to successfully parlay their cultural currency into lucrative relationships with major corporations outside of the music business to create such cross-platform synergy.

By 1987, Murphy had replaced Richard Pryor as the top comedian in America. His films had generated revenue of Spielbergian proportions. Placed in a broader context, Murphy's box office dividends by 1987 nearly eclipsed the combined financial returns of George Lucas's *American Graffiti* (1973) and *Star Wars* (1977). The importance of these economic factors is crucial in apprehending the enormity of Murphy's industry influence. He reached an acme previously unattained by a Black performer. His unprecedented economic dominance formed the very axis on which the Black Pack revolved. Within this cultural context, at the height of his industrial prestige, Murphy executed a distinct performative turn that bewildered many white film critics. With the entirety of the mainstream entertainment complex at his disposal, Murphy publicly proclaimed his alliance with a renegade group of humorists, the Black Pack.

Having solidified the legibility of his brand as Hollywood's preeminent "Black buddy" in formulaic white comedies, Murphy's union with the Black Pack is symptomatic of a paradigm shift. The unveiling of his Black Pack association also coincides with rumblings and growing disquiet within segments of the Black bourgeoisie. Murphy was publicly chided for being what some detractors considered apolitical regarding the broader struggles of Black America and the marginalization of Black creatives in Hollywood. Outspoken filmmaker Spike Lee issued a pointed critique, declaring, "Eddie needs to flex his muscles that can help Black people get into this industry. Clout isn't just getting the best table at Spago."[22] In a rare interview with *Spin Magazine* conducted by Lee himself, Murphy offered a candid glimpse into his political philosophy. He revealed, "My politics are much more covert [than yours, Spike]. I am very Black and I have a strong Black consciousness, but I am about gradual change and dialogue that is much more civil."[23] This recherché insight into Murphy's ideology and social politics is essential to truly understanding the strategic interventions of his Black Pack cycle.

For the first time in his career, Murphy began exercising creative and authorial control over his work, creating projects with Afro-centered overtones. His Black Pack films subtly weave in a political dimension and social depth. His strategy serves as a counterpoint to Hollywood's historical repression of Black narratives. The fraternal camaraderie within the Black Pack collective signaled Murphy's growing acceptance of a sense of social responsibility that accompanied his unprecedented cultural and industrial power. He eschewed the "safety" of status-quo filmmaking despite the seduction of his celebrity status and attendant perks. Instead, he wielded his comedy to align with a politically engaged cinema, making visible a variety of social tensions largely ignored in Hollywood. Murphy's approach to Black resistance humor diverges from the confrontational style of his predecessor, Richard Pryor, or the skewering barbs of Paul Mooney. Instead, Murphy employed a strategy of imaginative reinscriptions, subverting Hollywood formulas through films that centralized Black themes and characters. His Black Pack productions supplied audiences with a tantalizing glimpse at the potential of a Black creative utopia—a type of aspirational film practice that challenged normative industry values and catalyzed the burgeoning Black media boom of the 1990s.

In Murphy's next six films—except, to a lesser degree, *Another 48 Hrs.* (1990)—the technique of reinscription is used as his primary performance ritual of resistance. Extending Franz Fanon's *Black Skin, White Masks* analysis, Edward Said gives insight into reinscription as a creative device for strategic opposition. Said argues that to gain mainstream acceptance and appreciation, oppressed groups must "rechart and then occupy the space in imperial cultural forms reserved for subordination, to occupy self-consciously, fighting for it on the very same territory once ruled by consciousness that assumed subordination of the designated inferior Other. Hence, *reinscription*."[24] Throughout the Black Pack cycle, Murphy's articulation of social consciousness pivots on the geometry of renegotiating Black alterity. Operating within the regulatory structures of Hollywood, Murphy's Black Pack comedies offer reinscriptions of Blackness that hybridize Black Power tenets through symbolic and visual signifiers while maintaining an appearance of accommodation. This infiltration-like approach proved rather effective. His Black Pack output championed Black empowerment from inside the commercial sphere and provided opportunities for the emergence of fresh Black voices in the media industry.

Murphy's Black Pack films, specifically *Coming to America*, *Harlem Nights*, and *Boomerang*, decentralize whiteness in Hollywood narratives and shift focus to society's farthest margins. By elevating the margins, these films reinscribe Blackness, openly celebrating its inherent value, beauty, entrepreneurial drive, power, sex appeal, and cool. This collection of movies is provocative and widely popular. Their enduring appeal is evident in their continued celebration within many Black communities. Even the films' lines of dialogue evolved into catchphrases within Black vernacular—"Sexual Chocolate!" and "His momma name him Clay, I'm a call him Clay!" (both from *Coming to America*) and "Strangè, girl" (from *Boomerang*) readily come to mind. Across generations, audiences remain unquestionably drawn to Murphy's iconic Black Pack characters like Prince Akeem and Marcus Graham. Black communities, to be sure, revel in the alternative cinematic universe Murphy crafted, a sentiment reflected in the films' impressive box office returns and robust VHS and DVD sales and the enthusiastic reception of *Coming 2 America*, a sequel that arrived three decades after the original.

Soul Glo Activator

Floating high on the success of *Beverly Hills Cop II*, Murphy lobbied Paramount Pictures to appoint Robert Townsend as director for *Eddie Murphy: Raw*. The project marked Murphy's second stand-up concert film, following the triumph of his riotous HBO special *Eddie Murphy: Delirious* (1983). Filmed live at New York City's iconic Madison Square Garden, *Raw* represents Murphy's seminal stand-up performance. Further demonstrating his commitment to the Black Pack ethos, he also championed the inclusion of Keenen Ivory Wayans as cowriter for the movie's opening sequence. Townsend and Wayans, fresh off their collaborative efforts on *Hollywood Shuffle*, readily embraced the opportunity. The film opens with a nostalgic flashback depicting a precocious young Murphy (Deon Richmond) entertaining his family during a Thanksgiving dinner. Also featured in the scene is a preteen, Tatyana Ali, as Eddie's sister and Samuel L. Jackson as Eddie's uncle Ray. The creative alliance with Murphy, Hollywood's comedic wunderkind, proved pivotal, serving as a springboard for Wayans's and Townsend's careers. Upon its theatrical release on December 18, 1987, *Raw*

FIG. 2.3. *Eddie Murphy: Raw*, 1987.

skyrocketed to the number-one spot at the box office. The film earned over $50.5 million, cementing its position as the highest-grossing stand-up comedy concert film in cinema history.[25] Despite its commercial triumph, the film faced scathing rebukes from women's rights and LGBTQ+ organizations for rampant sexist and homophobic material in Murphy's routine. As film and media critic Bambi Haggins explains, "The sexual politics of Murphy's stand-up does [not] challenge the status quo but it reaffirms it as well by reasserting Black masculinity through the degradation of Black women (and women, in general) and annunciating the beginning of a backlash against feminism."[26] Moreover, in her book *Black Looks: Race and Representation*, bell hooks lends a critical eye to Murphy's work, notably drawing attention to the patriarchal depictions of women and Black queer men in his material. She contends that his humor trafficked in harmful tropes that relied on the objectification of women, reducing them to mere sexual objects or caricatures. Additionally, hooks argues that Murphy's treatment of Black gay men often situated them as the butt of jokes, portraying them as weak, effeminate, and cowardly. She notes that Murphy's humor mirrored the broader cultural homophobia of the time, normalizing the marginalization of queer communities in mainstream media and reinforcing social hierarchies. Through their critiques, both hooks and Haggins challenge audiences to consider the deeper implications beyond the surface-level enjoyment of Murphy's comedy, asking us to consider how the laughter they evoke might come at the expense of those already marginalized by society. The elements of sexism and homophobia arguably expose a performer indulging in the excesses of his newfound fame, prioritizing unfiltered humor and bravado over political correctness. Such pointed critiques levied against *Raw*, in particular, influenced a new direction in Murphy's next film, an attempt to recalibrate his public image.

While the proverbial iron was hot, Murphy, ever the strategist, saw an opportunity to strike. He understood the power of momentum and continued championing his Black Pack crew. Riding the wave of popularity from *Raw*, he produced an HBO special, *Uptown Comedy Express* (1987), recorded live at the Black-owned Ebony Showcase Theater, a vibrant cultural hub in the heart of South Central Los Angeles. With a discerning eye, Murphy curated a stellar lineup for the show, handpicking a veritable who's who of rising comics. The cast included Black Pack mainstays Robert Townsend and Arsenio Hall, as well as Marsha Warfield and a fresh-faced Chris Rock in his HBO debut. *Uptown Comedy Express* was a ratings coup and generated lucrative VHS sales. Murphy had created a mainstream platform for upstart Black comics to showcase their talent at the highest level. For HBO, this success echoed Murphy's previous special, *Delirious*—offering a small glimpse into the emerging power of the Black Pack and the expansion of Murphy's role as a cultural tastemaker and industry force.

Eager to begin working on his next film, Murphy held brainstorming sessions with Arsenio Hall. During one of their phone calls, Murphy divulged the concept for a new project. Together, they developed an idea that would blossom into *Coming to America*. Murphy acknowledged, "I needed to be something different. A character who talks loud and goes wherever he wants to go—I had to get away from that."[27] In a moment of candor, Hall concurred with Murphy's assessment, stating, "I told [Eddie] it was time to get rid of the smoking guns and car chases [from his previous films]. People think from some of the lines in *Raw* that Eddie hates women and gays. But that's not who he is. [I told Eddie] he needed to show [his] shyer, more sensitive side."[28] Hall's enthusiasm soared when Murphy unveiled his new concept—a contemporary fairy tale centered on a wealthy African prince venturing to the United States on a quest for true love. At the pinnacle of stardom, Murphy wielded unprecedented authorship and creative control over his studio-backed projects. The location of *Coming to America*'s pitch meeting distinguishes Murphy's position at the top of Hollywood's food chain. Ned Tanen, then president of Paramount Pictures and one of Hollywood's most influential figures, did not summon Murphy to his office to hear the actor's pitch as most presidents would. Instead, the studio head traveled to Murphy's office on the Paramount backlot to hold the meeting.

As Murphy and Hall pitched the movie to Tanen and his team, one studio executive interrupted them, declaring, "Stop, stop. This is great. You guys go write."[29] Murphy, credited with developing the film's story, penned the first twenty-five pages of the screenplay before enlisting the talents of his two favorite staff writers from *SNL*, David Sheffield and Barry Blaustein, to complete the script. Murphy also advocated for the inclusion of beleaguered director John Landis to helm the film's production. Landis previously directed Murphy in *Trading Places*. Despite his recent flops, Paramount acquiesced to hiring Landis. However, the Landis-Murphy working relationship during *Coming to America*'s production was the source of constant tension, even escalating to the point of physical altercations. Landis, harboring a vision of the film as more "universal" (a euphemism for "white" in the insular lexicon of Hollywood), wanted to steer the project away from its initial conception as a distinctly "Black film." Landis and his production team envisioned *Coming to America* as a modern extension of classic Hollywood romantic comedies like *Roman Holiday* (1953) and *It Happened One Night* (1934). Despite their ongoing philosophical clashes, Landis, recognizing Murphy's exceptional talent, encouraged him to play multiple characters in the film. He knew this would truly showcase Murphy's prodigious comedic and performance versatility. Eddie loved the idea. He was undoubtedly inspired by Richard Pryor, whose entertaining performance in Michael Schultz's *Which Way Is Up?* (1977) saw Pryor seamlessly portray a trio of roles. In *Coming to America*, Murphy's performance hinges on his portrayal of Prince Akeem Joffer, heir to the throne of the fictional African nation of Zamunda. In addition, Murphy also masterfully embodies an eclectic ensemble of characters, including Clarence (a pontificating barbershop owner), Randy Watson (an inept R&B crooner), and Saul (an elderly white Jewish man). Murphy's astounding comedic performance on screen and his ability to, as Racquel Gates suggests, "slip in and out of various characters and [embody] their varied individual and racial subjectivities, is the radical move in the film."[30] Murphy's uncanny ability to flawlessly transfer between multiple roles is the breakthrough feature of the movie. In fact, playing numerous characters became his trademark filmic strategy in the 2000s with films like *Norbit* and, of course, *The Nutty Professor* franchise. Murphy's virtuosic multiperformance in *Coming to America* was further amplified by the artistry of Rick Baker, whose visionary work in special-effects makeup renders Murphy and Arsenio Hall virtually unrecognizable in their secondary roles. Baker's transformative techniques garnered him an Academy Award nomination for the film.

FIG. 2.4. Eddie Murphy as Randy Watson in *Coming to America*, 1988.

FIG. 2.5. Eddie Murphy as Clarence in *Coming to America*, 1988.

FIG. 2.6. Eddie Murphy as Saul in *Coming to America*, 1988.

The story world of *Coming to America* unfolds in the wealthy and beautiful African nation of Zamunda, where Prince Akeem, the royal heir, is disenchanted with his life of empty opulence and seclusion. On his wedding day, an extraordinarily extravagant affair and national holiday, Prince Akeem unexpectedly defies tradition. He rejects the bride his father, King Jaffe Joffer (James Earl Jones), has chosen for him. As per tradition, Akeem does not meet his wife until the wedding day. When they finally meet, Akeem, after interrupting the ceremony to chat with his future wife (Vanessa Bell Callaway), realizes they have no natural chemistry. In a quest to find a more genuine and meaningful romantic connection, Akeem disperses the wedding and embarks on a journey to Queens, New York City, with his loyal aide Semmi (one of Hall's multiple roles), to find the prince a queen. In New York, Akeem poses as a poor immigrant and begins his search for a spouse who will love him for the person he is rather than for his status as crown prince of Zamunda. While attending a pageant during "Black Awareness Week" in their new Queens community, Akeem encounters Lisa McDowell (Shari Headley), a grounded, captivating, and intelligent woman from an upper-middle-class Black American family. Her upwardly mobile father, Cleo (James Amos), owns a neighborhood restaurant, "McDowell's," a thinly veiled and legally dubious knockoff of the fast-food chain McDonald's. During Akeem's American odyssey, he takes a job as a janitor at McDowell's to become closer to Lisa, but she barely notices him.

The unique charm of *Coming to America* stems from its assemblage of visual metaphors celebrating Black cultural specificity, interwoven humorous explorations of class tensions, and the heterogeneity present in Black communities. Murphy strategically positions the audience to encounter a constellation of Black experiences in the film, disputing assertions of a monolithic Black community. We meet a wide array of Black people in the picture, from the colorful working-class characters inside the "My T Sharp" barbershop, which provides the film with some of its most sidesplitting and iconic moments, to the enterprising McDowell family, who represent an upwardly mobile vision of Black social progress in the post–civil rights era. Murphy also makes visible the multifaceted world of Black religious expression rendered through Reverend Brown (hilariously played by Hall), a Baptist minister who never stops preaching, even outside of the pulpit. Nor does Murphy shy away from lampooning the aspirations of the petit bourgeoisie through characters like the self-centered pretty boy Darryl Jenks (Eriq La Salle), Lisa's boyfriend, whose Jheri-curled family owns the

"Soul Glo" Black hair care company and embodies the crass materialism of the nouveau riche. While at a private party at the McDowell mansion, Darryl arrogantly informs Lisa's father, Cleo, that he and Lisa are engaged to be married. Ever the doting father, Cleo announces the engagement to all the guests during a champagne toast. The only problem is, Lisa was never consulted. Darryl never proposed to her. He essentially went behind her back and lied to her dad, leaving Lisa in the dark about his plans. Blindsided and outraged, Lisa storms out of the party, fed up with her relationship with Darryl and with being taken for granted. Enter Akeem, "Johnny on the spot," poised and ready to listen, comfort, and sweep Lisa off her feet. Throughout the film, Akeem goes to painstaking lengths to hide his true identity and wealth from Lisa and her disapproving father, who believe Akeem was a goat herder back in Africa. The more time they spend together, the more Lisa falls for Akeem despite his ostensibly low socioeconomic status. Her genuine affection for him confirms to Akeem that Lisa is the woman he desires to marry. But when the opulent King Joffer arrives in Queens searching for his son, it blows Akeem's impoverished cover. Soon, the McDowells discover their goat-herding janitor is actually an African prince. In the end, Akeem comes clean about his circumstances, and Lisa ultimately joins him in Zamunda to live happily ever after. The film presents a vibrant tableau of richly textured characters who showcase the multiple ways Black people live and love in the world. In doing so, Murphy's film invites audiences to revel in the pleasures of its inside jokes and calculated exaggerations, provoking culturally affirming laughter as an antipode to the debilitating optics of the Reagan era.

In *Coming to America*, Murphy deploys a satirical arsenal of reinscription and social inversion that explores prevailing notions of class and social mobility. The film's comedic taxonomy (also evident in *Harlem Nights* and *Boomerang*) functions as a centrifugal force, outmaneuvering the white hegemonic gaze—studio executives and film critics—with koan-like illuminations of Black pride. Murphy's comedic strategy in the movie articulates a politicized Black identity, veiled in jocularity and visual metaphors. However, during production, both Murphy and Hall anticipated adverse reactions they imagined *Coming to America*'s premise would elicit from white critics. Throughout the 1980s, media portrayals of Africa were overwhelmingly skewed toward despair. In the American social imagination, the continent was seemingly synonymous with little more than poverty, famine, and the heartbreaking images of starving children with distended bellies—a trope relentlessly exploited in various charity television commercials.

Historically, representations of Africa in Hollywood movies have perpetuated white-manufactured stereotypes of primitivism through films like the 1930s *Tarzan* series, *Tarzan the Fearless* (1933) and *The New Adventures of Tarzan* (1935), and even Paul Robeson's later disavowed role in *Sanders of the River* (1935). Such racist depictions crystallize the erroneous trope of the atavistic, uncivilized "savage African" within the U.S. social imagination. *Coming to America* offers a glaring counterpoint, presenting a vision of Africa that challenges the extremely polarizing banality of Africa and, by extension, Black American inferiority. Yet amid its progressive intent, an argument can be made that the film's emphasis on monarchy raises questions about the romanticization of patriarchal ideals that reify Western values. At the same time, progressive portrayals of Africa rarely find depiction in Hollywood pictures. As Ada Gay Griffin points out, "Those aspects of our culture and history that come most often to our attention, usually because they have been popularized by or expropriated by the dominant society, tend to line up along the side of assimilation and, as a consequence, are available as vehicles for our oppression."[31] *Coming to America*, then, as a cinematic experience, provides Black audiences with a pleasurable space of levity and social detachment, free from the burdensome demands of literal interpretation. The film functions, as Fredric Jameson might argue, as both an expression of the dominant social order and a form of utopia. It offers a means of coping with and challenging popular culture in a moment of crisis.[32] By creating a modern fairy tale centered on a prosperous African family from a stable and wealthy African nation amid the distorted symbolic landscape of Reaganism, Murphy disrupts conventional narratives and, predictably, draws the ire of white critics. At a publicity event promoting *Coming to America*, Murphy playfully mimicked a hypothetical white critic's response to the film: "I just don't find any of it believable. Everyone knows Africa is a continent in crisis, here [Murphy's portrayal of Africa] is beautiful and everyone is running around happy and I just don't buy this movie."[33] However, within systems of domination, as James C. Scott argues, the art of disguise becomes a crucial tool, what he calls the "weapons of the weak" that enable marginalized groups to enact everyday forms of resistance and oppose regimes of power under the radar.[34] *Coming to America* exemplifies this strategy, offering a seemingly innocuous comedy that subtly challenges ingrained stereotypes.

By recognizing Murphy's oppositional framework, one can begin to see his Black Pack films' interventions. Each project operates on its own internal logic rather than predetermined white notions of what Black cinema should

FIG. 2.7. Eddie Murphy, James Earl Jones, and Madge Sinclair as the royal family of Zamunda in *Coming to America*, 1988.

be. To that extent, in order to challenge authority, marginalized artists often adopt the tools of disguise, folklore, and subterfuge. Houston Baker terms this approach the "deformation of mastery," a method of interpreting Black expressive culture that rejects societal constraints.[35] Baker contends that for Black artists to address racial politics *and* gain recognition in a mainstream context, they may employ the strategies of "mastery of form" or the "deformation of mastery." Here, "form" signifies not a rigid literary structure but rather a mode of performance. Through this lens, resistant Black artists can choose to excel within a specific form (exhibiting mastery) or opt to reject established forms by offering disruptive styles that challenge the status quo (deformation of mastery). Murphy's socially inverted premise in *Coming to America* illustrates this concept, rejecting Hollywood's usual derogatory visions of Blackness and delivering an underserved audience a knee-slappingly funny film that utilizes deformation of mastery to deliver its resistant message.

Although *Coming to America* stands as a symbolic rebellion against Hollywood's racist archive, it also carves out a pleasurable space of social detachment for Black viewers yearning for a lost ontology. The film constructs a "better world" for Black audiences, free from the confines of literal interpretation. According to Racquel Gates, "*Coming to America*, primarily through Murphy's influence, takes a standard Hollywood formula, one that was designed to appeal to all audiences, and reforms it into a culturally Black film—a film that continues to have particular resonance with Black viewers."[36] The movie is set in an all-Black milieu, both in Queens and in Zamunda, where the political system of whiteness is never granted the time of day. This subtle brushstroke subverts the established power dynamics differentiating *Coming to America* from Murphy's interracial buddy comedies. Thus, Procrustean criticisms labeling the film's portrayal of Africa as "unrealistic" fail to grasp Murphy's deliberate rejection of literal representation in favor of deforming the Hollywood industry's racial formulas. The movie avoids bleak and derisive Black depictions that often plague commercial cinema, opting instead for a playful and socially conscious comedic form that celebrates Black life.

Murphy turns the tables on the establishment by merging Black American traditions with reconceptualized visions of Africa that embrace the philosophy of Afrofuturism and its concepts of ancient Black royalty. Black artistic expression has consistently imagined liberatory realities where Black communities thrive in self-governance, free from the constraints and afflictions of the dominant society. Mark Dery describes this form of expression as Afrofuturism, which extends from literature to encompass philosophy, music, fashion, film, television, and ever-evolving forms of critical thought.[37] From the visionary worlds crafted by Octavia Butler and Samuel R. Delany to the intergalactic sonic journeys of Sun Ra and the funk of George Clinton's Parliament, Afrofuturism's philosophies and aesthetics have long shaped Black cultural expression, self-representation, and cultural identity. *Coming to America*'s engagement with Afrofuturism defies Hollywood conventions and rewrites Black cinematic language. The film's idea of Black royalty signifies the elevation of communal values and a powerful ancestral connection that predates the horrors of Western enslavement and colonialism. In the literature of Afrofuturism, Black royalty extends back to the dawn of human civilization and stands in opposition to Western ideals. Murphy applies these tenets to commercial cinema as a rhetorical weapon, simultaneously critiquing American film and forging a connection with Black viewers. Through the liberating power of Afrofuturism, revolutionary laughter, and irreverence, he celebrates Black nobility as a counterpoint to its historical erasure.

Opening weekend greeted Murphy and the studio with the warmth of tremendous financial returns. *Coming to America* debuted at number one at the box office, holding the top spot for two consecutive weeks. The movie's rapturous response earned it nearly $300 million against its $36 million budget, becoming the highest-grossing film for Paramount Pictures in 1989 and the third biggest Hollywood release of that year.[38] More significantly, the film established itself as the highest-grossing Black movie of all time—a record it held for a remarkable three decades. *Coming to America* moves beyond a mere attempt at cinematic revisionism, emerging instead as a subtle social comedy infused with Black pride and Afrofuturist sensibilities. The film's curious inconsistencies are not haphazard but rather measured acts of cultural contestation, showcasing Murphy's deformation of mastery in commercial filmmaking. By reclaiming Africa as the Motherland, a place of ancestral significance, wealth, and breathtaking beauty, *Coming to America* aligns with principles of Afrofuturism with its alternative visions of history, civilization, and human origin, ultimately offering a comedic reclamation of Black dignity that holds immense significance in many Black communities today.

Their Eyes Were Watching Harlem

By 1989, there was considerable buzz around several Black film directors in Hollywood. The excitement was spurred by the standout cinematic efforts of Spike Lee with *She's Gotta Have It* (1986), his first studio film; *School Daze* (1988); and the instant classic *Do the Right Thing* (1989). At the same time, the triumphant directorial debuts of Black Pack members Robert Townsend (*Hollywood Shuffle*, 1987) and Keenen Ivory Wayans (*I'm Gonna Git You Sucka*, 1988) further fueled attention to Black directors. The success of these films seemed to herald a new era of Black cultural advancement in the industry. Studio executives began revisiting the financial logic prevalent in the Blaxploitation era, producing low-budget films—ranging from $3 million to $10 million—centered around Black-oriented action themes. Despite having relatively paltry production budgets by Hollywood standards, these films showcased the potential for substantial returns. The industrial logic of Hollywood cinema, ever adept at absorption and co-optation, occasionally deploys these tactics to boost corporate profits. This was the case following the success of Melvin Van Peebles's 1971 independent social revenge fantasy *Sweet Sweetback's Baadasssss Song*. By the late 1980s, the industry's flavor du jour consisted of constructing a production model around the co-optation of the emergent Black director as "celebrity auteur." This appropriation served a crucial function: to maintain cultural authority, the film industry requires the symbolic legitimization of Black talent operating within the established framework. Given Murphy's undeniable Black star power, it comes as no surprise that he was encouraged to direct his first feature. His competitive nature, as it were, refused to be outshined by his Black Pack contemporaries, who bore the multihyphenate titles of writer-producer-director-star. After all, Murphy's success blazed the trail for this upstart generation of Black cultural producers to explore a new comedic modernity on the Hollywood frontier.

Harlem Nights is Murphy's only directorial effort and the fourth project of his Black Pack cycle. The film is a comedic period piece set in the Harlem Renaissance era of the Roaring Twenties and 1930s—a moment highly regarded for its cultural expressions of Black artistry and creative excellence. Through meticulous attention to detail, Murphy brings to life elegant fashion, luxurious costuming, and an elaborate mise-en-scène to depict a Prohibition-era Harlem New York City. At first glance, the film does not outwardly appear radical in a traditional sense. However, by situating the narrative within historic Harlem, the mecca for Black cultural expression, Murphy decentralizes the white gaze, immersing the viewer in an exclusively Black world. This resistant cultural maneuver once again challenges dominant narratives, offering a glimpse into the realm of the "Black fantastic"—a space where Black subjectivity and imagination reign supreme. *Harlem Nights*'s emphasis on fashion, style, and sartorial splendor satisfies Black audiences' scopic desire to witness themselves on-screen in new ways. Rather than delivering a didactic message to jettison Hollywood's demeaning tropes, Murphy flips the script on that legacy by delivering representations of Black life that activate a sense of solidarity. The film luxuriates in a Black world of flapper dresses, fedora hats, opulent speakeasies, and a bygone Harlem elegance. More than mere spectacle, *Harlem Nights* caters to a long-denied Black desire. Harlem, a potent symbol within Black culture, becomes a character in the film. It's a mythical space, a site of creativity, intellectualism, and political radicalism where oppositional worldviews emerged and were celebrated.

First and perhaps most evident to viewers is the fact that *Harlem Nights* represents a hybridization of Hollywood genres. The film reinscribes the cinematic conventions of comedy, film noir, caper, and gangster films for engagement in a predominately Black environment. In so doing, the film expands "into the satiric realm of racial performance and [demonstrates] race as performative."[39] The movie also bears a certain residue of Blaxploitation, with its emphasis on gunfighting and action scenes and the prominence of a sexually desirable, ultracool Black hero who is free to dole out

FIG. 2.8. Eddie Murphy as Quick and Richard Pryor as Sugar Ray in *Harlem Nights*, 1989.

street justice mainly without consequence. After the financial victory of *Coming to America*, Murphy exercised even more creative control over *Harlem Nights*. He not only consolidates the talents of comedy icons Richard Pryor and Redd Foxx, but he also earns a quadruple hyphenate—serving as the film's executive producer, writer, director, and star. Murphy was eager to cast Foxx in what would be his last feature film role and his first movie appearance since *Norman . . . Is That You?* (1976) alongside his comedic hero, Pryor, despite Pryor's secret battle with multiple sclerosis. With *Harlem Nights*, Murphy orchestrates a historic convergence, capturing three generations of legendary American comedians on-screen together for the first and only time.

It was a dream come true for Murphy. Reflecting on the momentous occasion, he reveals, "Hollywood wasn't trying to hook us up. But I think it's historic that I get to work with these brothers. The privilege of working with Richard and Redd has been the greatest reward of my career."[40] The significance of this cultural moment was not lost on Pryor or Foxx. Pryor reflected on the experience in an interview, stating, "It's turning out to be more pleasant than I expected. . . . You walk around here and look at the people—have you ever in your life seen this many Black people on a movie set? I haven't."[41] Pryor's observations encapsulate the impact of Murphy's efforts to leverage his star power to develop a Black creative enterprise that was resistant to Hollywood's "old boys" network. Instead, his ambitious production practice jumpstarted a "new school" network where Black artists could generate liberating narratives dedicated to self-representation and cultural autonomy, interrupting the traditional economy of uneven exchange between American cinema and Black audiences.

Harlem Nights spins the tale of Sugar Ray (Richard Pryor), an aging nightclub owner, and his mercurial son, Quick (Eddie Murphy), battling a predatory white mob boss, Bugsy Calhoune (Michael Lerner), for control of their thriving speakeasy. When Calhoune realizes that Sugar Ray's nightclub is more profitable than his own, he sets out to acquire or destroy the Black establishment. Beyond a cursory reading of the film as a slick-looking crime comedy, Murphy offers a subtle critique of American race relations by exposing the machinations of the dominant culture's perverse desire to derail Black economic progress. We have seen this catastrophic impulse play out throughout American history, where economically thriving Black communities are entirely, viciously destroyed and burned to the ground and innocent Black citizens are violently massacred in public without consequence by evil white militias in cities like Wilmington, North Carolina (1898); Rosewood, Florida (1923); and Tulsa, Oklahoma's Black Wall Street (1921), among many others.

Harlem Nights also features a scene-stealing cameo by Arsenio Hall. His portrayal of the "Crying Man"—a clumsy, grief-stricken, vengeance-seeking yet comically inept henchman—leaps off the screen. Hall's character meets his demise courtesy of Quick in a jocular evocation of the iconic shootout in Brian De Palma's gangster epic *Scarface* (1983). *Harlem Nights* expresses a blues ideology that situates the viewer in a world that is always already entrenched in illegal activity—every character in the film is a criminal.[42] Yet the film recasts these Black underworld figures as blues heroes. Their criminal acts connote survival strategies within a hostile and unjust social system. Even a prominent female character like Vera (Della Reese), a madame managing the lives of "women of the night," is elevated to the status of a blues heroine. Vera's larger-than-life personality embodies strength, sensitivity, and audacity. She commands respect from everyone, particularly the men in the film. In one unforgettable scene, Quick questions Vera's integrity. She delivers a caustic rebuttal and challenges Quick to a fistfight in a dark alley, culminating in his hilarious beatdown. To salvage his pride, the embarrassed Quick regrettably shoots off her pinkie toe. The scene's humor is derived from outrageous behavior. The movie offers audiences a rare opportunity to witness Black characters unleashed to be funny and over the top.

Beneath Herbie Hancock's melodic soundscape, the sumptuous costuming (which received an Oscar nomination for Best Costume Design), and the hilarious one-liners lies a blues ideology rooted in cultural affirmation and Black empowerment. Despite the picture's multigenerational all-star cast that included Della Reese, Jasmine Guy, Robin Harris, and Arsenio Hall, the film was widely panned by white critics. The *Los Angeles Times* wrote, "Murphy may have gotten so tangled up in the myths and myopia of high-powered movie making that he can't get back the pungent, kick in the throat awareness earlier audiences loved."[43] This review represents a coded critique of the film's departure from the racial comfort zone established by Murphy's previous film persona as the subordinate Black sidekick protected by a white chaperone. The *Chicago Tribune*'s scathing assessment amplified this sentiment, declaring, "This is Eddie Murphy's shockingly embarrassing debut as writer-director. This 1930s Harlem nightclub comedy has gross amounts of racist dialogue directed at both whites and Blacks, a sexist portrayal of women as hookers, and the wasteful use of comic legends Richard Pryor and Redd Foxx as cohorts of Murphy's in an illegal casino."[44] These reviews, dripping with condescension, expose the white establishment's discomfort with Murphy's cultural moves away from Hollywood's racial norms to assert a politicized Black identity. The *Chicago Tribune*'s condemnation of *Harlem Nights* for containing "racist dialogue" proves a misguided application of the term. Kwame Ture (formerly Stokely Carmichael) and Charles V. Hamilton remind us that the words "racist" and "racism" are frequently used but are rarely understood in American discourse. Ture and Hamilton argue that "racism is the predication of decisions and policies on the considerations of race for the purpose of *subordinating* a racial group and maintaining control over that group."[45] That is to say, racism necessitates an essential power relation where decisions are made to subordinate and exploit a particular group. Absent of such power, Black Americans and other marginalized groups are not purveyors of racism; they remain its targets. Perhaps more to the point, much of the criticism levied against Murphy coincides with his public chastisement of the Hollywood industry as a presenter at the sixtieth annual Academy Awards.

On April 11, 1988, during the live worldwide broadcast of the Oscar ceremony, Murphy seized an unscripted moment before announcing the nominees for Best Picture. In a move reminiscent of Pryor's Oscar critique a decade earlier, Murphy candidly spoke out against the industry's discriminatory practices that preserve a systemic underrepresentation of Black talent, both on-screen and within the Academy itself:

> When they came to me and said they wanted me to present the award for Best Picture, my manager told me that the Academy had picked me, and my first

> reaction was to say, "No, I ain't going." And my manager said [*Murphy mimics his white manager's voice*], "But why, Ed?" [*Audience laughs.*] I said, "I'm not going because they haven't recognized Black people in motion pictures." He said, "What are you talking about? Black people win Oscars." I said, well, Black actors and actresses have won Oscars throughout, like, sixty years: Hattie McDaniel won the first one, then Sidney Poitier won one, and Lou Gossett won. And I'll probably never win an Oscar for saying this, but hey, I gotta say it. [*Pause*] Actually, I might not be in any trouble because the way it's going, it's like every twenty years we get one. So we ain't due until about 2004. [*Audience laughs.*] By that time this will all have blown over. I said, "I wasn't going," and my manager said, "You just have to go. You can't snub the Academy." So I came to give the award, but I just feel that we have to be recognized as a people. I just want you to know that I'm gonna give this award, but Black people will *not* ride the caboose of society. And we will *not* bring up the rears anymore, and I want you to recognize it.[46]

Murphy's extemporaneous rebuke of the Academy, Hollywood's most exclusionary institution, laid bare the racial fault lines that fracture the industry. For many in the white Hollywood establishment, Murphy's comments were dismissed as an ill-conceived "rant." For Black audiences, on the other hand, his words resonated as a daring act—a rare instance of a prominent Black celebrity publicly speaking truth to power.

Despite the criticism lobbed at *Harlem Nights*, the film soared to number one at the box office, bringing in an impressive $95.8 million in ticket sales.[47] The dissonance between the film's critical reception and box office performance exposes the limitations of white tastemakers dictating the preferences of Black audiences. The economic realities of Murphy's film further positioned him as a Hollywood mega-commodity. The critical mauling of *Harlem Nights*, however, reveals a fraught tension between the establishment's desire to return Murphy to his "place" in subordinated movie roles as a loud-talking, slightly suspicious character versus Murphy's desire for creative autonomy. This ideological clash presaged the demise of his Black Pack cycle. Unfortunately, *Harlem Nights*'s production and release arrived at the tail end of the legendary careers of both Pryor and Foxx. The critics who derided the film's alleged "wasteful use" of their comedic talents clearly overlooked this crucial context. They also failed to acknowledge the profound visual pleasure derived by Black audiences from witnessing their collaborative on-screen presence. The significance carried by Foxx, Pryor, and Murphy together on-screen conveys unarticulated implications. Their combined

FIG. 2.9. Redd Foxx and Richard Pryor in *Harlem Nights*, 1989.

cultural capital—as icons of American humor—infused *Harlem Nights* with profound levels of meaning. Black audiences experienced immense gratification witnessing these legendary figures united, performing with agency and commanding the screen. It was a visual affirmation of Black cultural heritage and achievement.

The film indeed offers amusing moments from both Foxx and Pryor. Still, to expect the high-energy dynamism of their youth disregards the realities of aging. Pryor's private battle with multiple sclerosis and Foxx's heart condition, which tragically claimed his life a few years later, tempered their performances. The television series *The Royal Family* (1991–1992) was another facet of Murphy's Black Pack strategy, stemming from the relationships he forged on the set of *Harlem Nights*. Murphy endeavored to help revitalize the careers of the financially strapped Redd Foxx and the underutilized Della Reese. Murphy exercised his influence at Paramount, and *The Royal Family*—his brainchild—provided a platform for Reese and Foxx to reprise variations of their *Harlem Nights* characters in a sitcom format. The show's story world centered on a retired couple whose tranquility is upended by the return of their divorced daughter and her children.

Harlem Nights, for many Black audiences, rather significantly operates as film as fun. The movie exists outside the realm of Hollywood hegemony, where white executives dictate the stories of the Black world. The film elicits laughter when "the comedic realm is denaturalized in important ways regarding racial performance, the occupation of space, and self-actualization."[48] *Harlem Nights* revels in subverting expectations, presenting Blackness in positions of power, and celebrating the pleasure derived from unfiltered language, irreverent humor, and cartoonish violence. The picture delights in the unburdened amusement enjoyed by similar white-led crime comedies like *Dirty Rotten Scoundrels* (1988) or *A Fish Called Wanda* (1989), a refreshing departure rarely afforded to Black motion pictures. At the film's end, Sugar Ray applies his sharp mental abilities rather than brute force to outmaneuver his adversaries. His resourcefulness culminates in Sugar Ray and Quick securing a significant sum of money. Their aim is to use the funds to transition into a legitimate business to aid their community and foster Black economic empowerment. *Harlem Nights* finds the effectiveness of its racial satire grounded in its capacity for self-creation through self-examination. Murphy's ventures into creating productions that centralized Black themes disrupted authoritarian sensibilities that longed for him to return to fast-talking characters devoid of social depth, historical grounding, or political agency.

Reversal of the Dog

Eddie Murphy's next feature, *Another 48 Hrs.*, though dismissed by critics, performed well with audiences. This sequel to his 1982 breakout film saw Murphy return to the interracial buddy genre that catapulted him to stardom. The narrative rehashes Murphy's vintage wisecracking portrayal of Blackness under the watchful supervision of a rugged yet dutiful white authority figure. With box office receipts exceeding $155 million, it suggests the establishment's satisfaction with the return of "their" Eddie Murphy—the one who fits neatly into a white milieu.[49] The subsequent ousting of Paramount Pictures CEO Frank Mancuso ended his thirty-year run and paved the way for his replacement, Brandon Tartikoff, longtime entertainment division president at NBC. A critical factor in his hiring was the friendly relationship Tartikoff shared with Murphy, dating back to the actor's days on *Saturday Night Live*.[50] His inaugural act as CEO was green-lighting Murphy's next project, *Boomerang*. There were, however, lingering anxieties among some studio executives who thought the film's predominantly Black cast presented a commercial risk for Paramount. But Tartikoff's imperative was clear: Murphy was their billion-dollar golden goose, and his continued appeasement was good for business.

Boomerang marked yet another shift in Murphy's comedic persona. For the first time, he took on the role of a romantic lead in a film steeped in a culturally specific Black context. Continuing his aspirational production model, Murphy petitioned Paramount to entrust the film's vision to a Black director. At Murphy's behest, Reginald Hudlin, the Harvard-educated writer-director behind the hip-hop-infused teen comedy *House Party* (1990), was hired to shoot *Boomerang*. Hudlin eagerly embraced the opportunity. During preproduction, however, Paramount executives, clinging to outdated notions of audience appeal, exerted pressure on Murphy and Hudlin to insert an arbitrary white sidekick into the film. This transparent attempt to safeguard against white anxieties was met with adamant resistance from Murphy and was ultimately rejected.[51]

Thematically, *Boomerang* extends the rebellious precedent established in *Coming to America* and *Harlem Nights*, situating Murphy within an exclusively Black cinematic milieu. He portrays Marcus Graham, the successful vice president of marketing at a major Black-owned cosmetics corporation in New York City. Marcus and his social circle represent a 1990s emergent class of Black urban professionals. The film amplifies Murphy's socially resistant cinematic brushstrokes, articulating a rising political consciousness and Black economic empowerment that counters Hollywood's historical denigration of Blackness. On the surface, *Boomerang* dazzles with its depiction of Black affluence and corporate success, yet beneath its sleek veneer lies a subtle, more complex exploration of class politics and the elusive nature of Black upward mobility in America. The film paints a portrait of Marcus Graham as a polished advertising executive who embodies the quintessential '90s New York buppie, navigating the business world—a Black man who has "made it" in a corporate sphere traditionally dominated by whites. Yet *Boomerang* is not merely a celebration of Black success; it is a critical examination suggesting the trappings of wealth and status do not need to come at the expense of cultural solidarity. The film defies conventional Hollywood narratives as an understated meditation on Black identity in a capitalist society—a society that offers the promise of upward mobility but demands a relentless performance of class politics to sustain it. At its core, *Boomerang* also celebrates romantic and platonic Black love, articulating a deformation of mastery from within a hostile system. Murphy's cinematic disruption is achieved by not only centering Blackness in the movie's story line but also showcasing Blackness as the epitome of success, beauty, cool, and cultural richness.

The revolutionary laughter the film evokes is tethered to its performances of class politics and social inversion—that is, its embrace of an aspirational Black world, or as Danielle Fuentes Morgan might describe it, its celebration of "the multiple autonomous ways of being Black—that prevents psychic death, or being objectified and flattened."[52] With *Boomerang*, Murphy recognizes the crucial role cinema plays in constructing social horizons and defining the parameters of the possible. The film's unapologetic Black vocality posits Murphy and his castmates as purveyors of pop culture who defy convention. They represent a class of Black professionals in America—a class historically relegated to the cinematic margins, yet here, they claim a space within the upper echelons of corporate power. The movie revels in its portrayal of Black executives who are as polished and sophisticated as their white counterparts, yet it does not shy away from the performative aspects bound up in their success. Every tailored suit, every chic hairstyle, every immaculately appointed office space, every (Black) power move is a testament to the characters' hard-won success and a reminder of the tenuous nature of their status in America. These characters aren't merely business executives; they are symbols of the Black middle class, maneuvering through a corporate environment that is as much about strategy as it is about style. The stellar ensemble cast, which includes future Oscar winner Halle Berry, Robin Givens, and rising comics Martin Lawrence and Chris Rock, is not just funny and fashionable but also intelligent, financially empowered, and undeniably attractive—a compelling assertion of Black agency in the '90s cinematic landscape. Murphy and his castmates come alive on-screen as multidimensional human beings, reflecting the heterogeneity of Black communities. Each character stands in stark contrast to the ultraviolent Black portrayals widely circulated in Hollywood flicks of the 1990s. *Boomerang*, like *Harlem Nights*, presents its central characters in sartorial grandeur, self-consciously exuding elegance and sophistication. The film's opulent fashion, trendy costuming, and luxurious production design activate Black visual pleasure, while Murphy's emphasis on aesthetic refinement and "Black cool" functions to reclaim the dignity of Black bodies on-screen that have been habitually "othered."

Another one of the film's disruptive innovations materializes in its reversal of patriarchal power dynamics. *Boomerang* attempts to, but ultimately falls short of, a full engagement in a third-wave feminist-leaning sensibility. The movie spins the tale of Marcus Graham, an infamous womanizer, nattily clad in Armani togs and Bruno Magli loafers, who personifies male chauvinism. His romantic interest in women notoriously evaporates after sexual intimacy, reducing his dates to mere conquests. Marcus's incessant pursuit of sexual validation masks a deeper emotional void and insecurity. His behavior earns him the label of a "dog"—a term denoting men who objectify women for sexual gratification. Following a corporate takeover at his place of employment, Marcus quickly learns he is being denied a promotion and will be forced to work under the leadership of a new boss, Jacqueline Broyer (Robin Givens), an intelligent and attractive Black woman. This narrative twist mirrors the dynamic established in Doris Day and Rock Hudson's romantic comedy *Lover Come Back* (1961). In the film, Day and Hudson play rival New York City ad executives who overcome Hudson's chauvinism and questionable business tactics to end up happily married. *Boomerang* enlivens and reinscribes this formula against a buppie backdrop with Murphy as the leading man caught in a love triangle. The film deforms socially constructed gender roles by ensuring that Marcus's infamous chauvinism meets its match. Jacqueline's professional success and moral relativism regarding casual sex challenge traditional notions of female agency. Her nonchalant attitude toward conventional romance and gender expectations expresses security in her self-assured independence, power, and modernity. An emblematic scene that underscores this power reversal occurs while Marcus attempts to woo Jacqueline with dinner at his swanky Manhattan apartment. However, rather than succumbing to his romantic advances over a candlelit meal, she requests that they dine in front of the television set to satiate her passionate interest in watching the New York Knicks basketball game, an activity typically associated with male interests. As Jacqueline is entirely engrossed in the NBA action, she ignores Marcus, and his powers of seduction are rendered useless, a metaphor for the erosion of patriarchal authority in the face of her independence.

Jacqueline later rejects his offer for a postprandial espresso, instead requesting a beer, further destabilizing audience expectations of gender norms. *Boomerang*'s exaggerated portrayal of Marcus's chauvinism illuminates entrenched cultural beliefs surrounding heteronormative sexuality. To the film's credit, Marcus is forced to experience his own objectification firsthand through Jacqueline's reciprocal treatment. Her lack of emotional attachment to Marcus and the act of her bragging about their sexual encounters to her female colleagues subvert patriarchal power, leaving Marcus feeling degraded and exploited. His eventual transformation is ultimately driven by a new relationship with the grounded and vivacious creative director Angela Lewis (Halle Berry), an artsy, intelligent, and sensual modern Black woman. The source of energy and tension in *Boomerang* appropriately arises in its challenge to outmoded notions of womanhood, particularly through the restrictive lens of objectification.[53] Through the reversal of patriarchal power, Marcus is forced to confront the inadequacies of his

FIG. 2.10. Robin Givens as Jacqueline and Eddie Murphy as Marcus watching the NBA in *Boomerang*, 1992.

FIG. 2.11. Halle Berry as Angela and Eddie Murphy as Marcus in *Boomerang*, 1992.

crass behavior toward women. The film's appeal lies in its rejection of the social construct that defines women as sexual objects. It attempts to embrace a feminist-leaning sensibility that suggests that chauvinistic adherence to patriarchal beliefs ultimately undermines a man's capacity for a genuine connection with a woman. The movie endeavors to depict Black women as multifaceted individuals, fully equal to their male counterparts and endowed with intelligence, agency, and power. However, *Boomerang* does stumble, particularly in its underdeveloped handling of the conflict between Marcus and Angela. Throughout the film, Marcus finds himself in lust with Jacqueline, yet over time, he falls head over heels in love with Angela, creating a twisted love triangle—an entanglement. While the portrayals of Angela and Jacqueline were cutting edge for the time, after further consideration, sadly but predictably, both characters appear to succumb to a binary argument that a truly independent, liberated woman must take on masculine characteristics. Jacqueline expresses the warped patriarchal notion that a truly powerful woman should embody aspects of traditional masculinity in order to win while playing a "man's game." In other words, to succeed as a "real Black woman," she must *act* like a man and *think* like a man, signifying two sides of a rusty patriarchal coin.[54] Angela, on the other hand, is sweet and endearing, all the things Jacqueline is not, which is why Marcus ultimately chooses her. Angela's soft feminine energy helps Marcus grow, both in his understanding of love and in his maturity in relationships. But Angela quickly dumps him after discovering his affair with Jacqueline.

At this point in the narrative, Marcus's forced introspection compels him to acknowledge his personal failings and ultimately recognize his genuine love and affection for Angela. His emotional journey climaxes in a heartfelt pursuit to win back her trust, leading him to locate her office at a new company, where she is now a high-powered corporate art director. Here, the movie stumbles. Visibly hardened by heartbreak, Angela far too quickly dismisses Marcus's infidelity and rekindles her relationship with him, undermining the film's reversal of power. Put differently, the movie's obligatory happy ending comes at the expense of a good woman. For the picture to end cheerfully, Angela must be forgiving and take Marcus back in spite of the heartache he caused her. A more nuanced depiction would require Marcus to undertake a more arduous journey to reclaim her trust, with Angela demonstrating a greater resolve in holding him accountable for his actions. Perhaps she would choose to love herself first, focus on her own goals and desires, and let fate be the deciding factor in their relationship. In the absence of such tension, the film's resolution inadvertently privileges masculinity over the complexities of genuine reconciliation. As bell hooks argues, Black men who cling to sexist ideologies and patriarchal fantasies "need to know that a concrete engagement with feminist thinking would allow them to examine the ways their acceptance of patriarchal notions of masculine identity undermine their capacity to live fully and freely."[55] That said, *Boomerang*'s negotiation of progressive sexual politics is a bit clumsy.

Nonetheless, the film's broader merit, and perhaps its most astute innovation, lies in its ability to offer audiences a radically alternative vision of Black culture and professional success. Murphy deforms conventional Hollywood formulas by employing comedic reinscription, foregrounding an upwardly mobile Black social consciousness in a racially inverted environment where the Black characters are the primary movers and shakers and arbiters of their own social destinies.

To its credit, *Boomerang*'s production of humor also delivers koan-like criticism of the invisible architectures of systemic racism. The film's critiques are delivered through crafty satire, primarily executed in three pivotal scenes involving Marcus and his friends, the quirky Gerard Jackson (David Alan Grier) and the impulsive Tyler Hawkins (Martin Lawrence).[56] The first occurrence plays out at a fine-dining restaurant when a white waitress approaches their table to take their order. As she describes the menu, the waitress mentions the day's special, which includes asparagus spears. After she walks away, Tyler immediately draws his friends' attention to her use of the word "spears" instead of asparagus "tips." He argues that her choice of words represents a racial microaggression, associating their Blackness with primitive stereotypes of "spear-wielding" Africans. Tyler's observation hilariously draws attention to the deceptive ways in which racial biases permeate everyday interactions for Black people.

Another instance of the film's critical brushstrokes transpires while Marcus and his friends shop in an upscale Fifth Avenue clothing store. As they enter the boutique, an arrogant white salesclerk, of course, cryptically follows the three Black men around the store, eyeing them suspiciously like criminals. He finally approaches the gentlemen and condescendingly informs them that the store offers no layaway plans. He also tells them that they don't keep any cash in the store—as if the Black men are there to commit robbery. The clerk erroneously, and quite obviously, presumes Marcus and his friends are incapable of affording the expensive items at such a high-end establishment. The smug clerk's racist microaggression toward Black customers, despite them already donning expensive attire, underscores white assumptions of Black inferiority. The comedic sentiment in the scene comments on the absurdity and irrationality of racism and whiteness as a system of power that operates, in most instances, to impede Black social and economic progress.

One of *Boomerang*'s most succinct and hysterical commentaries on race unfurls with Tyler and his buddies Marcus and Gerard as they hang out and shoot pool. Tyler explains the underlying symbolism embedded in the game of billiards. He argues the game is a veiled expression of whiteness and

FIG. 2.12. Martin Lawrence as Tyler, Eddie Murphy as Marcus, and David Alan Grier as Gerard in *Boomerang*, 1992.

systemic racism. The domination of the white ball over the colored balls (red, yellow, etc.), he argues, is a metaphor for the power dynamics of race in the West. With politically Black wit, Tyler points out that victory in billiards hinges on the white ball removing the black ball from the equation, emphasizing the game's subliminal reinforcement of racist hierarchies. The humor in this sequence challenges America's racial contract, peeling back layers of social anxiety. While the characters' conversation appears jocular, beneath the veneer of comedy, the jokes land a critical punch that calls out the history of racist treatment in America. All three of these scenes exemplify Murphy's cultural maneuvers, using racial satirization to revise the terms of engagement established by Hollywood and activating the plausible deniability of humor to offer an appraisal of America's ancient network of racism.

Before its release on July 1, 1992, *Boomerang* encountered a barrage of negative reviews from white critics who misrepresented the film as a "reverse racist" vanity project for Murphy. The *Los Angeles Times*, for instance, pronounced that Murphy had lost his comedic edge, asserting, "Marcus Graham is no hustler, no scrambler after respectability, he is a polished and successful director of marketing."[57] The review further argued, "This film takes pains to create a reverse world from which white people are invisible except when comic relief is called for. Aside from an insipid waitress, a bumbling racist store clerk and four beefy young slaves (the credits coyly lists them as escorts) who are enthusiastically whipped by Strangè as they pull her chariot through New York's World Financial Center (don't ask), the only pale American face prominently visible belongs to Capt. James Kirk of the starship Enterprise."[58] Such misguided appraisals ignore the century-long history of Hollywood cinema's exclusion, caricature, and racial distortion under the rubric of white nationalism. Several reviews, including one in the *New York Times*, expressed similar disdain for *Boomerang*'s politically Black reinscriptions of Hollywood formulas, dismissing the film as the pretentious, self-indulgent by-product of Murphy's presumed celebrity ego. Harry Allen astutely explains this type of response and its correlation to the burden of representation forced upon Black people, arguing that "any filmmaker can use any filmic strategy to make a point, as long as that strategy is coherent. And Black filmmakers are burdened with the rope chain of 'reality' in ways that white people simply aren't."[59] Yet the negative reviews did not impede the overwhelming support *Boomerang* garnered in many Black communities.

When considering the film's musical elements, composer Marcus Miller's jazz-infused score blends impeccably with the irresistible grooves of a soundtrack crafted by music superproducers Antonio "LA" Reid and Kenneth "Babyface" Edmonds, best known for creating hits for Whitney Houston and Mariah Carey. The *Boomerang* soundtrack was a phenomenon in its own right, selling a staggering three million copies, reaching number one on the R&B charts and number four on the Billboard Top 200. It impressively featured three top-five singles and launched the career of R&B singer Toni Braxton with her empowering anthem "Love Should Have Brought You Home." The soundtrack's other singles were "End of the Road" by Boyz II Men, which peaked at number one on the charts; "Give You My Heart" by Babyface and Toni Braxton; and "I'd Die without You" by P. M. Dawn, which hit number two and number three, respectively, cementing the *Boomerang* album as one of cinema's highest-selling film soundtracks. Still, misreadings of Murphy's Black Pack films as commercial failures or vanity-driven missteps reflected a rising blowback against the ideological shift these productions express. Despite its critical panning, *Boomerang* was another commercial juggernaut for Murphy, earning over $131 million at the box office.[60] The film's enduring popularity in Black communities and its substantial financial track record testify to Murphy's culturally affirming vision. However, the picture also signifies a demarcation point, marking the culmination of Murphy's innovative era of Black Pack cinema.

The negative white blowback to Murphy's Black Pack output reveals the persistent mechanisms of power within Hollywood and its tangled practice of repression. His Black Pack films are refined brushstrokes that provide multifaceted visions of the world through a Black gaze, from Madison Avenue boardrooms to the lively banter in Black barbershops. These cultural productions thrive in sequestered spaces in a Black world that exists outside of the dominant society. Murphy's engagement with Blackness in these films is not beholden to "official" industry narratives. He ambitiously cultivates a resistant comedic space within a hostile system that tends to marginalize Black voices. Racquel Gates argues that "Murphy himself challenges the idea that one must be independent and outside of Hollywood in order to offer a Black-centered perspective. Though he may have found success within the Hollywood industry, and often supported its ideological constructs in his own [non-Black Pack] projects and performances, this does not fully account for his politics or how his work reflects them."[61] Murphy's ambitious production model enlarged Black cinema and media as a cornerstone of creative freedom that was never allowed to fully develop or reach its potential. During this brief and energetic Black Pack period, as Gates correctly points out, Murphy was able to bend the "very structures that Hollywood typically uses to ensure white privilege and Black marginalization in order to ultimately subvert them and destabilize whiteness in his film and television projects."[62] Murphy's Black Pack productions highlight a refined sense of political engagement in their apparent departure from his earlier cinematic persona as the streetwise sidekick. Free from the constraints of typecasting and Hollywood containment measures, Murphy's Black Pack cycle put forth a radical vision of Black comedic modernity and cultural reclamation.

Hiring predominantly Black casts and championing Black filmmakers and creatives in key below-the-line positions also demonstrate solidarity and Murphy's aspirational production model. His calculated power plays behind the scenes achieve what I call *cultural prestidigitation*.[63] That is to say, Murphy cunningly utilized his high-level Hollywood access and A-list influence to activate a cultural and artistic sleight of hand, creating a temporary window for unprecedented opportunities for Black creative image-makers. The unifying theme of these three films is Black-oriented subject matter that catalyzes subversive pleasure among viewers, whereby the process of social impact unfolds in the act of the subversion itself, underscoring the absurdity and arbitrariness of American racial politics without heavy-handed didacticism. Murphy's Black Pack motion pictures challenge, interrupt, and deform Hollywood formulas that seek to relegate Black stories and experiences to the furthest margins of the cinematic frame. In *Coming to America*, *Harlem*

Nights, and *Boomerang*, Murphy self-consciously engages in nonconfrontational radical Black comedic frequencies. Each of his Black Pack productions articulates the notion that "autonomous portrayals of Blackness not only lead to justice on the level of the individual—the idea that it is just to present yourself in your own terms—but also naturally opens into collective in-group justice that illuminates the many valid ways of being Black."[64] From this frame of reference, one might analogize Murphy's role as the leader of the Black Pack to a comedic incarnation of the Dan Freeman character (played by Lawrence Cook) in the Blaxploitation-era film *The Spook Who Sat by the Door* (1973). Both Murphy and Freeman gain access to the heart of their adversaries' institutions through infiltration. Then they strategically utilize the knowledge and resources acquired while working within the system to disrupt it, introducing rebellious Black vocabularies to their respective communities. Murphy's cinematic language of racial reversals and social inversion centers Blackness as a celebration of creative freedom, directly challenging the industry's established cultural hegemony.

The cultural and economic success of Murphy's Black Pack productions interrupts Hollywood's status quo and remains his most significant cinematic achievement. *Coming to America*, *Harlem Nights*, and *Boomerang* transcode ideas of cultural affirmation and Black Power nationalism as an expression of post-civil-rights-era momentum. This collection of films undermines the centrality of whiteness in cinema, situating audiences within a Black gaze of Afrofuturist tales of the Black world and all its attendant richness, rituals, symbols, and mythology. This critical and commercial breach distinguished Murphy as a subversive pop-culture visionary who thwarted traditional systems of production. His Black Pack oeuvre temporarily destabilized the white gaze that profoundly overdetermines the fate of Black cultural expression in the Hollywood industrial complex. Through the rituals of Black resistance humor, these films expose the inherent absurdity of racial constructs, underlining the distinctions between Black self-presentation and industry-imposed depictions of Black identity. It is only reasonable, then, to recontextualize Murphy's cinematic legacy by acknowledging the oppositional gaze that undergirds his sui generis Black Pack cycle. These films, appropriately enough, instigated a breakthrough in articulating Black possibility on-screen, demonstrating that entertainment can indeed have social relevance and that comedic resistance comes in many forms.

3

The Mothership

Hollywood Shuffle and the Arrival of Robert Townsend

Reflecting on the pivotal role of humor in our society, the esteemed director Billy Wilder, known for his sharp wit as well as for garnering seven Academy Awards for his classical-era Hollywood films, once quipped, "If you're going to tell the truth, make it funny, because otherwise they'll kill you."[1] Wilder's remarks, though seemingly lighthearted, carry a profound recognition of the duality of humor as a shield and sword for truth-tellers. A brief review of history reveals numerous examples of the tragic irony embedded in Wilder's words—those who dared to speak truth to power often faced severe consequences. Yet humor affords a means to temper the sting of truth, making it more palatable and fundamentally more survivable. This insight into the rebellious power of humor finds a potent exemplar in the career of Robert Townsend.

As an actor, comedian, and later a writer-director, Townsend deployed comedy not only as entertainment but as a weapon of resistance. His body of work, which is crucial to the cultural and comedic innovations of the Black Pack in the 1980s and '90s, underscores the vital role of humor in both critiquing and surviving a racist social structure, offering necessary counternarratives that celebrate Black resilience and creativity in the face of adversity. Townsend's independent filmmaking strategies, developed amid political and economic challenges, showcase humor's capacity to challenge oppressive systems while simultaneously creating spaces for Black joy. His self-reliant approach to cinema revived the spirit of rebellion that drove early twentieth-century film trailblazers like Noble Johnson, a movie star and cofounder of the Black-owned Lincoln Motion Picture Company, or Theresa "Tressie" Souders, one of the first Black women to step behind the camera as a film director. Yet despite dismissals by some critics as kitsch, the comedic tools in Townsend's Black Pack arsenal provoke far more than cheap laughs. He achieved mainstream success as an alchemist of Black resistance humor, transmuting anger, critique, satire, and playfulness into piercing social commentary. Townsend's landmark debut, *Hollywood Shuffle* (1987), harnesses a powerful comic energy that blends the evocation of controlled aggression with the discerning gaze of righteous anger and judgment, simultaneously embracing the levity of play and the joy of revolutionary laughter. The film's humor captures the era's comedic zeitgeist and showcases a Black social consciousness that acts as a barometer for the powerful and cutthroat nature of the Hollywood machine, offering a candid and hilariously sharp assessment of the nation's racial delusions.

From the earliest days of motion picture making, Black filmmakers forged independent pathways in the shadows of Hollywood's colossal studios, successfully maneuvering outside mainstream modes of production. Black cinema pioneers like Johnson, Souders, and the most eminent early Black film director, Oscar Micheaux, were emboldened with a sense of responsibility and moral obligation to communicate the social and political realities of their time. Townsend's intrepid strategy in producing *Hollywood Shuffle* extends the legacy of these early Black directors whose films critiqued America's racial politics and uplifted the Black cultural image. It is also true that the historical repression of Black cinematic voices in the commercial film business has resulted in waves and troughs of independent Black films. This has led to a catalog of underseen masterpieces like William Greaves's *Symbiopsychotaxiplasm: Take One* (1968), Charles Burnett's *Killer of Sheep* (1977), Kathleen Collins's *Losing Ground* (1982), Billy Woodberry's *Bless Their Little Hearts* (1984), Wendell B. Harris Jr.'s *Chameleon Street* (1989), Julie Dash's *Daughters of the Dust* (1991), and Haile Gerima's *Sankofa* (1993). Townsend's social satire, predictably enough, initiated a new cycle of tepid Black (exploitation) comedies that swept through the Hollywood industry like a sandstorm, reaching critical mass in the 1990s with pictures like *Livin'*

Large (1991), *CB4* (1993), *How to Be a Player* (1997), *Good Burger* (1997), and *I Got the Hook-Up* (1998). The commercial success of *Hollywood Shuffle* was also a driving force that accelerated the development of the upstart Black Pack crew of comics and their migratory production patterns across film and television. By channeling Black resistance humor in the movie, Townsend derides and exposes the industry's racial hypocrisies.

Before Steven Soderbergh's independent hit *Sex, Lies, and Videotape* (1989) and on the heels of Jim Jarmusch's *Stranger Than Paradise* (1984) and Spike Lee's *She's Gotta Have It* (1986), the frustrated actor-turned-director Robert Townsend created a stingingly resistant film comedy that introduced the world to the "Hollywood Shuffle Players," many of whom emerged as future comedy stars, including Keenen Ivory Wayans, Damon Wayans, Anne-Marie Johnson, and John Witherspoon. Townsend's film was a platform for rising comedic talent to communicate oppositional worldviews that were both funny and politically Black. *Hollywood Shuffle*'s culture of production—that is, the material environment and behind-the-scenes conditions the cast and crew experienced during the moviemaking process—is legendary in film industry lore. Before the advent of digital filmmaking technology and the ubiquity of cell phone video, Townsend's debut feature was shot in a fast-paced guerrilla mode and self-financed on a handful of credit cards, solidifying his rebellious comedic style and gregarious directorial persona. The film remains strikingly relevant as a biting satire of Hollywood's devalued depictions of Black people. The movie combats misrepresentations of Black communities and, in the process, humanizes its members by disrupting how these communities are perceived in the social and cultural imagination.

The revolutionary laughter *Hollywood Shuffle* elicits is sidesplitting and subversive. It also cultivates a sense of community rooted in shared ethnicity and the desire to alleviate Black communities from cultural and political exclusion. Townsend's approach to the production of humor aids in constructing the foundation of what Rebecca Krefting describes as cultural citizenship. For Krefting, "building cultural citizenship involves taking control of a public image created by others to maintain hierarchies; it is about empowering otherwise marginalized social identities, a means of locating and asserting oneself within a specific social, cultural, and political matrix in order to counteract inequitable treatment, develop community, acquire rights, build identity, and experience a sense of shared cultural belonging."[2] *Hollywood Shuffle*'s confrontational humor defies the vulgar role of white social domination in the commercial film business, challenging the political dynamics of power in what writer Nelson George describes as "postsoul" America.[3] This chapter offers a production study that contextualizes, archives, and analyzes *Hollywood Shuffle*, its political economy, its recalcitrant comedic voice, and the institutional issues and forces at stake for Black entertainment creatives in the 1980s and '90s. By exploring this crucial landmark in Townsend's career, we draw more profound insights into an unruly masterwork of Black resistance humor as an affective template of dissent that ignited his career and triggered the momentum and social velocity required to galvanize the arrival of the Black Pack.

It is not so ironic that the motion picture industry and its technologies of hegemony matured during the same period of American history, from 1890 to 1915, that witnessed the nightmare horrors and brutality of systemic racism, extrajudicial murders, lynchings, and legal discrimination against Black citizens. Film historian James Snead astutely reminds us that "early American films depended unthinkingly on theatrical precursors, propagating racial caricatures borrowed from the popular vaudeville and minstrel shows. Black skin (often represented by blackfaced whites) came to be linked with servile behavior and marginal status."[4] These conditions of hostility precipitated the naissance of "race movies" or, perhaps more aptly, Black silent-era films. The Black silent film movement emerged as an independent force that peaked in the 1920s and, in many ways, denotes an interesting parallel to Townsend's production model on *Hollywood Shuffle*. Black silent-era cinema centered on Black stories and characters portrayed by Black actors, produced by Black filmmakers working in predominately Black motion picture companies that distributed films in Black-owned theaters that catered exclusively to a voracious Black moviegoing audience. Inside this alternative reality of esteemed and segregated Black communal spaces, an oppositional politics formed as a rebuttal against racist and terrorizing image production in films like Thomas Edison's *Ten Pickaninnies* (1903) and D. W. Griffith's notoriously denigrating *The Birth of a Nation* (1915). The release of *The Railroad Porter* (1912) by William D. Foster, through his Black-owned Foster Photoplay Company, marked the establishment of one of the country's first independent Black film studios. Foster's success with *The Railroad Porter*, coupled with George and Noble Johnson's formation of the Lincoln Motion Picture Company and the debut of their two-reel film, *The Realization of a Negro's Ambition* (1916), signaled the advent of the nation's first Black cinematic movement. The early Black silent movies often emphasized unity, pride, and an upwardly mobile social consciousness. Many of these films showcased Blacks succeeding against tremendous odds in an openly racist society. Micheaux established the Micheaux Film and Book Company in 1918 and directed approximately forty films in thirty-three years, entirely outside of the Hollywood studio system. However, most of the companies responsible for producing the over five hundred Black silent-era movies were profoundly undercapitalized and suffered from a paltry distribution network. By the onset of the Great Depression, the advent of "talkies" adversely impacted Black film companies, and several of the silent era's top Black actors were wooed into Hollywood. So despite their innovations and achievements, most early Black filmmakers were subjected to Hollywood's surplus repression and its attendant and intractable restrictions of cultural domination.[5]

Hollywood Shuffle's politically Black comedic energy lambastes the voluminous history of racial caricatures in American media. Townsend brings to the forefront of popular culture a Black worldview that eschews inequality. His jokes invigorate audiences with a wickedly funny take on the racist conditions that impact what audiences see on commercial screens. The film's incendiary humor springs from a cultural and political consciousness that tackles issues of equity and social justice. By exploring the surplus repression of Blacks in Hollywood, we gain insight into the institutional conditions that inform Townsend's social critique and the way his work is commodified and transformed during the Black Pack period. Yet very little critical treatment is given to Townsend's resistant comedic persona, his production model, or his ability to develop a strategy that intertextually integrated with many Black audiences across multiple media platforms (stand-up, film, television, video). *Hollywood Shuffle*'s unorthodox production model was essential to the Black Pack's ability to generate corporate profits and activate the ancillary market revenue that was vital to their commercial success. Ironically, satirizing Hollywood proved to be the cultural move that allowed Townsend to cross over into the mainstream. His creative alliances with fellow Black Pack members Keenen Ivory Wayans and Eddie Murphy buoyed Townsend's career. Together, they capitalized on a new industry logic fueled by the rise of HBO as a premium cable channel and the emergence of Rupert Murdoch's Fox network as television's fourth major broadcaster. Despite its resounding box office triumph, *Hollywood Shuffle* passes judgment on the industry and still erupts as the urtext of the Black Pack, setting the stage for the comedians to consolidate, break through, and create other mainstream productions. Although the Black Pack and the major studios often had antithetical motives, they became partners, and for nearly a decade, both parties profited. Townsend's aggressive self-promotion, particularly how he engaged news media outlets in circulating his well-crafted production mythology, aided in solidifying *Hollywood Shuffle* as one of the top independent films of the year—and as one of the movie industry's legendary success stories.

One Black Movie a Year

To truly grasp the Black cinematic condition shaping the late 1980s, it is essential to acknowledge the intricate interplay among the ideological, aesthetic, and political-economic dimensions of race woven into the fabric of the American film industry. In the decades following the civil rights movement, the nation transitioned into a new phase of its history. The 1960s, primarily recognized as the apex of the Black liberation movement, marked a cultural moment when student-led marches, voting rights legislation, and strategic aggression challenged centuries-old notions of what it meant to be an American. By the 1970s, with post-Watergate paranoia gripping the country, the national mood soured as a major economic crisis beleaguered the Carter administration. The struggling U.S. economy also weakened the resolve of Hollywood executives to return to the glory days of producing prestigious "social problem films" like *Guess Who's Coming to Dinner* (1967) or *In the Heat of the Night* (1967). A decade prior, such films challenged the industry's status quo of racial representation. Concurrently, 1970s television programming limited Black actors largely to roles in sitcoms where the characters were confined to working-class ghettos on shows like *Sanford and Son* (1972–1977), *Good Times* (1974–1979), *What's Happening!!* (1976–1979) and *That's My Momma* (1974–1975). The exception, of course, was Eric Monte's *The Jeffersons* (1975–1985), whose lead character, George Jefferson (Sherman Hemsley), was allowed to "move on up" to Manhattan's ritzy Upper East Side following his success as an entrepreneur.[6] For Nelson George, the 1980s struggle for Black liberation saw several strident victories, failures, and ambiguities. George describes this cultural moment as the postsoul era—a period that "defines the twisting, troubling, turmoil-filled, and often terrific years [when America] witnessed an unprecedented acceptance of Black people in public life . . . and to a remarkable degree considering this country's brutal history [Blacks] were accepted as citizens, if not always as equals."[7] The arrival of superstar comedians like Whoopi Goldberg and Eddie Murphy, alongside the success of television programs like *The Cosby Show* (1984–1992), *227* (1985–1989), *Amen* (1986–1991), and *A Different World* (1987–1993), appeared to point toward Black progress in media culture.

At the same time, the 1980s provided a seemingly endless procession of nightly television news stories of Black Americans that were overwhelmingly dreadful: inner city crime, drug trafficking and addiction, broken families, teenage pregnancy, crack babies, welfare queens, failing schools, abject misery. Meanwhile, the Reagan administration's "Morning in America" campaign manufactured and glamorized the appeal of a wholesome and folksy vision of the country in the public imagination—outwardly ignoring the harsh economic and social realities faced by millions of Black citizens. Reagan's vision of America held largely adverse implications for Black people, indicating a regression into shadowy policies of second-class citizenship and overt denials of social justice and civil and human rights. As such, the gains and achievements of the postsoul era as described by George were extremely short lived.

FIG. 3.1. Robert Townsend as Corporal Ellis and Howard Rollins Jr. as Captain Davenport in *A Soldier's Story*, 1984.

In September 1984, Norman Jewison directed *A Soldier's Story*, an adaptation of the Pulitzer Prize–winning play by Charles Fuller. The film later won three Academy Award nominations. The movie's narrative depicts the murder investigation of a Black military officer during World War II and features a dynamic ensemble cast of talented Black thespians, including Denzel Washington, Adolph Caesar, Howard Rollins Jr., David Alan Grier, and Robert Townsend. After filming on location in Arkansas, Townsend returned to his Los Angeles apartment, exhilarated by the rare experience of working with a stellar Black cast on a major Hollywood film. As an up-and-coming actor,

Townsend naively brimmed with positive expectations regarding the impact *A Soldier's Story* would have on his career.[8] Despite hopeful expectations, the only auditions Townsend received after his role in this studio-financed prestige film were grossly stereotypic characters: muggers, drug addicts, pimps, and other woeful social deviants. Dejected, Townsend took a meeting with his talent agent, who candidly explained to him that in Hollywood, "every year they do one Black movie, and you just did it."[9] This unfiltered candor forced Townsend to come to terms with the structural inequalities inherent in Hollywood's discriminatory insider networks that historically locked out Black cultural producers from major executive-level decision-making roles.

After cutting his teeth as an improv performer at the mecca of Chicago's Second City, Townsend began his acting career with minor roles in two Chicago-based Hollywood films, *Cooley High* (1975) and *Mahogany* (1975). He subsequently moved to the East Coast and spent years navigating the Black theater scene in New York City. His penchant for mimicry and impersonations allowed him to land work as a voice actor in television commercials and a minor role in the cult classic crime drama *Warriors* (1979). During this period, Townsend gave a memorable audition for the sketch series *Saturday Night Live* but was unwittingly beaten out by his future Black Pack collaborator Eddie Murphy in what turned out to be Murphy's career-defining opportunity. After moving to Los Angeles, Townsend made his comedic rites of passage by appearing on *The Tonight Show Starring Johnny Carson*—the Holy Grail for up-and-coming comics. As an actor in Hollywood, he found himself deeply frustrated with the utter lack of diversity in the roles that were available to Black performers.

To commiserate, Townsend reached out to his friend, fellow actor, and future Black Pack pioneer, Keenen Ivory Wayans. The two met years prior on the comedy scene in New York. They bonded over shared ambitions to make names for themselves as actors. Wayans was the first to make the transition to Los Angeles and was soon similarly aggravated by the limiting and demeaning roles he regularly auditioned for. Townsend and Wayans experienced firsthand the types of containment strategies major studios had in place for Black talent in the 1980s. In fact, since the early days of Hollywood movies, depictions of Black life have been predominantly relegated to two categories: invisible or grotesque. Such racialized image production is associated with negative values in our society and indelibly etched into America's cultural imagination. Donald Bogle's typology of toms, coons, mulattoes, mammies, and bucks is perceptive in its outline of Hollywood's condescending bias when depicting Black people on screen. Bogle argues that well-constructed and reductive racial fallacies are passed down in various iterations throughout motion picture history.[10] This type of misrepresentation furthers the repression of Black lives along the scales of power in America. Both Townsend and Wayans felt they had reached Hollywood's glass ceiling for Black actors (*not* named Eddie Murphy). Determined to showcase his talent, Townsend leveraged the money he earned from *A Soldier's Story* to direct a short film. He wanted the project to serve as his calling card to studio executives, demonstrating his ability to create quality work from behind the camera.

Over a period of three days in 1984, Townsend directed himself, Wayans, and a patchwork group of Black actors in *Sam Ace: Private Eye*, a parodic treatment of the hard-boiled detective, lampooning Dashiell Hammett's famous sleuth Sam Spade and classic film noir titles like *The Maltese Falcon* (1941), *Murder My Sweet* (1944), and *The Big Sleep* (1946). Shot on black-and-white film stock, Townsend portrayed "Sam Ace," a Black private investigator—a character and image largely absent from the silver screen. The Black private detective would later find further exploration in two television series: *Sonny Spoon* (1988), starring Mario Van Peebles, son of director Melvin Van Peebles (who also costarred with Mario on the program), and *A Man Called Hawk* (1989), starring Avery Brooks as an urbane, chess-playing, art-collecting, pistol-toting gumshoe. In literature, Walter Mosley's World War II era character Easy Rawlins first appears in the 1991 novel *Devil in a Blue Dress* and stands out as the most popular fictional Black private eye. *Devil in a Blue Dress* was later adapted for film in 1995 as a Denzel Washington vehicle, featuring a scene-stealing performance by Don Cheadle.

Shortly after wrapping the Sam Ace project, Wayans and Townsend wrote a second short film intended to ridicule the overinflated self-importance of white movie critics. Townsend and Wayans's efforts resulted in "Sneakin' in the Movies." The project's comedic energy flows from Townsend and fellow actor Jimmy Woodard's mock-serious joke-telling style and exaggerated street parlance that turns the table on the Hollywood system, slyly denouncing its repressive racial hierarchies. In "Sneakin' in the Movies," Townsend and Woodard portray Tyrone and Speed, a streetwise version of TV personalities Siskel and Ebert. Tyrone and Speed embody a socially resistant "homeboy" vernacular as a rhetorical strategy that shatters the pretentiousness of the white movie critic archetype. The homeboys secretly enter a movie theater without purchasing tickets and review films from a Black outsider's perspective. They introduce themselves by breaking the fourth wall and speaking directly to the audience:

FIG. 3.2. Tyrone (Jimmy Woodard) and Speed (Robert Townsend) in "Sneakin' in the Movies," *Hollywood Shuffle*, 1987.

TYRONE [WOODARD]: Peep this, each week me and my boy, we go to different theaters and stuff and sneak in and check out the movies.

SPEED [TOWNSEND]: Then we come back and tell ya'll what's up and, like, if ya'll should pay money and shit.

The homeboys' slacker personas demonstrate a willingness to subvert social rules. Their refusal to pay for movie access puts Tyrone and Speed at risk from the theater's management and local authorities. Yet their rebellious act is not haphazard. Instead, it serves a utilitarian role that articulates a neo-Marxist critique of the instabilities of racial capitalism. Townsend and Woodard's exaggerated performance style showcases a rich understanding of movie clichés that unmasks Hollywood's maintenance of artistic, social, and cultural repression of Black talent. By acting as cultural intermediaries in "Sneakin' in the Movies," Tyrone and Speed disarticulate the powers of dominant cinema through their against-the-grain readings of each film. They view the movies before Black communities can consume them. This previewing opportunity allows Tyrone and Speed to provide an a posteriori assessment for the benefit of Black working-class communities. They disturb the normal process of consumption in a capitalist system by digesting the films before the products can reach their communities, actively helping "The People" avoid wasting money on movies not aligned with community interests. The homeboy critics, in that respect, perform an act of resistance, openly disrupting the system's imperative for profits. They inject themselves into the regulation of

FIG. 3.3. Dirty Larry sequence in "Sneakin' in the Movies," *Hollywood Shuffle*, 1987.

public conversation to exert influence over a commercial system that has a history of economically exploiting Black Americans through racial capitalism. In this context, Tyrone and Speed draw from a Black cultural heritage that evokes communal aspirations and a shared history while exposing Hollywood's true center of power—which is, of course, the almighty dollar.

The first film the homeboys review is *Amadeus Meets Salieri*, a Eurocentric period piece about the composer Mozart. Tyrone and Speed ridicule the movie as complete "bullshit." They also review *Chicago Jones and the Temple of Doom* and *Dirty Larry*, both spoofs of popular movie franchises *Indiana Jones* (1981) and *Dirty Harry* (1971). They blast *Dirty Larry* as unrealistic in its portrayal of exaggerated Black criminality pitted against the valiant "white savior" trope. The two critics take particular exception to Dirty Larry proclaiming his cliché catchphrase "Go ahead, make my day" (a direct appropriation of the slogan popularized by Clint Eastwood in *Dirty Harry*) to a group of heavily armed gang members. The homeboys defiantly point out that "brothers with guns" would not simply stand idly by listening to Larry's remarks.

Tyrone defiantly asserts, "As soon as he said 'make my day,' boom! [*pretending to shoot a pistol*] Do fifty bullets in your ass make your day?" Their final review is of the film *Attack of the Street Pimps*, which they proclaim to be a "good movie." They discuss the picture using a parody of pseudo-highbrow language, arguing, "The director captured the essence of street life and a horror-type situation." The homeboys conclude the movie "was full of stereotypes, but it was well directed." To recap their reviews, Tyrone and Speed appropriate Siskel and Ebert's "thumbs-up, thumbs-down" ranking system and employ their own panache. They give *Amadeus Meets Salieri* a thumbs down; they give *Dirty Larry* the "finger"; and *Attack of the Street Pimps* gets a "high five." With "Sneakin' in the Movies," Townsend demonstrates his propensity for symbolic reversal and social inversion as his trademark approach to Black resistance humor—that is, stereotype-slaying, culturally coded humor with a critical bite.

After completing a small role in the movie *American Flyers* (1985), Townsend collaborated with Wayans on another short project called "Black Acting School." The production was completed in six days over the course of two weekends at Nichols Canyon in Los Angeles. The project radiates with politically Black comedic energy that captures the nuances of the racially charged processes of production and performance embedded in Hollywood film and television. "Black Acting School" satirically depicts the demeaning manner in which Black performers are often stripped of dignity for a chance to work as actors in Hollywood. Townsend portrays Bobby Taylor, a Black actor classically trained in Shakespearean theater, who incredibly (and hilariously) transforms on-screen from playing a dimwitted Enslaved "sambo" butler with a slow southern drawl to revealing his true identity as an accomplished character actor who actually speaks with a posh British accent. He is one of many gifted Black thespians struggling to make a living in the inhospitable confines of Tinseltown. But he manages to find a viable solution to their chronic underemployment. To achieve professional success, Bobby and his talented colleagues are "reeducated" by white instructors at the Hollywood Black Acting School. This fictional institute specializes in training aspiring Black actors in the art of portraying one-dimensional racial caricatures. The instruction they receive makes the actors more marketable, safer for white consumption, and perhaps more importantly, viewed as far more employable in the eyes of studio executives. Bobby, the institute's spokesperson, lays out the merits of the Black Acting School in an infomercial-style format, enthusiastically promoting the school's approach:

> BOBBY: I had to learn how to play these slave parts, and now you can too at Hollywood's first Black Acting School! Learn Jive Talk 101 [so] you too can be a Black street hood.

The school's white instructors blithely demonstrate the many self-denigrating ways Black actors must often conform to neominstrelsy performance styles to gain the approval and attention of white gatekeepers.

FIG. 3.4. Robert Townsend as Bobby Taylor in "Black Acting School," *Hollywood Shuffle*, 1987.

Townsend's humor simmers with defiance and deep social awareness of the political and professional injustices that haunt Black actors in the ruthless, cutthroat movie industry. The jokes lay bare the complexities and perversions of Hollywood's racial obsessions and its bizarre fascination with manufacturing buffoon-like characterizations of Black people. Throughout the sequence, Bobby continues to sell the viewer on the school's immense value. The white instructors, who have perfected the racist on-screen conventions of modern-day "blackface," are paid to teach the techniques, gesticulations, and linguistics that sustain Black marginality in Hollywood. Their eagerness to train Black actors on how to "act Black" signifies that the exploitative and demeaning history of racial caricatures that litters American cinema was not, in fact, invented by Blacks themselves but rather fashioned within the musty and insidious dungeons of the white racial imagination. Bobby then turns his attention to conducting an interview with a successful graduate of the program, the muscular and eloquent Ricky Taylor (Grand L. Bush), a Black actor who proudly offers a testimonial about his career achievements since studying at the school:

> RICKY: I've played nine crooks, four gang leaders, two dope dealers, and I've played a rapist twice. [*Smiles proudly*] That was fun. Currently, I'm filming a prison movie. I play this tough con who tries to fuck this new inmate.

"Black Acting School" brilliantly echoes Townsend's and Wayans's real-life frustrations in Hollywood, sarcastically chastising the industry's bizarre

FIG. 3.5. Students and teachers in the "Black Acting School," *Hollywood Shuffle*, 1987.

fascination with racial tropes, Black pain, and depravity.[11] Their jokes offer a wellspring of social and political consciousness, using humor as a catalyst for addressing the persistent racial issues and forces at play in American media. The power and comedy in this sequence lie in its capacity to illuminate systemic contradictions, urging us toward a more equitable future. Each joke lands like a body blow—vicious uppercuts wrapped in punchlines, Black American humor laced with righteous anger. Townsend's provocative performance style amplifies and exposes the impossibility of Black actors occupying entertainment industry spaces unscathed. It also clarifies the disturbing ways the politics of whiteness and white racial fantasies in Hollywood film and television have become essentialized, packaged, marketed, sold, and recycled as "authentic" Black experiences. In "Black Acting School," Townsend and Wayans express a commitment to Black cultural citizenship. Indeed, this cultural citizenship operates as "a process manifested in particular types of cultural practices that embody symbols, discourses, practices, values and identities by which a subordinate community establishes a social and cultural space within which to affirm its collective sense of identity, solidarity, common historical experience and struggle to reclaim their rights."[12] Townsend's and Wayans's production of humor in this sequence challenges and disrupts the conditions of their cultural subordination in the industry. They keenly satirize the painful concessions and mind-numbing career choices that Black performers are often pressured to make in order to work and survive in Hollywood. The scene raises important questions about the ethical dilemmas that are inevitably attached to those choices. To its credit, "Black Acting School" also underscores the alarming eagerness of some Black performers to be accepted by the industry and their disturbing willingness to conform to white racial fantasies. Townsend asks the viewer to think critically about Black characters on-screen. Still, he does not let Black performers off the hook for their participation in the recycling of racial caricatures.

After completing "Black Acting School," Townsend and Wayans met to discuss their next move. They soon were forced to acknowledge the major financial and distribution limitations of short films in the commercial marketplace. They determined that they had accumulated enough footage from their three short projects to constitute the foundations for a full-length feature. So Townsend developed a story line around his "Black Acting School" character, Bobby Taylor—a young actor who aspires to make it big in the movie industry. Bobby's aspirational journey becomes the unifying premise of *Hollywood Shuffle* and the connective tissue binding the footage Townsend and Wayans previously shot. When Bobby lands an audition for the lead role in a slick new studio flick, *Jivetime Jimmy's Revenge*, he thinks the film, despite its terrifyingly stereotypical overtones, is precisely the opportunity he needs to skyrocket his career. The tension in the film surfaces as he is confronted by a series of choices to either maintain his integrity or "sell out" for fame and fortune. In taking on the role of Bobby Taylor, Townsend develops a doubly subordinated character. This strategy allows him to examine the plight of being Black in the United States and in the Hollywood context, confronting the psychological and social obstacles that overdetermine the politics of racial difference.

Over the next several months, Townsend struggled to allocate the necessary funding needed to finish the feature. He had already invested $60,000 of his own money bankrolling the short film projects, and any revenue generated from his television work had been depleted. In an attempt to raise capital to complete the production of *Hollywood Shuffle*, Townsend embarked on a Midwest comedy tour, returning to his roots on the stand-up stage. When he arrived back in Los Angeles, he received several preapproved credit card offers in the mail. It was an epiphanic moment. In a later interview with the *Los Angeles Times*, Townsend recalled, "I realized that in this society there is nothing you can't charge."[13] So he applied for five bank credit cards and two department store credit cards and began his crash course in "guerrilla film financing."

Townsend's unorthodox financial approach highlights a by-any-means-necessary production model. His strategy underscores the lack of access to capital and traditional economic resources that often plagues Black filmmakers. Spike Lee's career trajectory offers an interesting parallel. Lee also employed creative "outside-the-box" financing methods to address the capital-intensive realities of film production. His first feature, *She's Gotta Have It*, engaged a "kick-starter" strategy to raise his total production budget to $175,000. The film grossed over $7 million at the box office, catapulting Lee into mainstream prominence and solidifying his position as the first "celebrity auteur" of Hollywood's new Black film boom.[14] Decades later, *The Sweet Blood of Jesus* (2015), Lee's remake of Bill Gunn's Black horror classic *Ganja and Hess* (1973), was also independently financed through the web-based crowdfunding platform Kickstarter. Even at Lee's level of stardom and celebrity, his challenge in gaining studio funding for his projects exhibits the intractable and protracted nature of the continued repression of Black creative voices in the commercial movie business.

As cowriters of *Hollywood Shuffle*'s screenplay, Townsend and Wayans offer audiences a glimpse into the devastating psychic toll that Black performers must pay to cross bridges of conformity for a chance at riches and stardom. Their objective was to create a film imbued with the social edge to satirize and reappropriate the industry's clownish racial tropes. They honed a double-voiced style of Black resistance humor that proved adept at unmasking the complex discriminatory practices prevalent in the movie industry. The film's amorphous, nonlinear narrative fluctuates between fantasy dreamlike sequences and segments set in the "real world." This fluid structure infuses the film with a free-flowing aesthetic quality evocative of an improvisational jazz composition. *Hollywood Shuffle* challenges contrived media misrepresentations of Black people with an incendiary force stylistically parallel to the clarity and command of an intricate tenor saxophone solo by John Coltrane or an elaborate collage from the hand of Romare Bearden.

Guerrilla Financing

Townsend's financial resourcefulness while producing and directing *Hollywood Shuffle* is, in many ways, a testament to Black American resilience and pliable adaptability. His creative strategy of using whatever materials and tools were at his disposal aided his efforts to exceed traditional film industry limitations. The plan was straightforward. He purchased the wardrobe with his Saks Fifth Avenue card. Painting supplies and materials for art design and set decoration were charged to his Montgomery Ward card. Props and furniture were charged to Townsend's Sears card, and craft services were charged to his Visa. He had no upfront budget to compensate actors or crew members, so he promised deferred payments if the film sold to a distributor and regularly rallied the cast and crew at local gas stations to fill each person's vehicle with fuel. That expense was charged to the Visa. He rented a camera package, lighting, and grip equipment with his MasterCard.[15] In addition to shooting on leftover studio film reels handed down from Norman Jewison, Townsend cunningly secured a 10 percent discount on film stock from vendors after purchasing UCLA T-shirts for himself and the crew and posing as grad students.[16]

Since *Hollywood Shuffle*'s guerrilla style required the movie to be shot "on the run," Townsend decided to use two production vans: one for equipment and wardrobe and the other to transport performers. Locations were scouted in advance, invaded without warning, typically in early morning hours, and vacated quickly before police could ever arrive to question Townsend about his lack of movie permits. The film's production culture exemplifies a spirit of collaboration and community. It is also true that *Hollywood Shuffle* not only showcases the writing and acting talents of Townsend and Wayans but serves as a platform for many of their comedy peers who were talented yet chronically underemployed in the industry. One of the by-products of the movie's budgetary restrictions required the cast and crew to spend more time together in preparation for filming, which aided in community-building. Since Townsend could only afford to shoot one take per scene, he coerced the actors into long rehearsal periods. This intense preparatory process was an effort to maximize time efficiency during filming and take full advantage of the unnervingly finite amount of film stock he had available for cinematography. As Townsend recalls, "When it came time for me to shoot my film, the first time I looked at a camera I didn't know what I was looking at because I didn't really understand composition and everything. I got this whole crew together and I never directed, when someone says 'Townsend, come over here and look at this shot' I was nervous. I wanted to work as a director and when you really want something there's no obstacle."[17] *Hollywood Shuffle*'s financial constraints and Townsend's by-any-means-necessary mindset required the crew to wrap principal photography after filming only fourteen total days over a three-year span. His collaborative and communal style forged a production culture that pushed boundaries and reflected a larger vision of Black cultural resistance and social impact. After production wrapped, Townsend had incurred $40,000 in credit card debt. In the end, by implementing his guerrilla financing strategy, the film's total cost of production barely reached the size of an average Hollywood film's insurance budget.

To further cut costs, Townsend completed the movie's final edit at a postproduction facility in the San Fernando Valley that, oddly enough, specialized in editing pornography flicks. Subsequently, he rented the theater of the Writer's Guild of America (WGA) in Los Angeles to screen *Hollywood Shuffle* for studio executives, hoping to attract a major distributor. He also charged the theater rental fee and the cost of a lavish postscreening buffet to his credit cards and invited representatives from every studio in Hollywood to attend. Inside the studio ranks, he invited everyone from presidents and vice presidents to secretaries and production assistants.[18] Townsend's advanced screening had an excellent turnout; the reaction from the crowd was electric. However, not all the attendees understood the symbolic meaning of the movie. During the postscreening party, several studio executives approached Townsend, eager to distribute the picture. But these executives had one stipulation: they asked Townsend to cut a promotional trailer for the film that emphasized the "jive-talking" stereotypical scenes to appeal to a "broader" (white) audience. These executives were engaging in what Brandon Manning calls "consumptive laughter," a concept that refers "to the ways dominant culture often uses laughter to reduce, essentialize, and disregard Black experiences."[19] This is, of course, the same laughter that became the impetus for Dave Chappelle's departure from his sketch comedy series three decades later. Consumptive laughter, Manning argues, attempts to flatten "Black rebellious humor and the ways in which the audience is implicated in issues of social critique and representation."[20] Townsend's encounter with the "out-of-touch" studio executives at the postscreening party reveals the historical dialectic and tension among racist laughter, Black performativity, the white imagination, and the shrewd ways the industry perpetuates the visual language of oppression.

It was, however, Townsend's conversation that night with Samuel Goldwyn Jr. that changed the fate of *Hollywood Shuffle*. Samuel Goldwyn Sr. founded Goldwyn Pictures, a company later acquired in 1924 by theater magnate Marcus Loews, who also purchased Louis B. Mayer Pictures, consolidating both companies to create Metro-Goldwyn-Mayer, or MGM Studios.[21] In 1979, Samuel Goldwyn Jr. founded the Samuel Goldwyn Company, an independent film and television distribution firm. After viewing *Hollywood Shuffle* at the WGA screening, Goldwyn Jr. had a positive reaction to the film and saw its potential to turn a profit. Goldwyn also understood the movie's broader concerns. He indicated that the "film is about the future of Black actors." When Townsend heard Goldwyn's remarks, he thought to himself, "Somebody understands me."[22] Despite *Hollywood Shuffle*'s thematic and satiric ambitions, the film's postscreening reception exposed the tightrope Townsend walked, navigating the nuanced connection to his artistic creation in an anti-Black world while also contending with an industry that not only misinterprets Black life but actively sidesteps the processes of meaning-making within Black culture. Not long after their initial conversation, Townsend and Goldwyn struck a deal for *Hollywood Shuffle*. And as a show of confidence and good faith, Goldwyn wrote Townsend a check for $40,000 to cover the credit card debt he incurred financing the production. Additionally, Goldwyn arranged for the film's cast members to finally get paid for their work on the movie.

Hollywood Shuffle premiered at the Santa Barbara International Film Festival on March 7, 1987, and was released in theaters nationwide on March 20, 1987. The movie was produced for roughly $100,000 and earned a whopping $5.2 million at the box office during the first ten months of its release.[23] It was a breakout hit and a success with critics and audiences alike, announcing the arrival of Townsend's snarky humor into the mainstream cinema conversation. He worked deliberately to cultivate the aura of an upstart "celebrity auteur" who placed a sizable bet on himself by targeting underserved Black audiences as a viable market segment. A crowning achievement in Black social satire, the commercial triumph of *Hollywood Shuffle* situated Townsend in the public sphere as a charismatic humorist who exposed the film industry's racial neurosis, prompting audiences to critically examine dominant cinema ideologies. As Darryl Dickson-Carr points out, Black Americans were historically "forced to create various complex coded languages and expressions that allowed for indirect expression of their frustration. Bitingly satiric humor was as much a part of these codes as any other rhetorical element, written into a language of indirection that often satisfied those who held power even as it stymied them."[24] From this perspective, Townsend's irreverent brand of Black resistance humor entertains viewers, encourages self-reflection, and motivates a reappraisal of deeply held assumptions. Under very challenging circumstances, Townsend managed to create a film with a radical edge born out of sheer frustration from the industry's repression of Black cinematic voices. The film's achievement, in many regards, is predicated on its reappropriation of white-engineered stereotypes of Black people. By sacrificing professionally and financially, Townsend was able to promote the film's culture of production as the lore from which legends are born. His sacrifice paid off at the box office, and he was hailed as a multitalented rising star in comedy.

The Industry's New Logic

Three key developments in the 1980s entertainment industry aided in accelerating the social diffusion of *Hollywood Shuffle* and the Black Pack's cultural productions at large: first, the increased market saturation of videocassette recorder (VCR) technology and home videotape rentals; second, the expansion of HBO as a premium cable network; and third, the emergence of Rupert Murdoch's Fox Broadcasting Company as the fourth major television network. VCR technology and home videotape circulation radically altered patterns of American media consumption that had previously been stable for decades. At the onset of this shift, Sony's Betamax and JVC's video home system (VHS) emerged as the two dominant formats for videotape cassettes. VHS soon became the technological leader in consumer-level production of VCRs and videotapes. For millions of Americans, VCRs offered what Frederick Wasser calls a "technology of choices," or a new way to watch films at home with more temporal control and the ability to record and collect television programs.[25] Wasser argues that VCR technology provided consumers "not only more choices over what movies and television shows to watch but also over when to watch the shows. This was a new and decisive form of consumer control over TV programming."[26] The primary reason consumers craved more choice and control over the temporal flow of their entertainment was the growing importance of "harried leisure," a phrase that describes the time crunch experienced by a rapidly expanding affluent sector of the American labor force in the 1980s.[27] However, major film studios initially opposed the videocassette market, citing concerns over potential copyright and intellectual property issues. But the success of VCRs ultimately augmented the film industry's profits. Soon, major video rental franchises like Blockbuster and Hollywood Video sprang up in cities across the country, generating robust financial activity by offering consumers the chance to buy or rent movies on videotape. By the mid-1980s, feature film rentals were the primary function of VCR usage in the United States.[28]

In 1988, one year after the public arrival of the Black Pack, theatrical film revenues in Hollywood increased by 70 percent from videocassette sales.[29] This meant that, for the first time, Black audiences could enjoy repeat viewings of new and exciting Black Pack films, like *Hollywood Shuffle* and

Coming to America, from the comfort of their own homes. The desire to collect and share television shows materialized with consumers' increased access to new movies at home. One unintended consequence accompanying this shift in viewing habits was the rise in video piracy or bootlegging within the consumer market. Many Americans began duplicating videotapes to collect, archive, and share movies and TV programs in their communities in a previously unheard-of manner. VCR technology and the development of home video systems paved the way for an entertainment phenomenon that deepened the Black Pack's cultural cachet through rituals of repeat watching, collecting, and community circulation among audiences. Videotape duplication (i.e., bootlegging) became a way for average consumers to exert control over their favorite movies, allowing anyone to become their own film curator, collector, or archivist. This new ability fundamentally changed the way viewers accessed visual media.

Adjacent to the rising prominence of home video technology, the expansion of the cable network HBO was also crucial to the ascent of Townsend and the Black Pack collective. On October 1, 1975, HBO became the first cable channel to deliver its service via satellite when it aired the heavyweight championship boxing match between Muhammad Ali and Joe Frazier live from Quezon City in Manila, Philippines.[30] The legendary battle, dubbed the "Thrilla in Manila" by Ali, went fourteen jaw-dropping rounds. Ali won the fight in what is widely regarded as the greatest heavyweight boxing match of all time. Millions watched HBO's broadcast, and the network began using satellite distribution as its competitive advantage. HBO aired its first comedy special, *On Location*, featuring Robert Klein, on New Year's Eve 1975. The program brought the comedy club experience into American homes and, as Bambi Haggins and Amanda Lotz point out, "exposed the hottest and hippest of A-list comic talent in stand-up concert specials that spotlighted those already on the top of the comedy club marquee."[31] The series boasted stand-up appearances by popular comics like Freddie Prinze and Redd Foxx. Likewise, George Carlin's first HBO special aired in 1977. He performed an updated version of his famous "Seven Dirty Words" routine on the campus of the University of Southern California. *On Location* helped cement HBO as a viable network where comics could deliver incisive and controversial material without fear of corporate reprisal. The channel's early emphasis on boxing and edgy comedic programming aided it in establishing brand loyalty in many middle-class Black households. The network's dedication to the comedy genre, particularly stand-up specials, was a significant selling point for Black subscribers. According to *Time* magazine, "By most estimates, Black viewers make up a greater percentage of HBO's subscribers than of the general population."[32]

Two stand-up specials featuring Black comics on HBO in 1983 exploded in American popular culture: *Bill Cosby: Himself* and *Eddie Murphy: Delirious*. While the Murphy and Cosby specials each utilize observational comedy, drawing inspiration from daily life and human experiences, their approach to the production of humor significantly diverges. Murphy's routine crackles with vibrant energy. He uses wit, celebrity impressions, and physical humor while tackling taboo topics like sex and race. In contrast, Cosby's routine is warm and inviting, weaving relatable stories into a clean and accessible performance. Despite their divergent styles, each special showcases the power of stand-up comedy to entertain, challenge, and leave a lasting impression on audiences. Cosby parlayed the success of his family-friendly HBO special into a role as America's number-one TV dad on NBC's breakout sitcom *The Cosby Show*. In *Delirious*, Murphy, clad in a flashy red leather outfit, established his comedy rock star image and became a landmark success. HBO also introduced its subscribers to the comic talents of Whoopi Goldberg with her stand-up special *Whoopi Goldberg: Direct from Broadway* (1985). In her routine, Goldberg's insightful characterizations of subaltern folks highlight Black resistance humor.[33] Her comedy offers a critical lens, dissecting the complex intersectional realities of Black womanhood and the pervasive attempts to silence and marginalize Black women's experience in American society. Goldberg later joined forces on HBO with comedians Billy Crystal and Robin Williams to create *Comic Relief* (1986–1998), a stand-up telethon that raised money to combat homelessness.[34] The specials were, as Wayne Federman puts it, "the comedy world's turn to step up for a cause—just as musicians had with *Live Aid* and *Farm Aid*."[35] All four of these comedy specials tremendously helped HBO's subscription base expand in the 1980s.

The Mothership Connection

If one could point to a singular defining moment that solidified the genesis of the Black Pack, it would be Eddie Murphy and Robert Townsend establishing a formal collaboration after a private screening of *Hollywood Shuffle*. For Townsend, it was vital for Murphy to watch the film (and more importantly, enjoy it). After all, Townsend dedicated an entire scene in the movie to lampooning the unintended consequences of "The Murphy Effect" on Black actors in Hollywood. In the film's "Eddie Murphy" sequence,

Townsend's character, Bobby Taylor, receives a call from his agent after auditioning for a movie. The agent reveals that Bobby didn't land the role because the film's producers were specifically looking for an "Eddie Murphy type." Perplexed, Bobby asks, "So they want somebody to act like Eddie Murphy?" This inquiry triggers one of the movie's fantasy vignettes that unfolds like a satirical fever dream. The viewer observes a Hollywood casting call unlike any other: a corral of Black actors / Eddie wannabes waiting nervously—each dressed in leather suits (à la Murphy in *Delirious*). When the white director, writer, and casting agent (Eugene Robert Glazer, Dom Irrera, and Lisa Mende, respectively) enter the room, they inform the men that they are looking for an "Eddie Murphy type," boldly declaring to the actors in the lobby,

> *We want somebody who can act like Eddie Murphy, from head to toe. That's what we want.*
>
> *Someone who can dress like Eddie Murphy; to look like Eddie Murphy; to be Eddie Murphy; to give the actor himself a "Murphy-ectomy"; to have a Murphy-like quality, "Murphy-esque"—to be "Murphonic."*

This deft and sardonic hyperbole illustrates a lacerating commentary on Murphy's massive impact on the 1980s movie business. He was Hollywood's funny, fast-talking Black buddy. This sequence illustrates how the industry's white gatekeepers were irrationally fixated on replicating Murphy's dynamic persona, attempting to cast similar types of Black actors for the sole purpose of reaping the residual benefits of Murphy's popularity. Townsend, in other words, exposes the Hollywood machine's insatiable hunger for formula and its tendency to co-opt, recycle, pigeonhole, and reduce Black talent to a singular, marketable "type." This cyclical process restricts and stifles the rich creativity of Black cinematic expression. The vignette transcends sarcastic mockery and creates space for Townsend to artistically express reasonable claims of social, human, and cultural rights often denied to Black communities.[36]

The "Murphonic" sequence offers a Black resistant treatment of the ever-present burden of representation constantly weighing on Black artists. This psychic burden, an enormous albatross for so many Black performers, applies social pressure on them to contort and conform to Hollywood's newfangled versions of blackface minstrelsy in pursuit of fame and stardom. The film's irreverent humor exposes this hypocrisy and the gaps and disparities between the nation's promises to Black Americans and its failure to fulfill

FIG. 3.6. Robert Townsend as Bobby Taylor in the "Murphonic" sequence, *Hollywood Shuffle*, 1987.

those promises. With *Hollywood Shuffle*, Townsend ridicules racial capitalism and institutional repression with volcanic wit: a sledgehammer dipped in satire. After the private screening, it was no surprise that Murphy and Townsend found common ground and forged an immediate connection. Murphy greeted the film with great enthusiasm, impressed with its politically Black sensibility. The nucleus of the Black Pack formed as Murphy, Townsend, and Wayans began regularly hanging out, creating a dynamic and close-knit bond on their shared journey to comedic stardom. The camaraderie among the trio served as a launching pad for their near decade-long intervention against the industry's racial tendencies. *Hollywood Shuffle* not only offers audiences a hearty laugh (at the industry's expense) but also holds up a mirror to the many flaws that inundate the system. The audience laughs as those mirrored reflections sweat under the revelatory heat of truth. The movie is a call to action wrapped in jokes, and the revolutionary laughter it elicits stings, reminding viewers of what's ultimately at stake, both culturally and politically, in American motion pictures.

In a pivotal move, Murphy successfully petitioned Paramount executives to hire Townsend to direct his next project—the *Eddie Murphy: Raw* (1987) stand-up concert film. This effort cemented *Hollywood Shuffle* as the Black Pack's foundational urtext, or the "mothership," from which a constellation of secondary projects would spin off. Upon its release, *Raw* shattered box office records, raking in over $50 million and securing its place as the highest-grossing stand-up concert film in history. Townsend, seemingly overnight, had segued from struggling actor to celebrity film director, boasting two hit films in a single year. Moreover, Townsend's electrifying performance on *Uptown Comedy Express* (1987), the star-studded HBO special produced by Murphy, caught the attention of HBO executives, leading to a new collaborative business venture. Townsend was contracted to write, direct, and star in an hour-long special under the network's banner "HBO's Comedy Hour." This alliance blossomed into a series of sketch comedy specials for the network dubbed *Robert Townsend and His Partners in Crime* (1987–1991), the third cultural branch of the *Hollywood Shuffle* tree. Townsend's HBO specials became an extension of his community-building strategy. He filled the cast with Black Pack members Paul Mooney and Keenen Ivory Wayans, alongside Anne-Marie Johnson and Franklyn Ajaye, all familiar faces from *Hollywood Shuffle*. The specials carry forth a tradition of Black sketch comedy pioneered by Richard Pryor and Paul Mooney on NBC's *The Richard Pryor Show* a decade earlier. Each episode of *Partners in Crime* features an opening sketch performed in front of a live audience, followed by Townsend's stand-up routine interspersed with prerecorded sketches, stand-up acts by hot new comics, and live performances by some of the era's most prominent Black recording artists. This programmatic style proved influential, inspiring future shows like Fox's *In Living Color* (1990–1994) and Comedy Central's *Chappelle's Show* (2003–2006).

The energy and enduring appeal of *Partners in Crime* lie in Townsend's ability to engage audiences in the liberatory possibilities of an all-Black televisual space, particularly on a network best known for pushing the envelope. The HBO specials embody Townsend's satirical and parodic style and harness the same "insider" vocality that resonated so powerfully in *Hollywood Shuffle*. With *Partners in Crime*, Townsend carves out an irreverent space within the cable television universe that evokes revolutionary laughter from performances of social inversion, racial role reversals, and politically Black carnivalesque transgressions.[37] For example, the sketch "Townsend Talk" satirizes the tawdry sensationalism epitomized by flamboyant hosts like Geraldo Rivera and Morton Downey on the era's crude tabloid talk shows. No target was off-limits—from eccentric '80s pop stars to pervasive action flicks like *Running Scared* (1986), *Lethal Weapon* (1987), and *Tango and Cash* (1989). The sketch "Rock Cops," for example, takes aim at Hollywood's crazed obsession with the "buddy cop" genre, featuring Townsend and Wayans as "Michael Davis" and "Prince Jones"—a parodic reimagining of the iconic singers Michael Jackson and Prince as mismatched renegade cops.

"The Bold, the Black, the Beautiful" sketches were, however, *Partners in Crime*'s most popular comedic segments, a recurring socially inverted parody of 1980s prime-time television soap operas like *Dallas* (1978–1991), *Knots Landing* (1979–1993), and *Dynasty* (1981–1989). These sketches adopt a culturally affirming perspective, upending the conventional social order in America by situating its characters in an all-Black world where Black people are wealthy, sexy, powerful, and the arbiters of their own destiny. This comedic role reversal is witty and symbolic, exposing the contradictions of racial hierarchies while expressing the possibility for restructuring the social and economic disparities at the heart of American inequality. The "Bold" sketches unravel the exploits of a wealthy Black owner of a restaurant chain, Lake Arrington (Townsend); his unfaithful wife, Chandelier Arrington (Anne-Marie Johnson); and her lover, the corrupt Alderman Dexter Mitchell (Keenen Ivory Wayans). With its campy satire, the sketches lampoon the over-the-top melodrama prevalent in the popular white soap operas of the era, creating an all-Black socially inverted world. The sketches elicit tongue-in-cheek laughter for Black viewers that is at once comical and culturally empowering. By creating a counterimage to white prime-time soaps, Townsend's "Bold" sketches use a subtle, nonconfrontational style of Black resistance humor to produce new televisual representations intended to build community and cultural citizenship and celebrate Black social mobility. For Townsend and the Black Pack, their focus on building community and cultural citizenship through comedy aligns with their insurgent strategy to infiltrate and interrupt the capacious history of nightmare images that maintain Hollywood inequality. "The Bold, the Black, the Beautiful" segments are a social barometer, symbolically illuminating the nation's deeply embedded contradictions while subtly gesturing toward potential pathways for restructuring the social and economic landscape for Black Americans.

Partners in Crime's thematic impulse foreshadows the wave of visual culture focused on professional success and Black entrepreneurism that defined the cutting edge of Black film, television, and music in the 1990s. With *Partners in Crime*, Townsend not only produces new Black comedic frequencies, but the program leverages his mutually beneficial relationship with HBO to empower previously marginalized Black cultural practices and social identities, which Rebecca Krefting might describe as "a means of locating and asserting oneself within a specific social, cultural, and political matrix in order to counteract inequitable treatment, develop community, acquire rights, build identity, and experience a sense of shared cultural belonging" across multiple Black communities.[38] Townsend's comedy specials exude the confidence of an artist climbing toward their creative peak. His work on HBO won two Cable Ace Awards, including Best Actor in 1989 and Best

FIG. 3.7. Robert Townsend as Blake and Anne-Marie Johnson as Chandelier in *Partners in Crime*, 1988.

FIG. 3.8. "The Bold, the Black, the Beautiful" sketch on HBO's *Partners in Crime*, 1988.

Variety Special or Series in 1991. Beyond the accolades, the specials were a formal training ground, nurturing the talents of emerging Black comedians like David Alan Grier and Tommy Davidson as well as the younger Wayans siblings: Damon, Kim, Shawn, and Marlon. *Partners in Crime* also proved to be the necessary creative outlet Keenen Ivory Wayans needed to land his first directing opportunity, *I'm Gonna Git You Sucka* (1988). Equally significant, the rapidly expanding reputation of the Black Pack members signaled a crucial moment in the industry, the opening of a window for a new generation of Black cultural producers to gain a major financial investment in Hollywood.

Nights like This, I Wish Raindrops Would Fall

Townsend's next Black Pack production, the musical drama *The Five Heartbeats* (1991), was initially developed at Warner Brothers, but the studio ultimately passed on the project. The film later landed at 20th Century Fox. Townsend's relationship with the studio was tenuous from the start. He assumed the roles of executive producer, director, and lead actor and cowrote the screenplay with Keenen Ivory Wayans. However, the movie was not a raucous parody or satirical skewering; it was a soulful period piece drawing inspiration from the transformative R&B groups that defined Motown's golden age in the 1960s. This shift in genre and thematic focus sparked concern among 20th Century Fox executives. They were worried the film would not connect with audiences, given how Townsend's entertainment brand had become synonymous with raucous comedy.

The Motown record company, arriving at the height of the civil rights movement, emerged as a hitmaking factory in the '60s, churning out soulful anthems that forever altered the landscape of American music and popular culture. Under the visionary leadership of Berry Gordy, the label signed brilliant vocalists and musicians and cultivated a universal public appeal. Throughout the decade, Gordy painstakingly crafted the "Motown sound," writing catchy tunes along with gifted songwriters like Smokey Robinson, the smooth-voiced lead singer of the Miracles. Gordy assembled an all-star roster of legendary Black singers, including the Temptations, Diana Ross and the Supremes, Marvin Gaye, Stevie Wonder (who was signed to Motown at age eleven), the Four Tops, Gladys Knight and the Pips, and the Jackson Five. Motown's chart-topping tunes included hits like "Shop Around," "Please, Mr. Postman," "My Girl," "Heat Wave," "You've Really Got a Hold on Me," "Dancing in the Street," "My Guy," "Baby Love," "ABC," "I Can't Help Myself," and "Stop! In the Name of Love." The sheer number of hit records Gordy produced effectively became the defining soundtrack of 1960s America.

The Five Heartbeats adroitly channels the vitality of the Motown era while activating cultural citizenship and nostalgia. The film is an epic tale that spans three decades, portraying the rise and fall of a fictitious R&B quintet—patterned after soulful crooners like the Temptations, the Dells, the Spinners, and the Stylistics. The movie spins the tale of Donald "Duck" Matthews (Townsend), J. T. Matthews (Leon), Eddie King Jr. (Michael Wright), Terrence "Dresser" Williams (Harry Lennix), and Anthony "Choir Boy" Stone (Tico Wells), who form "the Five Heartbeats." On their journey to the top of the pop charts, the group struggles with issues of racism, betrayal, payola, and music industry corruption and the horrors of alcoholism and drug addiction, which have haunted countless music legends. The Dells, a real-life quartet from the '60s era, served as Townsend's technical advisers on the film and recorded all of the original songs for the soundtrack, including powerhouse tunes like "Nothing but Love," "A Heart Is a House for Love," and "Nights like This." The movie also boasts memorable performances from two Black Hollywood veterans: Diahann Carroll and Harold Nicholas. Carroll, in her first return to the silver screen since her Oscar-nominated turn in *Claudine* (1974), imbues her role with a wistful elegance. Nicholas, on the other hand, brings the weight of history to his performance as one-half of the famous Nicholas Brothers dance duo that broke racial barriers in the 1930s and '40s to become one of the premier Black acts in show business. The presence of Carroll and Nicholas in the film serves as a celebration of cultural heritage and a compelling reminder of the ongoing struggle for Black progress in the motion picture industry.

The Five Heartbeats's cinematic idiom transcends the genre of Hollywood musicals. The essence of the film's Black musicality harks back to the ancient call-and-response rituals embedded within African oral traditions. We hear the echoes of this lineage throughout Black music, from the fervent cries of gospel to the plaintive moans of the blues and the soulful pleas of R&B and the pulsating rhythms of funk to the unruliest anthems in hip-hop. *The Five Heartbeats*'s musical language and strong affective register are a compelling emotional conduit, engendering a strong sense of identification for many Black viewers. The film, with its talented cast, is a vessel for uncovering a trove of human truths through its memorable songs and performances. The actor Michael Wright electrifies the screen, dispensing the picture's most

FIG. 3.9. Leon as J. T., Michael Wright as Eddie, and Robert Townsend as Duck in *The Five Heartbeats*, 1991.

gripping portrayal as the group's lead singer, Eddie King Jr. Wright's dynamic performance embodies the character's internal conflict—a tortured soul and powerhouse crooner blessed with immense talent and charisma but burdened by inner demons. The cinematic world of *The Five Heartbeats* is nostalgic, a love letter to the unmatched genius of Black musical expression in America. When asked to encapsulate the film for *Jet* magazine, Townsend responded that the movie is about "true friendship [that] withstands the test of time, if you're really friends. It's about the bond. . . . It's a happy story, then it's a sad story."[39] At its core, *The Five Heartbeats* is a Black masculinist tale of cultural brotherhood, negotiating the choppy waters and emotional possibilities of lifelong friendships.

Released on May 29, 1991, in 862 theaters—significantly fewer than the 1,500 screens enjoyed by Townsend for his first studio picture—*The Five Heartbeats* encountered mixed critical reception and stumbled at the box office, amassing only $8.7 million against its $10 million budget. Despite these anemic financial returns, the film refused to fade into obscurity. Its fan base grew substantially, fueled by its home video release. VHS rentals and sales (and a heavy circulation of bootlegged copies) allowed the film to find a devoted audience and surge in popularity, catapulting it to the status of a Black cult classic. Twenty years later, the film's breakout star, Wright, reflected on this trajectory, sharing with reporters, "I don't mean to sound egotistical, but it's just mind numbing how incredible this movie's connection is with the viewer. I never imagined it would hold up so well, particularly since it was a box office disaster. People don't know that we only made about 7 or 8 million dollars, but [the film] took on life on cable or VHS, and people began to scarf the thing up, largely with bootleg [videotape] copies. Every household had a copy of this thing, and they wore it out."[40] Transcending its initial box office shortcomings, *The Five Heartbeats* stands as a cherished gem within Black popular culture. Its soul-stirring songs, its unforgettable characters and dance sequences, its hero's path to redemption, and a plethora of highly quotable lines of dialogue collectively cement the film's revered status in the illustrious canon of Black American cinema.

In his final picture of the Black Pack era, Townsend once again donned the roles of writer, director, and star for *Meteor Man* (1993), a superhero adventure comedy produced at MGM. The film boasts an all-star multigenerational cast of Black entertainers, including stars like Marla Gibbs, Bill Cosby, Robert Guillaume, James Earl Jones, legendary crooner Luther Vandross, the '90s preteen hip-hop boy group Another Bad Creation, and stand-up comic Eddie Griffin. The movie spins the tale of Jefferson Reed (Townsend), a mild-mannered Washington, D.C., elementary school teacher whose life takes a fantastical turn after he is struck by a meteor in a bizarre accident. Discovering that the celestial encounter has endowed him with superhuman abilities, Reed transforms into Meteor Man—a caped crusader on a mission to combat the scourge of gangs and gun violence in his community. In an interview with the *Los Angeles Times*, Townsend expressed his desire to create a film that "mixes magic in with real values and what's going on now in the cities. It's a fantasy [film] with a moral value. The time is ripe for a Black superhero."[41] Townsend envisioned *Meteor Man* as a narrative infused with a compelling social message, a Black superhero arriving at a moment when such representation was sorely lacking. While the social commentary undergirding it remains commendable, the film does not capture the edgy satirical bite of Townsend's earlier work in *Hollywood Shuffle* or *Partners in Crime*. Critics additionally lamented the absence of the exhilarating energy and emotional resonance that permeated the musical tapestry of *The Five Heartbeats*.

Meteor Man's theatrical release coincided with a period in Hollywood where studio executives were noticeably invested in (or some might argue perversely fixated on) cranking out films that centered Black youth violence and urban nihilism. This strategy bears a striking resemblance to the industry's response to, and co-optation of, the revolutionary spirit in the groundbreaking film *Sweet Sweetback's Baadasssss Song*. In the wake of *Sweetback*'s unexpected independent success, Hollywood studios rushed to capitalize, rolling out a string of cheaply made Black action flicks. These films, later categorized as the Blaxploitation cycle, provided new career opportunities for Black talent; however, many of these movies tended to dilute *Sweetback*'s potent social and political impulses, replacing it with a focus on inner city crime, exemplified in pictures like *Superfly* (1972) or *Black Belt Jones* (1974).[42] The significance of Blaxploitation films, however, rests in the sense of cultural affirmation and campy fun they engender, centering Black characters and celebrating Black music and fashion.

In a similar vein, the comedic buoyancy of *Hollywood Shuffle* and Spike Lee's *She's Gotta Have It* was immediately followed by a new slate of studio-backed Black films in the 1990s. These new motion pictures were popular and diverse, with titles ranging from *Waiting to Exhale* (1995) to *Bebe's Kids* (1992). This industrial moment also announced the advent of a new subgenre often referred to as Hollywood's "hood film" cycle. These movies emphasized narratives rooted in the harsh realities of Black poverty, inner city crime, drugs, and violence. Townsend created *Meteor Man* as a deliberate counterpoint to the rising proliferation of the hood flicks, epitomized by titles like *New Jack City* (1991), *Boyz n the Hood* (1991), and *Straight Outta Brooklyn* (1991). Such cinematic offerings fetishize the bleak realities of gang violence and drug culture spawned by fatalistic U.S. social policies during the Reagan era and the devastating repercussions of the Iran-Contra scandal in Black communities. However, the commercial success of hood films meant they raked in substantial box office receipts and triggered an increase in their production and market saturation. Townsend believed the liberatory promise of the 1990s Black media movement was gradually giving way to a deceleration of social progress. He felt that the cinematic landscape of the Black Pack era, once loaded with prospects for narratives of cultural transformation, was being overshadowed by a surge of hood flicks that perpetuated Black social stagnation. The once stentorian calls for Black Power slowly subsided, and as Ed Guerrero argues, "The great collective aspirations of the Black freedom struggle, across the political spectrum from nonviolent action to 'by any means necessary' militancy, [had] eroded into an ambivalent, self-focused consumerism of brand-name jeans and sneakers, and intracommunal annihilation through gun-drug-gang violence."[43] Paradoxically, many hood film directors publicly positioned their hyperrealistic portrayals of brutality and urban violence as cautionary tales intended to deter audiences from replicating the destructive behaviors depicted on-screen. Upon further scrutiny, however, it is impossible to ignore how such graphic depictions emerge from within a long-standing Hollywood tradition that dictates "acceptable" performances of Blackness. For Townsend, the hood film framework limited the range of narratives that sparked studio interest, thereby limiting the roles made available to Black actors. Even with "cautionary" intent, the persistent focus on graphic violence in hood flicks failed to generate meaningful discourse on how to dismantle the systemic forces that perpetuate such cycles of despair. While undeniably powerful and reflecting a harsh reality of truth, these films, for the most part, offered no clear path forward or any discernible prospects for social change.

Acutely aware of the potential psychological toll that Hollywood's hyperstylized portrayals of urban violence could have on Black youth, Townsend envisioned *Meteor Man* as a stark contrast. He described the movie as a "fairy tale for [Black] children": "[Black people] in this kind of movie are always the sidekick, the second banana. They never save the day. What effect does that have on a child's self-esteem? With this film, hopefully they'll be a generation of children that will have a hero that looks just like them, that is 100% hero."[44] The Black superhero in cinema has a complex lineage. Early iterations emerged during the Blaxploitation era, with films like *Shaft* (1971), *Foxy Brown* (1974), and the lesser-known *Abar: The First Black Superman* (1977) each fusing superhero motifs with inner city iconography and action-adventure tropes. By the 1990s, the Black superhero took a comedic turn with *Meteor Man*, *Blankman* (1994), and NBA Hall of Famer Shaquille O'Neal's *Steel* (1997), films that, regrettably, sputtered at the box office.[45] The decade, however, was not without commercially successful Black entries in the genre. Both *Spawn* (1997) and *Blade* (1998) achieved mainstream recognition and launched lucrative sequels, setting the stage for the rise of Marvel Studios as a cinematic goliath a decade later.[46]

When *Meteor Man* was released on August 6, 1993, despite its aspirational social message, it severely underwhelmed and failed to gain traction. The movie bombed at the box office, earning a disappointing $8 million return against its $30 million production budget. While the film sought to create a social inversion of the Superman archetype, it struggled to find its footing. Its execution was marred by a didactic tone, lackluster energy, and trite visual style. Even the performances, crucial for comedic impact, fell short of the director's usual snarky tone. Ultimately, *Meteor Man*'s aim to deliver a powerful social message was blunted by its critical shortcomings, leaving it to languish in Hollywood netherworlds, never fully connecting with its intended audience.

Following *Meteor Man*'s discouraging box office blues, Townsend set out to recapture his irreverent carnivalesque mojo by returning to sketch comedy,

FIG. 3.10. Robert Townsend as Jefferson Reed / Meteor Man in *Meteor Man*, 1993.

a genre that served him well on HBO. This time, however, he ventured into broadcast television, joining his Black Pack comrade Keenen Ivory Wayans on Fox. Three years prior, Wayans's own sketch series *In Living Color* broke out as a runaway hit for the network. On September 12, 1993, *Townsend Television* debuted on Fox. His new foray into sketch comedy blended prerecorded sketches and musical performances, hoping to recapture the success of *Partners in Crime* for a broader audience, featuring a cast comprising John Witherspoon, Paula Jai Parker, Barry Diamond, and Roxanne Beckford. Each episode contained Townsend's signature stand-up routine and sketches satirizing movies and television commercials. But the show's production of humor was largely deficient of the renegade energy and satirical force that distinguished series like *Partners in Crime* and *In Living Color*. Recurring sketches such as "Nigel Spider," for instance, hint at Townsend's past glory, rehashing the hard-boiled detective persona he previously mastered in *Hollywood Shuffle*. In essence, the program felt oddly tame and failed to capture the cultural zeitgeist. Its ratings were abysmal, and the series faced an untimely demise, lasting only ten episodes before its cancellation; it was the final project of Townsend's Black Pack period.

The fact remains that *Hollywood Shuffle* stands as a key achievement in American independent cinema. The film subversively captures the frustrations simmering in Black performers navigating the limitations imposed by the Hollywood industrial complex. During his run with the Black Pack, Townsend proved to be a master of comedic expression and strategic promotion. *Hollywood Shuffle*'s humor makes visible the unarticulated dominance of white hegemony over the representational politics in Black film and television. Townsend critiques this dominance as both laughable and dangerous. His lacerating wit calls into question the broken promises of the American dream within the context of Hollywood, engaging comedic expression through the insightful lens described by art historian Tina Campt as "a Black gaze." His humor compels the viewer to confront the radical questions put forth by Campt: "What would it mean to see oneself through the complex positionality that is Blackness—and work through its implications on and for oneself?"[47] In *Hollywood Shuffle*, Townsend and Wayans use a Black gaze to show us where the trouble resides in the American cultural imagination. They interrogate the media landscape's power dynamics, offering a counterpoint to the dominant gaze and advocating for more nuanced portrayals of Black life on-screen. The film's comedic strategy exemplifies Townsend's trademark style of Black resistance humor, simultaneously evoking joy, laughter, aggression, judgment, and play. By centering race, the film delves into an exploration of the Black condition in the commercial realm, calling into question the American pathology that perpetuates systems of inequality. Rebellious and cautionary, the movie challenges viewers to reconfigure prevailing beliefs about systemic injustice, deriding how whiteness functions (often invisibly) as the defining source of power in the United States. Through its humorous vignettes, *Hollywood Shuffle* captures the struggles of Black actors who are pressured to "sell out," compromise, and conform to white-manufactured, racially charged caricatures in order to advance their careers. It is ironic, perhaps, that the film's success stems from the consumptive laughter it generates and its "ability to leave white audiences space to create their own meaning and laugh away what remains as either nonsensical or absurd."[48] This consumptive laughter, however troubling it may be, was Townsend's gateway into the studio system, an arena previously closed to him. Thus, *Hollywood Shuffle*'s critical and commercial victory ultimately crystalized his comedic persona as the multihyphenate "Renaissance man" of the Black Pack.[49]

When considering the underlying social commentary in the film, Ed Guerrero succinctly describes a fundamental crisis faced by so many Black entertainers in Hollywood, writing, "The American star system is a fickle game demanding some serious personal tradeoffs and sacrifices in order for one to succeed even marginally and thus enjoy its substantial rewards and privileges."[50] *Hollywood Shuffle* brings this tension to the forefront, vividly illustrating the complex choices Black performers are forced to navigate.

The rising cultural cachet of the Black Pack in the late 1980s played a central role in Townsend's ability to forge key relationships with upstart media corporations like HBO and Fox. As his business relationships flourished, it is important to note that like most expressive art in postmodernist times, Townsend's work thrived on the brink of uncertainty of corporate support and commercial viability. The popularity of his early Black Pack ventures afforded him an unprecedented opportunity to carve out space for himself on stage, cable television, film, and broadcast television, in comic books, and in ancillary markets like VHS.[51] However, his unwavering commitment to Black resistant comedy eventually gave way to (seemingly inevitable) commercial limitations—a regrettable tax imposed on Black humorists who incorporate social politics into their comedic repertoire.

Townsend's Black Pack efforts represent the most endearing and significant achievements of his career. His productions, overflowing with an infectious energy, dared to envision a future that balanced the contradictory lure of 1990s supercapitalism with a commitment to Black social responsibility. Townsend created space for audiences to question institutionally racist practices by leveraging the social power of comedy as a weapon of resistance, rendering Black life on-screen from a fresh perspective that was provocative and exhilarating. *Hollywood Shuffle* is, without question, a tour de force of American comedy, leaving behind an enduring legacy. Its prophetic humor bristles with the social awareness of a broken and corrupted system. The film makes us laugh, but its truths hurt. So, we laugh . . . to make it hurt less. In the end, *Hollywood Shuffle*'s jokes are a forceful conduit—a Molotov cocktail of highly flammable satire, wit, and social critique holding up a mirror to the precarity of the Black world and the racial fissures that divide American media culture and society.

4

The Hipness Litmus

The Arsenio Hall Show, *In Living Color*, and Black Pack TV

In the seminal book *The Fifties: The Way We Really Were*, Douglas T. Miller and Marion Nowak offer a blazing critique of television's injurious racial history, asserting that "the TV industry avoided even the pretense of maturity regarding racial matters. Racism was both disseminated and encouraged by the medium. . . . It was easy for TV producers to imagine a world without Blacks."[1] This searing indictment lays bare the troubling realities of network television programming as a medium that influences social control and cultural power and has historically rewarded discrimination through its considerable and deliberate omissions, astonishing contradictions, daunting stereotypic imagery, and subtle co-optation of dissenting voices. Television's ubiquitous technology remains unrivaled in its capacity to preserve the intractable racial anxieties that persist as America's pastime. The nature of television's power, of course, lies not in its brute force but in its seemingly invisible ability to engage in a colonization of consciousness, influencing public perception to maintain existing power structures and maximize capital gains for giant corporate entities.[2] Network television and its affiliates thrive in a lucrative business environment, with advertisers vying for airtime and paying top dollar to promote their products during top-rated programs. From the very beginning, white TV network gatekeepers established a restrictive mode for broadcasting Blackness—a phenomenon that I refer to as *Black televisuality*. My line of thinking here flows from John T. Caldwell's concept of "televisuality," which he uses "to describe an important historical moment in television's presentational manner . . . and changing form of cultural representation, a mode of operating and a ritual of display that utilizes many different individual looks."[3] As a technology of cultural hegemony, television has traditionally exploited the nation's racial fixation, mobilizing tropes and narratives akin to what Toni Morrison might describe as "playing in the dark."[4] Therefore, "Black televisuality" refers to an often-restrictive presentational manner or, perhaps more succinctly, a manner of rendering Blackness on the small screen through the circumscribed aesthetic practices and ideological lens of the dominant culture, corporate interests, and the overall Hollywood machine. Network executives have historically defended this approach, describing television programs as neutral platforms that reflect American life. But as Christine Acham posits, "Although network television executives openly promised non-bias in television production, their rhetoric was overwhelmed by a reality in which Black participation was minimal at best and roles were typecast—a trend that has continued in much of network television."[5] It was Black musicians Hazel Scott and Billy Daniels who first broke television's color barrier. Scott and Daniels performed separately on fifteen-minute variety shows in 1950 and 1952, respectively. Four years later, *The Nat King Cole Show* (1956–1957) marked a significant milestone when the eponymous jazz singer and musician became the first Black host of a thirty-minute TV series. However, the show faced immediate criticism when national advertisers refused to sponsor a program featuring a Black host. So, of course, *The Nat King Cole Show* was canceled after one season.

Beyond the aforementioned variety series, Black televisuality has primarily been confined to the situation comedy genre. Some have argued that such creative isolation reinscribes dehumanizing notions that Black life is unworthy of "serious" or dramatic themes. TV's first Black sitcoms, *Beulah* (1950–1952) and *Amos 'n' Andy* (1951–1953), were both adaptations of popular radio programs. The radio versions were created by white men and starred white actors who portrayed Black characters using caricatured minstrel-style white impersonations of "black-voice." According to Robin Means Coleman, television's early Black sitcoms reflected the limitations placed on Black lives and stories in Hollywood and laid the groundwork for a second-class subgenre within the broader sitcom landscape. Coleman argues that Black situation comedies were marginalized "not only because of the featured performers, but also because the humor is based on race and a parody of Blackness."[6] Hence early Black televisuality in sitcoms privileged white middle-class values and sensibilities and highlighted crude interpretations of Black life through an anti-Black lens.

Beulah and *Amos 'n' Andy* introduced an ominous vision of Black televisuality to the airwaves, characterized by twisted, parody-like performance styles where Blackness itself was the butt of the joke—leaving little room for genuine humanity. *Amos 'n' Andy*, in particular, proved especially vexing. The program sparked considerable uproar within the Black bourgeois community. The NAACP publicly condemned the show for its portrayal of characters that were viewed as undermining Black dignity and social progress. The sitcom's depiction of the shiftless sambo caricature, for example, was embodied by the character "Kingfish," played by Tim Moore. *Beulah* featured the maid/mammy archetype played by, at times, three different actresses on the show: Ethel Waters, Louise Beavers, and Hattie McDaniel.

The 1960s ushered in a change in racial attitudes, albeit with limitations, generating an integrationist approach to Black televisuality. Bill Cosby's portrayal of an urbane secret agent on *I Spy* (1965–1968) and Diahann Carroll's turn as the wholesome widowed single mother on *Julia* (1968–1971) were breakthroughs for Black actors in leading TV roles. However, against the backdrop of the social and political turmoil of the era, *Julia* and *I Spy* presented sanitized, "whitewashed" characterizations devoid of racial nuance and Black ritual intonations. In the 1970s, despite the social pressure of the Black Power movement, television continued along the stubborn path of separate and unequal representation. By the 1980s, the American political landscape was increasingly polarized, and the media mirrored this division. Nightly news programs and the televised rhetoric of the Reagan administration amplified distorted images of Black communities overrun with "crack babies" and "welfare queens"—a stark contrast to, for instance, the country's number-one TV program, *The Cosby Show*, which featured the upwardly mobile Huxtable family's culturally affirming vision of Black success.

In the 1990s, two key Black Pack productions provided a vital caesura to the racially skewed landscape of American television. This chapter adopts a case study approach to archive and contextualize the creation and consumption of these programs: the late night talk series *The Arsenio Hall Show* (1989–1994) and the sketch comedy series *In Living Color* (1990–1994). Through an exploration of the production history of each program, I tease out their social, political, and aesthetic foundations and examine how their creators navigated the confines of the Hollywood industrial complex and its Black containment measures. By studying each program's pivotal disruptions to Black televisuality, we can draw valuable insights into how Arsenio Hall and Keenen Ivory Wayans asserted politically Black voices that advocated for changes to Hollywood's business-as-usual politics, policies, and economics. Each series fostered a Black gaze that defied the prevailing thematics of ignorance and pushed back against television's role in perpetuating limitations on Black creativity and influencing social trajectories along the axes of identity that shape cultural and social power in America. *The Arsenio Hall Show* and *In Living Color* mark points of rupture that offer audiences resistant negotiations of Black alterity on broadcast television. These programs boldly challenged traditional portrayals of Blackness and emerged as cultural artifacts that represent the Black Pack's vanguard television ventures. Both series thrived with a wily engagement of Black resistance humor that invited diverse publics to laugh at, think about, and grapple with the expression of Black images and language, the realities of racial exclusion, and television's routine circulation of dominant narratives that normalize whiteness as knowledge a priori.

Late Night Blackness: *The Arsenio Hall Show*

A discussion of late-twentieth-century television would be incomplete without recognizing the postmodern reflexivity of *The Arsenio Hall Show*. The program offered a fresh spin on the late night talk show format while wrestling with the fundamental paradox that confronts (at one point or another) Black film and television creatives in Hollywood. That is to say, how does one retain a distinct and original voice filled with rich cultural intonations while operating within a white corporate environment driven by bottom-line market economic logic and, oftentimes, an absence of understanding (or interest in understanding) Black expressive culture or the needs and desires of Black audiences. As a cornerstone of the Black Pack canon, *The Arsenio Hall Show* negotiates a space between social comedy and traditional American television mœurs. Beyond his signature jokes, flashy suits, fitted baseball caps, wide toothy grin, and boisterous laugh, comedian Arsenio Hall leveraged his late night TV platform to showcase multifaceted and oppositional expressions of Black identity.

Hall carved out a space aimed at celebrating the richness of contemporary Black culture and preserving the extensive heritage of Black excellence in entertainment. The program's deliberate focus on showcasing Black cultural trailblazers of the past and present like Muhammad Ali, Sammy Davis Jr., Michael Jackson, Whitney Houston, and Miles Davis served a dual purpose. Not only did the show offer a source of entertainment and spectatorial gratification for Black viewers; it was also a means to recuperate the Black American narrative from distorted media depictions. Hall's charismatic performance of Blackness propelled the show into the realm of a pop-culture phenomenon. He disturbed the norms of late night television by infusing the format with elements of hip-hop culture. In the early 1990s, the show was synonymous with Black cool and served as a critical platform for the Black Pack's increased visibility. Hall activated a new style of Black televisuality, and his nightly broadcasts were a forum that offered resistant possibilities for the expression and transmission of often suppressed Afro-centered aspirations, ideologies, culture, tastes, music, and fashion.

For decades, *The Tonight Show Starring Johnny Carson* (1962–1992) reigned supreme as the undisputed king of late night television. The program served as a launchpad for rising stand-up comics and a platform for established celebrities across entertainment, politics, and literature to promote themselves and their work. In a bid to challenge Carson's dominance, the newly launched Fox network entered the late night fray with *The Late Show* (1986–1988). Fox enlisted the comedic talents of Joan Rivers, who had previously garnered attention as a guest host for Carson, to lead its new venture.[7] This foray into late night television was a cost-effective strategy for the fledgling network to establish a foothold. Despite high hopes, the relationship between Fox executives and Rivers quickly soured. She was fired within a year. After a string of guest hosts, Fox turned to the relatively unknown comedian Arsenio Hall to take over as Rivers's permanent replacement in the summer of 1987. Hall signed a thirteen-week deal to host the show. His energetic and engaging personality resonated with audiences, leading to a noticeable increase in ratings. But Hall left the program at the end of his contract to begin filming his supporting role in the blockbuster Paramount Pictures comedy *Coming to America* (1988) alongside his close friend and Black Pack compatriot Eddie Murphy.

For years, Arsenio Hall struggled to gain traction in Hollywood. His comedic style was often deemed "too ethnic, too physical, or too up" by industry gatekeepers.[8] He met a young comic, Keenen Ivory Wayans, performing stand-up, and Wayans later introduced him to Eddie Murphy at the Improv comedy club. The comedians developed a strong bond around their shared ambitions. After joining forces with the up-and-coming Black Pack crew, Hall's professional fortunes changed. He landed a gig as the opening act on tour with the legendary singer Patti LaBelle and honed his hosting skills on the weekly music series *Solid Gold* (1980–1988). After his brief stint on *The Late Show* and with the phenomenal success of *Coming to America* at the box office, alongside his close ties to Paramount's top moneymaker Eddie Murphy, Hall negotiated a first-run syndication deal with Paramount Television to host his own series. *The Arsenio Hall Show* burst onto the late night scene on January 3, 1989, shaking up the televisual landscape with its in-your-face comedic ethos. Hall's arrival injected a much-needed jolt into a genre dominated by white male hosts on shows like *Late Night with David Letterman* (1982–1993) and *The Pat Sajak Show* (1989–1990). *The Arsenio Hall Show* became a vibrant counterpoint, offering a nightly parade of transgressive Black sensibilities and showcasing a range of voices that were absent from mainstream television. Behind the scenes, Hall emphasized hiring Black women and men in significant production positions. He jokingly dubbed himself the "Martin Luther King, Jr. of comedy."[9] In an interview with the *Los Angeles Times*, Hall openly discussed his strategy: "I set things up so that Black people are in key positions. I have five talent coordinators, and two are Black. Three of the four cameramen are Black."[10] Hall's hiring practices not only reflected a sense of social responsibility but evinced the cultural solidarity central to the Black Pack's entertainment agenda.

By 1989, the Black Pack's cultural footprint proved a dominating force, extending profitably across film, cable TV, music, stand-up, and home video. The launch of *The Arsenio Hall Show* marked a significant milestone—the Black Pack's first entry into broadcast television. The program immediately flourished, amplifying the Black Pack's influence and bringing an expansive nightly constellation of diverse talent into American homes. Hall's commitment to showcasing Black culture on such a large national platform did, however, position him as a controversial figure within the broadcasting terrain. His unconventional approach highlighted the complex racial dynamics and forces at play in the production of popular culture and the persistent tensions between market economics and television's troublesome representations of Blackness. Yet paradoxically, Hall's cultural contestations fueled the show's popularity and growth. The visual aesthetics and politically Black gaze of *The Arsenio Hall Show* positioned him as the antithesis of Johnny Carson. Unlike Carson's casual and conversational style, Hall's on-screen presence was flashy and gregarious. His production of humor was a unique blend of irreverence and social commentary, often laced with playful double entendres. According to Mel Watkins, historian of Black American humor, "Arsenio

Hall's wide-eyed, infectious laugh—sassy one minute, coy the next—helped catapult his late-night show to the top of the television ratings in the 1980s. It also helped take the edge off satirical potshots he aimed at celebrities ranging from Madonna to Jesse Jackson."[11] Hall's unapologetically Black subjectivity resonated with a new generation of young viewers (irrespective of race) who had no particular connection to the legacy of Johnny Carson.

The Arsenio Hall Show was edgy and hip from the onset. This was clearly evident in every detail of the program, even in its sleek set design on Paramount's sound Stage 29, which eschewed the traditional host's desk in favor of a more intimate arrangement with modern-styled sofas and ottomans. The show's nightly introduction by Burton Richardson was also quite distinctive. Richardson's announcement of "*ARSENIOOOOOOOO Hall*," extending the emphasis on the *O* syllable in "Arsenio," became a trademark feature of the program. The show also displayed a significant focus on hip-hop, referring to the house band as the "Posse" and playfully nicknaming a lively section of the audience the "Dog Pound." This rowdy group were encouraged to express their approval on the show not with customary applause but with loud barking and fists boisterously pumping in the air: "*Woof, woof, woof!*" Hall's comedic arsenal encompassed a range of techniques, including parody, ironic appropriation of stereotypes, and moments of profound social gravity. His nightly presence rearranged Black marginality and placed it at the center of popular culture. By privileging racial "otherness," the series gave viewers a nightly party-like atmosphere. In 1989, following his People's Choice Award win for Favorite Late Night Talk Show Host, Hall explained his strategy: "I didn't go after Johnny. Everybody's trying to compete with Carson. Nobody can compete with Johnny—he's like Mike Tyson. I went after everything Johnny leaves over. The people who watch Johnny—I went after their kids. Instead of competing with him, I just tried to find my own niche."[12] This approach also reveals the multifaceted nature of Hall's comedic mission and his role as an ambassador for Black culture within television's matrix of public interaction.

Hip-Hop: Money, Power, Respect

Beyond its entertainment value, *The Arsenio Hall Show* was a platform for Black solidarity, harnessing the boundary-defying electronic flow of television imagery to foster a sense of Black cultural affirmation. The series was a springboard for a blossoming hip-hop movement and its emerging talents.

Hall embraced a new generation of Black performers, including rappers, actors, and comedians, many of whom were ignored or deemed too controversial by the television industry's establishment. By centering marginalized and rebellious artists like Public Enemy or the rapper/actor Tupac Shakur, the show defied the racial politics of late night television and legitimized hip-hop as an indispensable form of Black cultural expression. Operating within the confines of the white-dominated industry, Hall's open embrace of hip-hop culture offered a fresh perspective on Black modernism, interrupting traditional narratives by determining (at least for one hour per night) how those narratives played out in the homes of Black viewers. Under the rubric of late night entertainment and bolstered by the Black Pack's cultural influence, Hall presented himself as a jocular everyman, paving the way for Black artists to capitalize on hip-hop's rising popularity and financial viability.

Hip-hop traces its origins back to the late 1970s, drawing influences from funk and soul music pioneers who "rapped" over live instrumentation. Visionary wordsmiths like the Last Poets and Gil Scott-Heron were integral in shaping hip-hop's early trajectory. Even James Brown, the legendary "Godfather of Soul," proclaimed in his song "The Payback,"

> I can dig rapping,
> I can dig scrapping,
> but I can't dig that backstabbing.

Brown's music, quite remarkably, became among the most sampled records in hip-hop, playing a vital role in the genre's evolution.[13] Starting in 1979, artists like the Sugar Hill Gang, Grandmaster Flash and the Furious Five, and Run DMC popularized early hip-hop soundscapes. By the mid-1980s, hip-hop culture fully materialized through its expressive street elements: graffiti art, deejaying, breakdancing, MC rhyming, beat-making, fashion, and beatboxing. Hip-hop also emerged, in part, from the disillusionment felt in Black communities following the perceived social failings of the civil rights and Black Power movements. The systematic targeting and assassination of radical Black leaders and activists, a slumping economy, and high unemployment rates disproportionately impacted Black communities, fueling a gnawing sense of alienation and disenfranchisement among inner city youth. According to Tricia Rose, hip-hop was born as a "cultural form that attempts to negotiate the experiences of marginalization, brutally truncated opportunity, and oppression with the cultural imperatives of African American and Caribbean history, identity and community."[14] One early example of hip-hop's angst and brash social commentary is Grandmaster Flash and the Furious Five's 1982 opus "The Message." The rapper Melle Mel vividly details the bubbling discontent and harsh conditions in Black inner cities:

> It's like a jungle sometimes it makes me wonder, how I keep from going under.
> Don't push me 'cause I'm close to the edge. I'm trying not to lose my head.

His lyrics question the material success of the civil rights movement with a mixture of anger and frustration, critiquing the social inadequacies of the American dream deferred. Besides music, hip-hop's diverse elements found expression on the silver screen in feature films like *Wild Style* (1983), *Breakin'* (1984), and *Krush Groove* (1985), further solidifying the genre's visual aesthetic in popular culture.

By the 1990s, *The Arsenio Hall Show* carefully curated a nightly lineup of hip-hop culture for mainstream consumption, enacting a symbolic reversal of authority in its role as a Black arbiter of television's cultural power. The program aired nightly at 11 p.m., a strategic move to capture viewers seeking an alternative to the nightly news. This timeslot gave Hall a head start on traditional programs like *The Tonight Show*, which began at 11:30 p.m. Paramount's programming strategy for *The Arsenio Hall Show* was to target "a young, urban, upscale audience 18 to 34 [year old demographic], which is a premium audience for the advertiser, and leave to Carson the older, less urban, more conservative crowd."[15] Former vice president of programming in Paramount's television division, Frank Kelly, admitted, "We get the benefits, obviously, that [Arsenio] is a Black host and we are going to do better in certain markets. But that's only in some markets; we have to look at the broad structure of (all) the markets he's going to be in and figure how to be successful across the board. The show is a big, big success. Paramount is very happy."[16] While this may be true, it is essential to state that Hall was only permitted to retain the symbolic, material, and cultural power his program afforded by maintaining high ratings that appeased advertisers.

Where Hollywood Meets the "Hood"

The Arsenio Hall Show was, no doubt, the epicenter of hipness for Black performers in 1990s Hollywood. The show was must-see TV. Hall was famous for "booking guests the competition wouldn't touch . . . as well as the usuals (girlfriend Paula Abdul, buddy Eddie Murphy); episodes [often] tackled serious issues, like gang violence; [and] Magic Johnson making his first appearance after announcing he was HIV-positive."[17] Hall was acutely aware of television's racially restrictive discourses. "Yes, I'm Black, very Black," he candidly told reporters. "And I've gone to the same schools as (white people) and read the same books. Now, can we go on and do the show?"[18] This statement accentuates Hall's understanding of the tangled dynamics that accompany his role as a Black talk show host on white airwaves. His efforts to expand the terms of Black televisuality were fortified by what Harlem Renaissance author Richard Wright might describe as a "double vision."[19] Wright lays out the concept of double vision in his novel *The Outsider*:

> [Blacks], as they enter our culture, are going to inherit the problems we have, but with a difference. They are outsiders and they are going to know that they have these problems. They are going to be self-conscious; they are going to be gifted with a double vision, for, being [Black], they are going to be both inside and outside of our culture at the same time. Every emotional and cultural convulsion that ever shook the heart and soul of Western man will shake them. . . . The political, social, and psychological consequences of this will be enormous.[20]

For Hall, the self-consciousness of Wright's double vision proved to be both a gift and a curse. The financial transactions at the heart of television's terms of engagement allowed Hall to reap the material benefits of his position as a Black cultural pacesetter. However, the corporate Hollywood system also produced an unavoidable sense of alienation and Sartrean "nausea," or the existential crisis one confronts when rebelling against an oppressive social order.[21] That is to say, Hall's double vision required him to navigate a social responsibility to "The People" (Black audiences) while operating in a system built on bad faith and inherent distrust in a commercial environment that views Black Americans under the rubric of suspicion. Despite these fundamental challenges, Hall's infectious comedic persona resonated with young viewers across racial lines and cultural divides. Opening each episode, announcer Burton Richardson welcomed viewers, touting the program as "the funkiest place on Earth—where Hollywood meets the 'hood." This description encapsulates the show's dual mission as a platform for lighthearted entertainment and the engagement of pressing social issues of the era.

One prime example was NBA Hall of Famer Earvin "Magic" Johnson's culturally significant appearance on *The Arsenio Hall Show* in 1991. More than a mere celebrity interview, the appearance served as a poignant real-life public service announcement on a national stage, raising awareness about

FIG. 4.1. Magic Johnson on *The Arsenio Hall Show*, 1991.

HIV/AIDS for all Americans. Hall's Magic Johnson interview went a long way in illuminating the risks and realities of living with and contracting HIV and AIDS, which, at the time, was perceived primarily as a problem in LGBTQ+ communities. Johnson's announcement that he was HIV positive sent shockwaves through Black communities, the NBA, and the nation. His message was a stark reality check, both powerful and sobering: practice safe sex; if a successful and admired figure like Magic Johnson could contract HIV, then anyone could be at risk. Stepping into the bright lights of Hall's late night stage, Johnson was met with a profoundly emotional five-minute ovation from the audience, a testament to the impact of his stunning revelation. Hall admitted his hesitancy to conduct the interview due to their close friendship. But Johnson insisted that *The Arsenio Hall Show*, with its culturally specific Black environment, was the only platform he felt comfortable conducting his first appearance after the stirring public announcement.

As Hall's popularity surged, he embraced a more diverse lineup of guests, welcoming celebrities like Roseanne Barr, Madonna, and Hulk Hogan to the show. One watershed moment aired in June 1992, when presidential candidate Bill Clinton joined the program. This appearance marked a critical turning point in American political culture. Governor Clinton's charisma was undeniable. But it was his participation in a seemingly "impromptu" jam session with *The Arsenio Hall Show*'s "Posse" that bolstered his appeal to a new demographic of youthful voters. Clinton showcased his skills on the

FIG. 4.2. Bill Clinton performing on *The Arsenio Hall Show*, 1992.

tenor saxophone, performing a bluesy rendition of Elvis Presley's "Heartbreak Hotel," which offered a shocking visual metaphor. The image of Clinton donning dark sunglasses and playing the sax tapped into a youthful, rebellious spirit then personified by the popular animated series *The Simpsons* (1989–) and its character Lisa Simpson, known for her moody blues riffs on the baritone sax. Following Clinton's musical display, Arsenio slyly quipped, "It's nice to see a Democrat blow something besides the election," a snarky jab at former democratic presidential nominee Michael Dukakis. Clinton's appearance on *The Arsenio Hall Show* showcased the future president's shrewd political savvy. Pundits debated whether his stint on the show was a calculated political move, pandering to the increasingly influential Black voting bloc. Clinton's subsequent victory in the 1992 election points to the efficacy of his outreach efforts. His appearance paved the way for a heightened convergence between presidential politics and late night entertainment. This synergy was fully realized years later with then senator

Barack Obama's multiple late night talk show appearances during his 2008 presidential bid.

Hall defined his singular niche as the epitome of cool within the late night talk circuit in large part by introducing new ways of hearing and seeing Blackness in the mainstream. His show self-consciously encouraged Black audiences to reject notions of themselves as second-class "raced" subjects in the United States. Nevertheless, Hall wasn't immune to the realities of network television politics. He routinely faced antagonism from what he termed the white "talk show mafia." A case in point: Hall's talent coordinator secured Black actor and dancer Gregory Hines as a coveted guest for the show, but Hines backed out at the eleventh hour. The *Los Angeles Times* subsequently reported that on the day Hines was scheduled for Hall's show, the so-called talk show "'Mafiosi' from *Late Night With David Letterman* had persuaded Hines to appear on their show first. [And] Hall had to find a replacement in a matter of hours."[22] In a race against time, facing Hines's last-minute cancellation, Hall played his trump card, calling in support from his Black Pack collaborator Eddie Murphy, who stepped in as a substitute guest for Hines. Murphy made several surprise appearances on the show during its run, and his on-screen chemistry with Arsenio was magnetic. They showcased their playful repartee and improvisational wit, connecting with viewers as they fired off fast-paced comedic riffs, rolling on the sofas while laughing at their own inside jokes.

The New King of Late Night

The Arsenio Hall Show's disruptive vision of Black televisuality was a far cry from the late night sea of white hosts perched behind polished desks in Brooks Brothers suits. With his increasing success, Hall jettisoned traditional late night habits and leaned into social commentary. In a defining moment for the nation, he tackled head-on the visceral emotions and widespread public outrage that swept through Black America following the acquittal of the four white police officers caught on video brutally assaulting Rodney King in Los Angeles. After a week of deliberations, the jury's verdict, delivered on April 29, 1992, sent shockwaves of anger and disbelief throughout the city, triggering the tsunami of unrest now known as the LA Riots. When faced with fires and looting, Mayor Tom Bradley imposed a dusk-to-dawn curfew and called in the National Guard. A day later, amid the crisis, Paramount executives were prepared to cancel Hall's taping and air a rerun episode. But Hall pushed back, adamantly insisting that his show was the ideal forum to foster a public dialogue about the tumultuous circumstances and events gripping the city and the nation. "I'm the guy who needs to do a show [right now]," Hall told journalists.[23] Gathering a diverse array of South-Central community members and enlisting the support of friends and colleagues, Hall transformed his program into a spur-of-the-moment town hall–style conversation. The emotional episode featured a surprising audience composition, with celebrities like Sean Penn, Sinbad, and Edward James Olmos sprinkled in the crowd. Hall opened the show with a powerful juxtaposition: a speech by Dr. Martin Luther King Jr. playing over video footage of the Rodney King beating and the subsequent uprisings engulfing the city. He then brought Mayor Bradley to the stage, providing a platform for the city's first Black mayor to address the horrifying predicament. The mayor spoke with candor about the trial, the racial composition of the jury, and his profound disappointment with the verdict, deeming it "senseless." As the episode progressed, Hall navigated through the audience, speaking with community members and celebrities alike. Many guests were impassioned and spoke eloquently about the LAPD, the officers' ludicrous acquittal, and the long-term implications of these events on race relations in America.

Hall's Rodney King episode provided a space for community members not only to listen but also to be heard, underlining the long-standing and bitter history of police violence against Black bodies and the absurdity and precarity of life in the Black world. No other late night program dared to confront sensitive and controversial topics in such a raw and unfiltered manner. At the same time, Hall consciously rode the wave of hip-hop's influence as an ever-evolving and increasingly viable commodity for economic growth within the financial matrices of corporate America. By embracing the hip-hop art form, *The Arsenio Hall Show* emerged as the definitive late night program for the "MTV generation." In its inaugural season, the show achieved what many deemed unthinkable—it surpassed Carson's *The Tonight Show* as the most popular late night series. During the 1989–1990 season, Hall's program audaciously claimed the throne on late night's Mount Olympus, a feat that brought an astonishing end to Carson's twenty-year reign.

Hall's penchant for bringing out surprise guests was a signature element of the show, sparking proverbial water-cooler conversations nationwide. One such occurrence unfolded during his interview with the legendary boxing champion and cultural icon Muhammad Ali, who, at the time, was grappling with the early stages of Parkinson's disease. Although Ali's speech was slowed, his charming wit and humor were undiminished. The atmosphere was electric as Hall introduced surprise guests "Sugar" Ray Leonard and the fresh-faced twenty-one-year-old boxing champ Mike Tyson. The emotional impact on Ali was palpable. The episode, a rare gathering of boxing royalty across three generations, resonated in many Black communities, offering a celebration of Black masculinity while fostering a sense of intraracial brotherhood, mutual respect, and admiration. Such genuine and heartfelt moments helped catapult the program to the number-one spot, an achievement it held for three seasons. In fact, Arsenio Hall remains the only Black talk show host to achieve this distinction.

Defeating the seemingly invincible Johnny Carson, beloved by white America, came with a hefty price. Hall's "mission [was] to bring worlds together on one couch."[24] However, his efforts were often met with ire and grievance from establishment forces. The *Los Angeles Times* described Hall's program as "the Blackest—late-night party in town, the kind of party many Americans [had] never been to. Its gossipy, in-joke humor, street-wise language and cutting-edge pop-culture references [were] so hip that the show [left] some [white] viewers feeling like uninvited guests."[25] The cultural moves playing out on *The Arsenio Hall Show* deliberately centered Black American experiences and decentered the white gaze. Hall's unapologetically Black perspective inevitably stoked animosity among a significant contingent of the show's white detractors. In one key instance, a TV critic at the *Washington Post* took aim: "As a middle-aged white man, you tune in [to Arsenio] and think: 'Now, am I meant to get this? Am I being an old fuddy-duddy if I don't get it?' I never thought of the Carson show and the Letterman show as for and about white people. (But) if I watch a show that I feel is for and about Black people, then I feel, well, this wasn't meant for me. I've been excluded. . . . I think Hall is going to have to widen his horizons a little if he wants a mainstream audience."[26] Lurking beneath this critic's apparent disorientation lies a potent undercurrent of America's racial anxieties couched in seemingly innocuous (but often dangerous) language. The critic's statement makes no effort to disguise the unmistakable odor of white privilege, which demands the world cater to the entitlement of white men. Such racialized attacks on *The Arsenio Hall Show* foreshadow a looming white backlash against Black Americans, one that would manifest in specious claims of "reverse racism" and "reverse discrimination" against whites. These accusations, often used to delegitimize affirmative action and other corrective policies aimed at alleviating systemic racism, served as a convenient way to deflect from centuries-long social inequalities that plague Black Americans. In the long run, pronouncements of the show as "too Black" exposed, perhaps predictably, the often-invisible mechanisms of institutional and structural repression that uphold the powers that be and perpetuate hierarchies of social, economic, and cultural control. Soon, mounting white resentment became a factor that accelerated the demise of *The Arsenio Hall Show* and its illuminating presence in the late night televisual landscape.

Prime-Time Blackness: *In Living Color*

By wielding unflinching satire as a weapon to lambaste social issues, celebrity culture, and politics, *In Living Color* gained commercial success and rapidly established itself as an equal-opportunity offender and a lightning rod for controversy. Debuting on April 15, 1990, the show was a contentious site for oppositional and raucous humor. The program rejuvenated the sketch comedy genre with its politically Black arsenal of irony, parody, and social commentary. The show's creator, Black Pack funnyman Keenen Ivory Wayans, assembled an ensemble cast of nine comedians—seven Black, two white. Wayans aimed to hire performers who were deemed industry outcasts or, as Wayans put it, comics whom Hollywood "didn't know what to do with."[27] His efforts altered the comedic substance and aesthetic appeal of sketch comedy, which, at the time, some industry insiders considered a dying form.

Under Wayans's stewardship, the series captivated audiences' attention with its vibrant irreverence and combustible humor. It also injected the rhythms and culture of hip-hop into the prime-time television discourse. In its debut season, Wayans's formula garnered *In Living Color* an Emmy Award for Outstanding Variety, Music or Comedy Series. The show propelled several cast members into superstardom, including future Academy Award winner Jamie Foxx, comedian Jim Carrey, "Fly Girl" background-dancer-turned-pop-star/actress Jennifer Lopez, Damon Wayans, David Alan Grier, and several of Wayans's other siblings: Kim, Shawn, and Marlon. Beyond its comedic success, *In Living Color* played a central role in establishing the newly formed Fox Broadcasting Company as a legitimate competitive force against the "Big Three"—ABC, CBS, and NBC—ultimately helping solidify Fox's position as the fourth major American television network.

In the late 1980s, as a member of comedy's emergent Black Pack, Keenen Ivory Wayans was instrumental in the creation of a number of commercial hits. He cowrote and costarred in *Hollywood Shuffle*, the film that solidified the Black Pack's earliest collaborative efforts. He also penned the opening sketch for *Eddie Murphy: Raw* and was a writer and costar for HBO's sketch series *Robert Townsend and His Partners in Crime*. Yet despite his contributions, much of the Black Pack's early recognition and acclaim went toward Murphy and Townsend, leaving Wayans essentially in their shadow. However, while working on the *Partners in Crime* series, Wayans wrote an original screenplay that caught the attention of executives at United Artists. Wayans signed a deal to direct and star in his debut feature, *I'm Gonna Git You Sucka* (1988). This film not only established him as a commodity in his own right but also showcased his talent as a multihyphenate filmmaker. The film cleverly blends the comedic stylings of *Hollywood Shuffle* and *National Lampoon*, crafting a wry parody of the 1970s Blaxploitation movement. *I'm Gonna Git You Sucka* spins the tale of Jack Spade (played by Wayans), an army veteran who returns home from military service to avenge the death of his brother. The movie skillfully spoofs the myriad clichés woven into the fabric of the Blaxploitation era: from its flamboyant sartorial displays to the larger-than-life personas of pimps and street hustlers, the enduring celebration of Black musicality, and the archetypal figure of the Black action hero who defiantly sticks it to "the Man"—that is, more aptly, the entrenched white establishment. The film gleefully skewers Blaxploitation classics like *Shaft* (1971), *Superfly* (1972), *Hammer* (1972), and *Three the Hard Way* (1974). It also proudly showcases a cast of stars from the era, including Ja'Net DuBois, best known for her roles in *Five on the Black Hand Side* (1973) and Eric Monte and Mike Evans's TV series *Good Times* (1974–1979);[28] NFL Hall of Fame luminary turned social activist and Blaxploitation icon Jim Brown; Bernie Casey, star of *Hit Man* (1972); Antonio Fargas, best recognized as the informant "Huggy Bear" on the TV police procedural *Starsky and Hutch* (1975–1979); and the Blaxploitation maestro himself, Isaac Hayes, composer of the iconic "Theme from Shaft," which clinched the Academy Award for Best Original Song in 1972. Simply put by Ed Guerrero, *I'm Gonna Git You Sucka* signaled that Black cinema had "reached the grand dialectal moment of self-parody."[29] The film's intertextuality enables Black audiences to see an older generation of Black performers on-screen in new and exciting ways. The fact that Blaxploitation-era actors portray the movie's central characters carries a social significance that triggers nostalgia and visual pleasure for many Black audiences. As Bambi Haggins astutely observes, *I'm Gonna Git You Sucka*'s "virtual role call of Blaxploitation stars . . . as middle-aged urban heroes in a literal fight against the (white) Man . . . provides additional spectatorial pleasure for those 'down' enough to recognize the stars' cultural cachet."[30] The film also features

FIG. 4.3. Jim Brown as Slammer, Isaac Hayes as Hammer, Bernie Casey as John Slade, and Keenen Ivory Wayans as Jack Spade in *I'm Gonna Git You Sucka*, 1988.

an attention-grabbing cameo by newcomer Chris Rock in his hilarious "one rib" scene, which demonstrates Wayans's multilayered and culturally coded approach to the production of humor. On one level, the film's jokes sparkle with sarcasm and levity; yet underneath the surface, it invites the possibility for multiple readings of its comedic material, eliciting laughter among audiences spanning a spectrum of social awareness.

I'm Gonna Git You Sucka was released on December 14, 1988. Financed on a paltry $3 million budget, the film went toe-to-toe at the box office with Universal Pictures's heavyweight comedy *Twins*, starring Danny DeVito and Arnold Schwarzenegger. Despite its meager budget, *I'm Gonna Git You Sucka* was a commercial hit, earning over $13 million in revenue and announcing Wayans as a rising star on the Hollywood horizon. Following this success, Wayans and his Black Pack writing partner Townsend cowrote the screenplay for the Motown-era musical *The Five Heartbeats*, a film that would become a cult classic of the Black Pack cycle. During Townsend's initial negotiations for *The Five Heartbeats* at Warner Brothers, Wayans landed a solo meeting with 20th Century Fox. The studio offered Wayans a network deal to create a series for the upstart Fox Broadcasting Company. Wayans declined. Undeterred by his initial refusal, the tenacious Fox executives persisted, sweetening the deal by granting Wayans carte blanche to create any show he desired on the network—a rare and tantalizing opportunity that proved too irresistible for him to spurn. Drawing inspiration from his previous work on HBO's *Partners in Crime* and the radical legacy of *The Richard Pryor Show* (1977), Wayans developed the sketch comedy series *In Living Color*. In an unprecedented move, he struck a deal with Fox to serve as the show's creator, director, writer, executive producer, and star—an unparalleled arrangement for a Black creative within the panoptical confines of network television production.

In Living Color debuted as tectonic shifts changed the geography of television. The rise of HBO as a premium cable juggernaut and the creation of the Fox Broadcasting Company temporarily opened new vistas of opportunity for Black performers and cultural producers who held mainstream aspirations. Fox, in particular, initiated targeted counterprogramming strategies to disrupt the traditional authority of the Big Three networks. Most notably, their market segmentation policy introduced a new logic to the industry. For an upstart network like Fox, market segmentation meant pivoting away from the pursuit of broad maximum viewership toward targeting the largest number of viewers within a particular audience segment deemed most valuable to their advertisers. By dominating smaller demographic segments, Fox executives recognized the potential to increase profit margins and solidify a strong foothold in the market. The network set its sights on the coveted "urban demographic," a corporate television euphemism used to designate Black audiences. Fox shrewdly capitalized on the box office momentum of Black independent filmmakers like Spike Lee and Robert Townsend and began using Black creative talent to produce television comedies at a low cost, tailored to this lucrative yet underserved niche market. This new industrial paradigm laid the groundwork for Fox (and later UPN and WB) to profit from, in essence, the exploitation of Black marginality—a stark reality that shaped the genesis of *In Living Color*. In the early 1990s, HBO and Fox forged alliances with promising Black comedic talent, utilizing the growing trendiness of hip-hop, Black culture, and thorny issues of race that served as lightning rods for public attention and controversy. Amid the allure of financial gain, a complex dynamic unfolded between Wayans and Fox—part of the historically delicate dance between white executives and the Black culture industry. Sociologist Ellis Cashmore delves into this complicated relationship, arguing that traditionally, "whites have intervened in Black culture, shaping it, changing it, packaging it, producing it, merchandising it, distributing it, franchising it and turning it into any shape that will turn a profit."[31] This pattern in the entertainment business still persists, offering a surefire pathway to financial success for white corporations and to a select few Black creatives who gain access to Hollywood's inner sanctum.

With *In Living Color*, Wayans stretched the boundaries of sketch comedy, infusing it with a confrontational style of humor steeped in a calculated

Black hipness—a magnetic allure that attracted the young urban demographic Fox so desperately courted. Almost immediately, the series found itself trapped in the crosshairs of criticism, drawing harsh scrutiny for what some perceived as its endorsement of regressive racial tropes and consumptive laughter at the expense of the Black working class and impoverished.[32] Such critiques cast a sobering light on the program and raise disturbing questions about television's alarming portrayals of Black identity. Indeed, *In Living Color* often found itself caught in a precarious dance of ambivalence even as it sought to challenge racism and white cultural hegemony. For Norma Miriam Schulman, the show's ambivalence is connected to the complex economic undercurrents at play within the realm of network television. Schulman suggests *In Living Color*'s ambiguity is a strategic maneuver used to navigate the treacherous waters of crossover appeal, "a quality deemed all important in a commercial medium for whom the aggregate minority viewing audience is insufficient in itself to the kinds of ratings that yield substantial revenue."[33] Despite these issues, *In Living Color*, like its predecessor, *The Richard Pryor Show*, still managed to activate a transgressive space for moments of Black resistance humor to leak into the broadcast television arena. *In Living Color*'s approach to the production of humor framed the social conditions of its creation and consumption in primarily racial terms and from Black points of view, interrupting television's traditional discourses. While Fox's strategy of market segmentation aided the show's commercial success, the network's cutthroat scheduling agenda ultimately created a strain on the relationship between Wayans and Fox executives over the program's syndication rights.

The Bad Boys of Television

The Fox Broadcasting Company was formed in 1986, bankrolled by Australian-born media titan Rupert Murdoch after his acquisition of the 20th Century Fox movie studio. Included in the deal were seven nonnetwork television stations. Following the sale, Murdoch found himself at the helm of a burgeoning empire, armed not only with the means of studio production but also with a vast film catalog of cinematic gems ripe for exploitation across his newly acquired TV stations. Before the establishment of Fox, American television was dominated by the Big Three networks: CBS, ABC, and NBC. The prospect of a fledgling fourth network daring to vie for viewership seemed nothing short of preposterous to industry insiders.

Undeterred, Murdoch enlisted the expertise of Barry Diller, former chairman and CEO of the Paramount Pictures Corporation, to spearhead the nascent Fox television network. Diller's tenure at Paramount boasted an impressive roster of hit movies and TV shows, including *Laverne & Shirley* (1976–1983), *Taxi* (1978–1983), and *Cheers* (1982–1993). Under Diller's leadership, Fox assembled a formidable team, with Jamie Kellner hired as the network president. Together, they embarked on an exhaustive campaign of consumer research, uncovering a pervasive sense of dissatisfaction among TV audiences with the offerings provided by the Big Three networks.

The insights gleaned from their data unveiled a litany of repetitive grievances echoed by viewers. The message was abundantly clear, as Fox research executive Andrew Fessel recalls: "[We knew] if we had innovative programming, if we had programming that focused on particular age groups, if we had programming that pushed the edge, if we had programming that we really stood behind, then we thought we could really appeal to a very strong need and interest that the consumers were indicating to us that they had."[34] Recognizing the opportunity to fulfill these unmet needs, Kellner assembled a dream team of the television industry's most promising talents. He hired Garth Ancier, then twenty-eight, and Kevin Wendle, then twenty-six, as top executives. Kellner poached both men from the clutches of NBC's programming department. With Ancier and Wendle at the helm, Fox implemented its bold programming strategy, meticulously targeting smaller segments of the television market. Their focus homed in on younger viewers residing in large urban metropolises. Under Ancier's leadership, Fox churned out a slew of hit shows, including the dysfunctional suburban family sitcom *Married with Children* (1987–1997), hailed as the antithesis to the saccharine *Cosby Show*; the eclectic variety series *The Tracey Ulman Show* (1987–1990); the teen police drama *21 Jump Street* (1987–1991); *The Simpsons*; and, of course, *In Living Color*.

Hot on the heels of the triumphant box office reception of *I'm Gonna Git You Sucka*, Wayans initially met with Fox anticipating a discussion to secure studio financing for his next feature. But the studio needed new shows for its TV network to carry out its alternative programming agenda. With the soaring influence and popularity of the Black Pack, Fox pinpointed Wayans's comedic voice as tailor-made to appeal to their target demographic. By hiring Wayans, the network wielded its corporate power to shape the cultural terrain, temporarily igniting a new aesthetic that molded the contours and trends of Black televisuality. Fox's directive for Wayans was clear: produce an ultracool show with an unmistakable edge. One network executive explained it simply: "The mentality of the show was rock and roll. The thing was our mentality was hip, not Black, not white. It was hip-hop, it was young urban."[35] *In Living Color* signifies both a departure from television mœurs and a convergence point for infusing the vibrancy of Black musicality and the aesthetics of hip-hop culture into sketch comedy. The show's fashion, color palette, art design, music, ideology, and widespread use of street vernacular were all rooted in hip-hop. Each episode featured resident deejay SW1 (Shawn Wayans) spinning vinyl records between sketches followed by dance routines from the hip-hop ensemble the "Fly Girls." This dance troupe, which included future pop star Jennifer Lopez, was choreographed by Rosie Perez, who had recently captivated audiences in the film *Do the Right Thing* (1989). Likewise, the show's theme song "'Cause That's the Way You Livin', When You're Livin' in Living Color" exuded the kick of a hip-hop anthem, performed by rapper Heavy D: "And how would you feel knowing prejudice is obsolete? And all mankind danced to the exact beat, and at night it was safe to walk down the street." The song's upbeat New Jack Swing groove, laced with Heavy D's mellifluous flow and insightful lyrics, captures the aspirational drive prevalent in early hip-hop. As sociologist Herman Gray observes in his analysis of *In Living Color*, "Rap and hip-hop are used deliberately but quite strategically in the program to generate identifications across racial lines."[36] The show's precisely constructed aesthetics—the music, the dancers, the deejay—were a driving force for the program's traction with young audiences. By the second season's premiere, performances by hip-hop's top artists became a much-anticipated finale to each episode.

The celebration of hip-hop culture on *In Living Color* unfolded against a backdrop of public scrutiny and criticism directed at rap music during the early years of the Clinton administration. Donald Bogle observes, "A new generation of African Americans was more conscious of its cultural roots in this Afrocentric era. Young rap/hip-hop artists celebrated Black life and culture and also examined . . . long held American social/political injustices and inequities."[37] During this "golden age" of hip-hop, artists like Public Enemy, Tupac, Queen Latifah, Nas, and many others wielded their creativity to condemn racism, amplify Black struggles and aspirations, and demand social justice—all while inciting listeners to party and dance. *In Living Color*'s production of humor and performance style leaned into hip-hop's rebellious spirit. For Bambi Haggins, *In Living Color*'s "engagement of hip-hop culture, like the multicultural movement, is presented simply and directly and fundamentally without any self-conscious critique."[38] However, after previewing the pilot episode, Fox executives grew apprehensive.

Fearing public backlash, the network's top brass deemed the pilot too provocative. Consequently, the program was shelved. Wayans's comedic approach proved as daring as it was indiscriminate; no one was spared from the show's barbs, skewering individuals across racial, sexual, and celebrity lines. Ironically, this edginess, initially deemed worrisome, became a catalyst for the program's eventual greenlight. When a VHS copy of the pilot leaked, Barry Diller circulated the episode among respected TV executives to assess the program. As Keenen Ivory Wayans explains, Fox "was actually very fearful of what I was doing. But they knew it was something different."[39] The buzz the videotape caused among industry insiders and the network's mission to increase revenue persuaded Diller to ultimately air the pilot.

In Living Color's midseason premiere on April 15, 1990, defied expectations, considering its comedic material frequently teetered on the edge of censorship. Fox took a gamble airing the unconventional sketch series with predominantly Black performers, hip-hop, and Black resistance humor as its centerpiece. The show, steeped in politically Black satire and parody, challenged the limitations of broadcast television and became a breakout program at Fox. For Gray, *In Living Color*'s "clever oppositional moves of resistance [were] disguised as signifying practices—parody, irony, shock, and most often, in-your-face interpretation—and dead-on critiques of the condition of life in modern America."[40] Wayans's ability to synthesize formal comedic techniques with nuanced intonations of Black resistance humor sparked discussions about consumptive laughter across ethnic and racial divides. While Wayans and Fox may not have intended to create a "Black show" per se, *In Living Color*'s cultural aesthetics and comedic style are apparent to the viewer. The program's outrageous satire and parodic voice, as Watkins observes, drew upon the "shuckin' and jivin', talkin' and testifyin', dippin' and grippin', slappin' and cappin' or simply dissin' [that] are all vernacular descriptions for African American inner-community verbal play."[41] After its first season, *In Living Color* was a crossover hit, ranking near the top in Fox's key demographic of eighteen- to thirty-four-year-old men, a rating much higher than the network's acclaimed animated series, *The Simpsons*.

Keenen Ivory Wayans's request for Black Pack firebrand Paul Mooney to join the show as a writer underlines his deliberate intent to confront racially charged themes. Mooney's writing introduced memorable

FIG. 4.4. The opening title graphics on the set of *In Living Color*, 1990.

characters like the militant jester Homey D. Clown and parodies of celebrities like Sally Struthers and her Christian Children's Fund commercials, Andrew Dice Clay, and Clarence Thomas. Even Black Pack member Arsenio Hall was parodied on the show by Wayans, donning a flattop wig, false teeth, and long prosthetic index fingers. The sketch "The Wrath of Farrakhan" is a noteworthy example of the show's skewering of American racial dynamics. It offers a politically Black exploration of the original 1960s *Star Trek* television series. The sketch unfolds as Minister Louis Farrakhan, leader of the Nation of Islam (hilariously played by Damon Wayans), beams aboard the starship *Enterprise*. Farrakhan addresses each of the multiethnic crew members, satirically illuminating the oppressive and exploitative conditions they suffer under the leadership of the white Captain Kirk (Jim Carey).

As Farrakhan boards the *Enterprise*, the bewildered Captain Kirk queries his second-in-command, Mr. Spock (David Alan Grier), about the intruder's background. Spock, ever the repository of knowledge, dryly explains that Farrakhan is "a former calypso singer . . . who later became the leader of a twentieth-century African American religious sect known as the Nation of Islam." This introduction sets off a multilayered, culturally coded comedic exchange. On cue, Farrakhan's imposing

FIG. 4.5. Damon Wayans in "The Wrath of Farrakhan," *In Living Color*, 1990.

security detail—the Fruit of Islam, clad in tailored business suits and bowties—solicits crew members with incense and bean pies as the minister launches into a fiery diatribe. Farrakhan proclaims his presence is a prophetic warning to alert the crew "about their enslavement upon this vessel." Captain Kirk rejects the minister's assertion, insisting members of the *Enterprise* crew enjoy complete autonomy. Farrakhan, however, remains unconvinced, setting the stage for a comedic clash of ideologies aboard the starship. He sarcastically declares,

> *It is that same lie that kept Elvis the king. That made that poor child La Toya Jackson think she could sing. It is that same lie that's got white boys rapping and the Fat Boys acting.*

With discontent intensifying and pressure mounting, Captain Kirk resorts to desperate measures. In a display of authoritarian panic, he attempts to vaporize Farrakhan with a laser gun. But Kirk's weapon proves ineffective against the minister. Emboldened by this turn of events, Farrakhan defiantly replies,

> *Put your puny weapon down, Captain. You cannot harm me. My people have survived four hundred years of slavery. Three hundred years of apartheid. And twenty-five years of* The Jeffersons *in syndication. [*Defeated, Captain Kirk runs away.*] [*Farrakhan smiles.*] I love it when I do that to them.*

"The Wrath of Farrakhan" lays out a staunch social critique, peeling back the layers of whiteness and its invisible political dominance. Damon Wayans's double-voiced humor orchestrates a Black ritual performance of symbolic role reversal. This comedic incursion upends traditional power dynamics, aligning with Black social consciousness while also appealing to "Trekkies."

Despite the show's ludic extrapolations and potential for resistance, the network remained hyperfocused on its Nielsen ratings. According to former Fox executive Andy Fessel, "We [didn't] even look at the household figures. Demos [were] really key to us."[42] Analyzing demos, or demographic data, revealed a gold mine: the show was pulling in a massive Black viewership. With *In Living Color*, Fox's Black audience share skyrocketed 187 percent compared to their general audience. Based on these consumer insights, Fox doubled down on its strategic pursuit to create alternative programming with Black talent. As Fessel explains, "We found that the African American audience was extremely wide, and it was a very effective or productive audience in terms of generating ratings points."[43] By capitalizing on the underserved Black audience, Fox gained traction in its ascendancy as the fourth major television broadcaster.

Fox's segmentation data unveiled a crucial truth: Black viewers were their secret weapon, and feeding the network's appetite for programming required fresh voices. Hence a new wave of Black cultural producers like Yvette Lee Bowser, Ralph Farquhar, and Mara Brock Akil were granted opportunities to craft multidimensional Black characters and narratives on the network. These Black creators envisioned a more inclusive entertainment landscape. Their momentum sparked a decade-long boom in Black television, with shows like *True Colors* (1990–1992), *Roc* (1991–1994), *Martin* (1992–1997), *The Sinbad Show* (1993–1994), *Living Single* (1993–1998), *Townsend Television* (1993), *New York Undercover* (1994–1998), *South Central* (1994), and *413 Hope Street* (1997–1998). As Keenen Ivory Wayans argues, "Fox changed the course of Black television *unintentionally*. They didn't go out to make Black shows. They went out to make alternative programming . . . and that's what they have to get credit for. By allowing that voice to be expressed, they discovered a whole new audience."[44] However, the notion of Fox "discovering" a new (Black) audience is, in fact, a well-documented pattern. Hollywood studios conveniently "discover" Black audiences in various starts and stops and waves of visibility and invisibility, all dictated by a studio's financial health. When profits wane, "new" Black audiences are remarkably "discovered" to revitalize revenue streams. Once market stability is achieved, the search for Black audiences predictably fades. In its pursuit of legitimacy, Fox's market segmentation directive shattered the Big Three's dominance. As Kristal Brent Zook observes, beginning with *In Living Color*, Fox soon aired "the largest single crop of Black produced shows in television history. And by 1995 Black-Americans (some 12 percent of the total U.S. population) were a striking 25 percent of Fox's market."[45] For many Black households, the network's programs, without question, constituted "must-see TV."

Despite *In Living Color*'s popularity, the series faced repeated criticism. Many detractors cited the show's portrayals of Black poverty and the working class as a source of contention. Some debated whether or not the program mobilized racial tropes with characters like the homeless vagrant Anton (Damon Wayans) and the unemployed, nosy inner city neighbor Bonita (Kim Wayans). Herman Gray argues that the show's portrayal of such characters left the poor and working class "exposed . . . as television objects of middle-class amusement and fascination . . . amusing social incompetents with whom few can or should identify and for whom most have little if any feelings."[46] The show's public reception was also complicated through the lens of consumptive laughter, considering its jokes were often interpreted in multiple ways, generating meanings other than what the creators intended. For Stuart Hall, media culture is always a battleground for constructing meaning and producing pleasure, which is often subjective based on an individual's perspective and experience.[47] A prime illustration of the show's complex meaning-making process lies in the recurring sketch "The Homeboy Shopping Network." These segments feature Iceman (Keenen Ivory Wayans) and Whiz (Damon Wayans), two petty thieves attempting to offload stolen goods to their TV audience before the police arrive. In each sketch, the Wayans brothers appropriate the caricature of the "inner city homeboy," transforming it into a subversive critique of media images that demonize Black men as inherently criminal. In the following excerpt, Iceman and Whiz find themselves in Hollywood, peddling a slice of the "good life" to their customers:

ICEMAN: Thanks to us, you too can enjoy the lifestyles of the rich and famous. That's right, for only $19.95, not only will you get maps of the stars' homes but blueprints and floor plans and security systems. [*Displays blueprints.*]

WHIZ: And as an added bonus, we'll throw in this key to the city. [*Reveals a crowbar.*] Yo, with this two-inch steel master key, no doors will be closed to you—windows neither!

ICEMAN: Who says you gotta be in film to get an Oscar? Not anymore. [*Removes an Oscar statue.*] That's right, use any sharp object to engrave your name here, then put it on the shelf, or the hood of your car.

WHIZ: Or be the envy of your neighborhood by wearing this as a funky fresh medallion. [*Attaches the Oscar to his gold chain.*] . . . Let me ask you this: How can I share some of that there celebrity type wealth?

ICEMAN: I'm glad you asked. Simply get yourself a cutout of your favorite star. [*Reveals a life-sized cutout of Bo Jackson wearing a dress.*] Put him in a compromising position then snap away. [*Takes a Polaroid picture.*]

WHIZ: I guess Bo knows cross-dressing too.

ICEMAN: You sell this photo to the *National Inquirer* or just blackmail the celebrity himself. Either way you slice it—

WHIZ AND ICEMAN: Mo' money, mo' money, mo' money!

The homeboys serve as a critique of America's rampant consumerism embodied on television platforms like the Home Shopping Network. Their sketches satirize television's techniques of persuasion, exposing the exploitative nature of capitalism's relentless manufacturing of artificial needs. The homeboys use oppositional humor to excoriate "the mass media as the voice of bourgeois hegemony, the instruments of capitalist reification, an overwhelming apparatus or 'influencing machine' broaching little resistance . . . [and] the media's 'total manipulation' of the 'false needs' and 'false desires' of its narcoleptic audience."[48] Critics argued that Wayans's satirical deconstruction of the "criminal Black man" trope straddled the fence of neominstrelsy. These critiques suggest the sketches do not go far enough to outwardly contest the socially constructed fallacies of Black criminality as a product created in the white political imagination. On the other hand, *In Living Color*'s parody and engagement with the rituals of Black resistance humor foreground the grotesque nature of stereotypes as a strategy of confrontation. Ella Shohat and Robert Stam caution against the search for so-called positive images on *In Living Color*, arguing the "show belongs to a carnivalesque genre favoring anarchic bad taste and calculated exaggeration."[49] The question of racial representation in the writers' room further complicated these issues. Of the thirteen writers on the show, only three were Black. This lack of diversity raises concerns about whose perspectives shaped the creation of the "street" characters that permeated much of the series.

FIG. 4.6. Damon as Whiz and Keenen Wayans as Iceman in "The Homeboy Shopping Network," *In Living Color*, 1990.

The Super Bowl Scuffle

One of *In Living Color*'s most remarkable industrial feats is its role in the evolution of the modern Super Bowl halftime show. The National Football League's Super Bowl, the season's final game, has long held the distinction of being the most-watched television program annually in the United States. In the 1980s and '90s, the game consistently garnered a viewership exceeding one hundred million people, establishing it as somewhat of an unofficial American holiday. At the time, the Super Bowl's halftime entertainment was rather dull and perfunctory, barely occupying viewers' attention during the game's intermission. In 1990, the NFL hired actors dressed as characters from the *Peanuts* comic strip to cavort around the field in an uninspired spectacle. Although Fox did not hold the broadcasting rights for the Super Bowl, network president Jamie Kellner knew the game's ratings would be so large that he suggested Fox capitalize on that audience by counterprogramming *In Living Color* during the game's mundane halftime show. According to David Peisner, "The conventional wisdom was it wasn't worth it for the other networks to sink money into programming opposite the game. There just weren't enough viewers leftover to make it worthwhile. But if Fox could get just a fraction of those Super Bowl viewers to turn the channel, Kellner argued, it'd be a coup."[50] Keenen Ivory Wayans was all in on the idea. The plan was for Fox to air a special live episode of *In Living Color* during the Super Bowl game's brief hiatus.

The network courted sponsors and unleashed a massive marketing campaign, flooding the airwaves with ads for the show's cool new "Super Halftime Party." Cast member David Alan Grier recalls, "It was prime for a takeover. Real simple. We were just going to do our show during halftime. And they started running ads all over Fox, wherever they could—'Be sure to tune in to *In Living Color*.'"[51] In preparation for the event, Kellner agreed to broadcast the live episode on a six-second delay to assuage the anxieties of network censors. In fact, "not only would Fox's Standards VP Don Bay be in the production booth with his hand poised over a button to bleep out any objectionable content, Kellner himself would be in the booth beside Bay, to watch over him."[52] On January 26, 1992, *In Living Color* went head-to-head with the NFL. When NFL commissioner Paul Tagliabue introduced the Disney-themed halftime act, Fox aired its special episode of *In Living Color*. That Sunday, the cast appeared live onstage in a party-like atmosphere with special guests Kirstie Alley, Blair Underwood, Pauly Shore, and musical guest Color Me Bad. The live episode highlighted the show's trademark sketches: "Men On," Jim Carey's "Fire Marshall Bill," and "The Homeboy Shopping Network." Keenen Ivory Wayans explains, "We wanted to put up a [countdown] clock on the screen so that people would know when to go back to the game. I was very confident that we would steal the show. It was such a perfect opportunity."[53] *In Living Color* dropped its edgy, youth-driven hip-hop aesthetic in front of Super Bowl halftime audiences and siphoned away roughly twenty-nine million viewers. It was an astonishing triumph that set the stage for the NFL's reimagining of the Super Bowl halftime show as the year's biggest music concert, an enormous spectacle featuring performances by the world's top singers: Michael Jackson, U2, Prince, Paul McCartney, Beyoncé, and so on. This shift serves as a testament to the cultural influence of Wayans's series at the height of its popularity.

Yet *In Living Color*'s breakout success was marred by constant friction between Wayans and network censors. David Kimmel argues, "Not since Joan Rivers and *The Late Show* in 1986 had something on the Fox schedule been such a continuing irritant to network operations. At first it had less to do with personalities than simply the nature of the program. There were ongoing negotiations with the standards and practices people at the network as to what would be allowed in the show and what went beyond the pale, even for Fox."[54] *In Living Color* had already drawn sharp criticism from gay rights organizations for its crude and insensitive depictions of the LGBTQ+ community. The recurring "Men On" sketches featuring two Black gay culture critics, Blaine Edwards (Damon Wayans) and Antoine Merriweather (David Alan Grier), were the focal point of much of this criticism, tension, and backlash. Each sketch presented Antoine and Blaine as flamboyant male "queens" dissecting pop culture using sexual puns and suggestive double entendres. Critics argued the characters' over-the-top mannerisms reinforced negative stereotypes about gay men. After the Super Bowl XXVI halftime episode, the network was threatened with defamation lawsuits over Wayans's and Grier's ad-libbed potshots that suggested actor Richard Gere and track and field star Carl Lewis were homosexual. Black queer filmmaking pioneer Marlon Riggs also criticized *In Living Color*'s portrayal of Black masculinity. Riggs, in his own film and television work, exposes the deep-seated biases around race and sexuality in American media. He spoke out sharply against the "Men On" characters, condemning what he described as the perpetuation of "a notion that Black gay men are sissies, ineffectual, ineffective, womanish in a way that signifies inferiority."[55] This depiction, he posits, not only caricatured gay men but also reduced their identities to a set of demeaning tropes. Riggs challenged the cultural acceptance of such portrayals, urging a reexamination of how media shapes perceptions of queer communities. He contends that the show's success reveals how mainstream media could exploit queer identities for humor while simultaneously upholding the very prejudices it claimed to satirize. Riggs's analysis urges a more nuanced understanding of how comedy can both reflect and reinforce social norms, particularly concerning marginalized communities. The continued presence of homophobia and transphobia in American comedy, evinced by contemporary controversies surrounding Dave Chappelle, demonstrates the persistent tensions and contradictions that remain within comedic spaces and the American cultural landscape more broadly. One of *In Living Color*'s most contentious moments involved the "Men on Fitness" sketch. While Blaine and Antoine are working out in a gym, a visually suggestive gag unfolds as a scantily clad body builder squirts water onto Antoine's face, simulating a lewd act too explicit for prime-time audiences, even by Fox's lax standards. The network reprimanded Wayans and censored the episode, further straining their relationship. After completing production on season 3, Damon Wayans left *In Living Color* over censorship disputes; Keenen's departure soon followed.

FIG. 4.7. Damon Wayans as Blaine and David Alan Grier as Antoine in the "Men On" sketches, *In Living Color*, 1992.

With Fox riding high in the 1990s, young urban viewers flocked to their edgy shows, leaving the Big Three networks scrambling. Flush with increased market share, Fox diversified its offerings with a new slate of white-themed programs. Enter the soapy indie-rock drama *The Heights* (1992). Fox placed significant hopes on *The Heights* when the show's fictional rock band generated a real-life chart-topping single, "How Do You Talk to an Angel?" But the song's popularity did little to buoy the show's ratings, which remained persistently low. Once the single's Billboard reign ended, so did the show's run. It was canceled after thirteen episodes. With *The Heights* no longer on the air, Fox had an hour-long void in its Thursday-night lineup. Newly appointed network executive Lucie Salhany received a directive from Fox's top brass to fill the one-hour gap with two sitcoms. However, Salhany made a bold move, opting to air back-to-back reruns of *In Living Color*'s first season. This scheduling choice set off a maelstrom behind the scenes. Keenen Ivory Wayans was livid about the network's unilateral decision to broadcast repeat episodes of the series. Legally, both Wayans and 20th Century Fox co-owned the show. From Wayans's perspective, the network breached its fiduciary responsibility as partners to protect the financial interest of the program. Kimmel points out that Fox, by "doing a third run of already repeated first season episodes was, in [Wayans's] opinion, destroying the potential value of the program in later syndication. Salhany's response to Wayans was that the variety series had no real value in syndication, so they were essentially arguing over nothing."[56] However, the decision demonstrably impaired *In Living Color*'s long-term prospects, diminishing Wayans's full earning potential. The network's draconian maneuvers were, perhaps, an attempt to exploit Wayans's perceived ignorance of the inner workings of the television business. By asserting supreme decision-making power, the network exposed Wayans's subordinated position, revealing one of the many ways that white corporate power overdetermines (and often undermines) Black media progress and financial interests in Hollywood. To that end, Wayans's concerns about the network's unethical business practices were a reasonable reaction to its literal domination of his intellectual property and its intentional diminishment of his future earnings.[57]

Salhany's assertion that *In Living Color* held no syndication value was, of course, inaccurate. As Timothy Havens explains, independent TV producers like Wayans financially "flourished because of the FCC's Financial Interest and Syndication Rules, which forbade the national networks from owning or profiting from the shows they broadcast. Because the real money in U.S. television had long been the local syndication markets, the FCC's rule effectively created lucrative markets for independent television producers."[58] Fox countered Wayans's valid grievances by invoking obscure contractual clauses allegedly granting them latitude to air additional runs of the show at their discretion—an argument steeped in legal semantics rather than equitable business practices. The decision to broadcast reruns of *In Living Color* did not solely rest with Salhany—she was authorized by Peter Chernin, the newly appointed head of the Fox Entertainment Group, who outranked both Salhany and Kellner. Unable to reach a resolution with network leadership, Keenen Ivory Wayans walked away from *In Living Color* in December of 1992. His resignation triggered the departure of the show's producers, Tamara Rawitt and Eric Gold, as well as his sister and castmate Kim Wayans. By the end of the next season, no member of the Wayans family remained on the show. Keenen Ivory Wayans's attorneys slapped the Fox network with a lawsuit, alleging their actions jeopardized his future financial interests in syndication rights, underlining the ongoing struggle for Black equality in the often cutthroat commercial landscape of television production.

Fade to Black

Wayans's legal action against Fox was resolved with an out-of-court settlement. The network agreed to buy out Wayans's interest in the show. However, the settlement terms prevented the disclosure of any financial details. By the fifth and final season, only Jim Carrey, David Alan Grier, and T'Keyah Crystal Keymàh remained from the original cast for the program's entire 142-episode run. The series' tepid final season lacked the energy and comedic flare that initiated the show's success. Producers relied heavily on special guest stars like Rodney Dangerfield and Chris Rock to resuscitate the show's slumping ratings. Following his departure from *In Living Color*, Keenen Ivory Wayans wrote, directed, and starred in his final production of the Black Pack cycle, *A Low Down Dirty Shame*, released on November 23, 1994. The action comedy featured Wayans as a wisecracking private investigator embroiled in a quest to find a missing fortune. Salli Richardson-Whitfield, Jada Pinkett Smith, and Charles S. Dutton rounded out the cast. The movie received a warm reception at the box office, earning $29.4 million on its $10 million budget.[59] The film's soundtrack, produced by Grammy-winning hitmakers Jimmy "Jam" Harris and Terry Lewis, further cemented the project's success. The soundtrack sold over five hundred thousand copies and ranked fourteenth on Billboard's hip-hop and R&B charts.

Concurrently, *The Arsenio Hall Show* was embroiled in a delicate balancing act as an emissary for Black expressive culture. Operating within the profit-driven landscape of late night television, Hall, the recipient of bitter attacks from the white establishment, faced increasingly frequent conflicts with Paramount Television executives. These struggles often centered on a reductive label of the show as "too Black" for mainstream audiences. The tension culminated during one of Hall's final monologues when he delivered a sardonic reference to Michael Fay, an American teenager who received international attention in 1994 after being caned for vandalism in Singapore. In his pointed jab, Hall targeted Marge Schott, then owner of Major League Baseball's Cincinnati Reds, infamous for her history of racist and homophobic remarks. Hall joked that since Schott "disses Blacks and gays, we should send her to Singapore and have Little Richard whip her wrinkly ass." Backlash from the joke added to the show's mounting troubles.

By the mid-1990s, the relentless pressures of hosting and executive producing the nightly series, compounded by the psychological costs of Black double vision, had exacted a heavy toll on Hall. As the program's ratings dipped, critics seized on the show's perceived hyperfocus on Black social issues as a convenient scapegoat. The nadir arrived when Hall booked the controversial Nation of Islam leader Louis Farrakhan as a guest. This decision proved a coup de grâce for the show. The announcement of Farrakhan's appearance triggered a torrent of vociferous reactions in the press. Hall rebuked the negative response, pointing out the racialized hypocrisy of his critics, who made no public outcry when white talk show hosts like Mike Wallace or Phil Donahue booked Farrakhan as a guest. Hall's episode opened with a stark visual montage of Nation of Islam leaders Elijah Muhammad, Malcolm X, and Farrakhan underscored by Hall's somber voice-over narration. His words were accompanied by the rhythms of radical hip-hop group Public Enemy to accentuate a defiant visual message. Hall appeared on-screen in a prerecorded introduction, self-consciously dripping in quintessential '90s hip-hop attire—a backward baseball cap, baggy overalls, and dark sunglasses. He candidly acknowledged the polarizing reactions to Farrakhan's appearance on the show, a complex interplay of admiration and outrage. Most responses ran along racial lines. On the one hand, many Black Americans were thrilled about the minister's appearance; on the other, many white Americans were furious about it. As the interview commenced, Farrakhan's opening remarks calmly addressed the controversy. The minister framed his presence as a threat to the established order: "The powers-that-be don't want me here because they are afraid that some truth will get out to help free the minds of Black folk." Farrakhan commended Hall for following through with the interview and displaying fortitude in the face of adversity and harsh blowback. The minister smiled and proclaimed to Hall, "You are a man of principles . . . and we are the victims of ignorance and oppression of our people. Our job is to teach Black people how to love themselves."[60] Three months after this stirring appearance, *The Arsenio Hall Show* broadcast its final episode.

Despite their inauspicious endings, *In Living Color* and *The Arsenio Hall Show* became the two most significant and successful television contributions of the Black Pack comedy cycle. Both programs dominated, electrified, and revolutionized American television for a brief but impactful period, defining the cutting edge of 1990s hipness while attracting massive crossover appeal. Although Wayans maintains he never set out to create an exclusively "Black show," *In Living Color* has become a cherished addition to the canon of Black cultural production. Wayans delivered a program that resonates across Black communities and beyond. The series reinvigorated sketch comedy, just as *The Arsenio Hall Show* reenergized late night, capturing the cultural zeitgeist and interrupting dominant television discourses. Armed with confrontational Black resistance humor, both programs critiqued social events and America's racial quandary with a distinctly Black vocality. Fueled by the aesthetics of hip-hop culture, each show provided viewers with a platform for comedic intervention, sparking cultural debates that circulated through the representational space of commercial television. These Black Pack productions also launched several '90s catchphrases into the American lexicon: "Two snaps up," "Homey don't play that," and the Arsenio "Dog Pound" bark became ubiquitous in popular culture. With the creation of *In Living Color*, Wayans was instrumental in paving the way for an expansion in Black visibility (albeit temporarily) on Fox, with stars like Martin Lawrence, David "Sinbad" Adkins, and Dana "Queen Latifah" Owens each landing sitcom deals. At its best, *In Living Color* embodies a rebellious ideological stance. The show's humor subverted, questioned, and undermined traditional American values, echoing the pioneering and daring spirit of *The Richard Pryor Show*. Paul Mooney, who famously wrote sketches for both programs, saw *In Living Color* as "a spin-off from *The Richard Pryor Show*": "We [Richard and I] were the first ones to land on the moon called color and provocative."[61] Keenen Ivory Wayans's comedic vision ridiculed the avoidance of stereotypes in our society by imploring audiences to laugh at political incorrectness. Thriving on the fringes of irony and pastiche, *In Living Color* was a fertile ground for exploring the complexities of race, class, and the possibility of subversion within a comedic framework. The show invited viewers to grapple with uncomfortable truths while reveling in cathartic laughter.

Similarly, *The Arsenio Hall Show* blossomed during its six-year run, appealing to a youthful demographic with its fresh, rowdy, and unapologetically Black approach to late night television. During his reign, Hall was the only host to outduel Johnny Carson in the late night ratings war. *The Arsenio Hall Show* drew energy and allure from its embrace of hip-hop culture and its nightly celebration of a range of Black musicians, filmmakers, artists, and comedians. By the mid-1990s, as the Rodney King uprisings and reactions to the verdict in the O. J. Simpson murder trial exposed the country's deep racial fault lines, *The Arsenio Hall Show* emerged as a hotbed for social commentary. While some have argued the show's "race talk" adversely impacted its ratings, Hall still challenged the traditionally white corporate sphere of television that functions to govern perception and the construction of meaning. During the taping of one striking episode, a group of white gay rights protestors from the group Queer Nation heckled Hall from the audience. In a heated exchange, Hall refused to shy away from the confrontation, addressing the protestors directly: "You didn't think I was gonna run from this, did you? This ain't Johnny. This ain't Merv. I'ma deal with this." Hall descended into the largely white audience, engaging with the protestors, who shouted, "Arsenio discriminated against gays!" Hall refuted their claims, defended his record on LGBTQ+ inclusion, and acknowledged his own experiences with discrimination as a Black man in America. However, even support from Black entertainers proved elusive for Hall. Spike Lee infamously took shots at the late night host, publicly labeling him an "Uncle Tom." Hall later recalled thinking, "Who am I doing this for—[white people] don't like me, and [Black people] don't like me. I might as well take my money and leave."[62] Feeling caught between the disapproval of both white and Black audiences, Hall decided to step away from the late night stage.

The Arsenio Hall Show's Black televisuality engaged late night dynamics as an evolving platform for exploring cultural identity through the transmission of language, imagery, music, and symbols—the very tools by which meaning is constructed. Hall fostered a cultural dialogue that challenged the prevailing narratives on race in the American mediascape. However, the impermanence of such victories should not be ignored. On May 27, 1994, *The Arsenio Hall Show* taped its final episode, a late night party extolling Hall's cultural influence. The star-studded event, a valedictory celebration, featured a roster of Black stars ranging from Whoopi Goldberg to James Brown. Archival clips of the program played in the background, offering a retrospective of the show's most impactful moments. Many of the era's prominent hip-hop artists, like Naughty by Nature, Yo-Yo, KRS-One, A Tribe Called Quest, Wu-Tang Clan, and MC Lyte, graced the stage in a collective tribute to Arsenio Hall, the Black "king of late night," to whom they were all undeniably indebted. As the show's final credits rolled, rapper Ol' Dirty Bastard, a member of the group Wu-Tang Clan, erupted in a spontaneous and impassioned outburst. He yelled repeatedly at the audience, "The Black man is god!" It was a proclamation at once haunting and emotional, serving as a poignant acknowledgment that America's nightly window into the polysemic world of Black expressive culture was closing, an eerie foreshadowing that Black voices and creators on broadcast television would, once again, soon be rendered invisible.

Coda

Black Resistance Humor into the Afro-Future

As our nation continues to wrestle with its enduring conundrum of race and inequality, I often find myself returning to the incisive wisdom embedded in the words of James Baldwin, particularly his sharp appraisals of Hollywood cinema in the profound book-length essay *The Devil Finds Work*. In his revelatory critique of the classic film *In the Heat of the Night*, Baldwin dissects the last scene, where Detective Tibbs (brought to life brilliantly by the incomparable Sidney Poitier) departs from the racially hostile town of Sparta, Mississippi, with the begrudging respect of its racist police chief, Gillespie (played by Rod Steiger). In this final reconciliatory moment, the film suggests these two radically different Americans, a Black man from the North and a white man from the South, have managed to, out of a tornado of racism and bigotry, forge a bond of mutual respect, even friendship. But Baldwin, always an astute observer of America's anti-Black contradictions, refuses to accept the film's tidy and saccharine Hollywood ending. Never one to mince words, Baldwin contends, "People who cannot escape thinking of themselves as white are poorly equipped, if equipped at all, to consider the meaning of Black: people who know so little about themselves can face very little in another: and one dare hope for nothing from friends like these."[1] Baldwin goes further with his blistering observation, asserting, "white Americans have been encouraged to continue dreaming, and Black Americans have been alerted to the necessity of waking up."[2] With that, he distills the essence of the fundamentally opposed aims and impulses that lie at the epicenter of the nation's racial dynamics—where the divergent realities of Black and white Americans are laid bare. The contrast between the illusions that sustain white America and the unforgiving realities that Black Americans must confront reveals the deep-seated tensions that fuel the nation's centuries-old struggle with systemic racism.

Yet amid our sobering challenges, Black people have long brandished wily satire and resistant humor as a means of survival—a way to navigate the absurdities of a society that persistently devalues them. And it is through laughter that Black Americans have, at times, found a way to cope with rage, subvert racial tropes, and assert their humanity. Looking back at a moment that underscores the enduring power of humor as a tool for social change, the cultural significance of the Black Pack has become more apparent with the passage of time. This unique network of Black American social humorists was deeply resonant in their cultural moment, and yet they were still ahead of their time, transforming anger into art that echoes as powerfully today as it did in the era of its creation. Their body of work is a testament to the power of storytelling and the enduring relevance of humor in our ongoing battle for equity and justice.

At their peak, the Black Pack enjoyed unparalleled mainstream success. For a fleeting moment, they were Hollywood darlings who leveraged their comedic talents to achieve public recognition while maintaining a keen focus on the specter of race, the inescapable shadow that shapes identity in America. Unlike many entertainers who seek to dilute their racial identities, the Black Pack, to their credit, did not succumb to the industry's temptation to "transcend" race with "colorless," flavorless comedy. Instead, they strategically sidestepped attempts to downplay race, opting to embrace Blackness unapologetically, utilizing America's racial preoccupations to their advantage. Central to their collaborative efforts was an ability to weaponize humor, converting it into a beguiling form of social commentary always contemplating and pointing toward a Black futurity full of agency, equity, visibility, and vocality. For the Black Pack, comedy was their cloak and dagger—a clever disguise that allowed them to infiltrate the bastions of commercial entertainment, confronting system-wide racism while posing as innocuous. By engaging multiple modes of Black resistance humor, they became, in essence, Hollywood's "spooks who sat by the door," traversing multiple media platforms and furtively pioneering an explosion of Black film and television.

The Black Pack comedians injected radical voices and lacerating wit into American culture. Propelled by the breakout star power of Eddie Murphy, the collective forged an organic alliance characterized by deep bonds of fraternal camaraderie and creativity, waging comedic war against Hollywood from within the very system it sought to critique. Their productions were not only cultural events but joyous celebrations that fostered shared memories and experiences for Black families and communities. They brought laughter and subversive pleasure to audiences, providing fresh perspectives on the legibility of Blackness in popular culture. It is also true that Hollywood studios, by their very nature, prioritize the maintenance of social order, profiting from the preservation of inequality. Disturbance of that order inevitably leads to a degree of dysfunction. The Black Pack canon, in that regard, is a disruptive intervention that momentarily recontextualized the social dimensions of commercial film and television. Their multitextured storytelling practices and comedic rituals of resistance upset dominant narratives with a critical Black gaze.

Throughout their transformative seven-year run, the Black Pack exercised considerable creative control over their productions—a rarity for Black cultural workers in Hollywood. Their autonomy, although ultimately ephemeral, allowed them to deliver, to an extent, an arsenal of Black resistance humor: reinscription, satire, parody, and irony as cultural maneuvers to question and unsettle, as much as possible, the formally constructed ways that institutional racism plays out in the Black lifeworld. And still, working within the framework of Hollywood racial capitalism, their productions were inevitably entangled in a complex exploitative process that co-opts social criticism and transforms resistance into market-driven commodities. This inherent contradiction reveals how the Black Pack eventually fell out of favor in Hollywood, despite their profitability. Once their subversive humor threatened to disturb dominant power relations, the establishment mobilized against them.

To some degree, the Black Pack project offers many Black audiences an opportunity to experience a momentary sense of empowerment and agency, access and mobility, freedom and power that eludes far too many Black Americans. These cultural productions are ripe for renegotiation and demand recognition for their significant impact on American humor. Their comedic material exists beyond simplistic positive or negative binaries. Rather, the Black Pack productions are cultural artifacts that bear "hidden transcripts" used to engage subtle yet compelling contestations of the racial condition. Moreover, their influence extends beyond punchlines and potshots. They advocated for increased representation in the Hollywood industry, championed inclusion for people of color in below-the-line production positions, and insisted Black cultural producers take their rightful place at the decision-making table.

Hollywood's '90s Black Explosion

In his study of the culture industry, Ellis Cashmore keenly discerns, "Black culture has been converted into a commodity, usually in the interests of white-owned corporations; [and] Blacks have been permitted to excel in entertainment only on the condition that they conform to whites' image of Blacks; and how Blacks themselves, when they rise to the top of the corporate entertainment ladder, have tended to act precisely as whites have in similar circumstances."[3] Cashmore's assessment underlines the rarity of the Black Pack's industry mandate as progressive creative image-makers in Hollywood. The Black Pack productions, though ideologically resistant, also proved financially lucrative. This economic reality, within the logic of the dominant system, granted them a temporary window to transgress, and their collaborations spurred a notable expansion of Black film and television production. Media giants like HBO, Fox, Paramount Pictures, New Line Cinema, and Miramax began investing more heavily in Black creative talent. Film comedies like *House Party* (1990), *Mo' Money* (1992), *CB4* (1993), *Fear of a Black Hat* (1993), *Friday* (1995), *Bad Boys* (1995), and *Soul Food* (1997) were among the beneficiaries of the Black Pack's cultural moves. However, along with the uptick in Black-themed comedies came the hyperviolent "hood film" fad. These movies were "less obviously politically focused, and in their violent nihilism (and sometimes self-contempt) they hardly suggest the possibility of social change."[4] Films like *New Jack City* (1991), *Boyz n the Hood* (1991), *Straight Outta Brooklyn* (1991), *Juice* (1992), and *Menace II Society* (1993) all depict Black struggles in the harsh realities of crime-ridden, drug-infested cities.

On the other hand, one can see how Black Pack productions like *Robert Townsend and His Partners in Crime*, *In Living Color*, and *The Arsenio Hall Show* cleared pathways for Black voices on television. The Fox network led the way. Black TV show creators like Yvette Lee Bowser, the first Black woman to develop a prime-time series with *Living Single* (1993–1998), and Ralph Farquhar's social problem sitcom *South Central* (1994) brought fresh perspectives to Fox. Yet as Kristal Brent Zook explains, "Rupert Murdoch not only found ways to profit from the cultural production and consumption practices of African Americans but he also manipulated, to the collective detriment of Black people, governmental infrastructures designed to balance the racially distorted playing field of media ownership. When such infrastructures threatened to limit Murdoch's monopolistic domination, in other words, he simply had them removed."[5] Meanwhile, as HBO's *Def Comedy Jam* (1992–1997) rose on cable, showcasing underground Black stand-up routines, it gave America an early glimpse of future stars like Bernie Mac, Dave Chappelle, and Chris Tucker. Airing on a premium channel provided the show with "the luxury of fewer restrictions on its content, allowing comics to perform as they would in a club, complete with expletives, sexually explicit content, and other material deemed offensive and inappropriate for major networks."[6] Similarly, BET's *Comic View* (1992–2008) offered Black stand-up comics a platform on basic cable. Although *Def Comedy Jam* and *Comic View* served as launchpads for Black talent, the programs' overreliance on ribald jokes and exaggerated performances of Black identity did very little to shift the status quo or ridicule the absurdities of systemic racism. By the mid-1990s, Black televisual voices were gradually quarantined. The launch of UPN and the WB as the fifth and sixth major American television networks mirrored Fox's segmentation strategy, introducing a surge of Black sitcoms like *The Wayans Brothers* (1995–1999), *The Jamie Foxx Show* (1996–2001), *Malcolm & Eddie* (1996–2000), and *Homeboys from Outer Space* (1996–1997). Backed by UPN, television star Kelsey Grammer produced the feminist-leaning sitcom *Girlfriends* (2000–2008), an exploration of Black female success, friendship, sexuality, and love from creator Mara Brock Akil. The network also produced *Everybody Hates Chris* (2005–2009), a quirky comedic take on Chris Rock's childhood upbringing. However, as Yuval Taylor and Jake Austen note, "Once established both Fox and the WB dropped their Black shows in favor of programs that appealed to white youth, who advertisers consider a more upscale demographic. UPN continued Black programming until it merged with the WB in 2006 to become the CW network."[7] This strategic shift once again points to the fundamental instability of Blackness in the Hollywood industrial complex, which predictably does not autocorrect.

The Politics of Thirst

By the mid-2000s, network television's lush gardens of Black programming suddenly resembled a desolate wasteland. *Girlfriends*, *The Game*

(2006–2009), and *Everybody Hates Chris* were among the last Black sitcoms on a major network by the decade's end. These programs continued to air on the CW after the merger, until *Girlfriends* was canceled in 2008, and the latter programs were canceled in 2009. The decline in production of Black-themed shows on major networks coincided with the rise of playwright-turned-mogul Tyler Perry, who built an empire on low-budget stage productions which he parlayed into the ubiquitous *Madea* film franchise and an overabundance of cable shows churned out for TBS, OWN, and BET. While the 1990s brimmed with a surge of optimism among Black film and television artists regarding creative opportunities, the industry's once-vibrant Black boom fizzled by the turn of the millennium, leaving little trace of the subversive energy and social velocity of the previous era. The rebellious humor that characterized the Black Pack production cycle gradually devolved into the rehashing of regressive performance strategies in films like *How High* (2001), *Soul Plane* (2004), *Madea's Family Reunion* (2006), and *Get Hard* (2015). The precipitous decline in Black-led shows on network television mirrored a systemic unraveling, plummeting from twenty-one programs in 1997 to a mere three by 2006. Ultimately, by 2009, the televisual landscape was totally barren, with no Black shows on a major network, exhibiting a representational collapse of catastrophic proportions.[8]

Shonda Rhimes eventually seized the Black popular imagination with the earthquake debut of *Scandal* (2012–2018) on ABC. The political thriller, headlined by Kerry Washington, ignited social media and marked a milestone as the first drama led by a Black woman on a major network. This success sparked a small flurry of Black productions with shows like ABC's *blackish* (2014–2022), *How to Get Away with Murder* (2014–2020), Fox's *Empire* (2015–2020), OWN's *Queen Sugar* (2016–2022), NBC's *The Carmichael Show* (2015–2017), *Abbot Elementary* (2021–), and FX's *Atlanta* (2016–2022), which triggered hasty declarations of a "new Black renaissance." This period, unsurprisingly, now appears little more than a breathlessly fleeting mirage. As of this writing, of the programs previously mentioned, only *Abbot Elementary* remains on a major network. Basic cable affords a different escape—the Tyler Perry universe, for instance, which is populated by shows like *Bruh* (2020–), *Sistas* (2019–), and *The Oval* (2019–), tends to cater to conventional notions of Blackness as abject, devoid of dissident perspectives or nuanced modes of expression. Such programs are fundamentally bound up in what I call the "politics of thirst," a cultural phenomenon wherein members of marginalized groups longing for representation may, because of scarcity, gravitate toward any mainstream media production with a semblance of familiarity, even if its ideology contradicts their own interests.[9] Storytelling is, most certainly, an intrinsic aspect of the human experience, serving as a mechanism through which we explore our identities, grapple with adversity, and contemplate the absurdities that accompany the human condition. For these reasons, Black audiences, historically disenfranchised and deprived of culturally affirming narratives, have developed a ravenous "thirst" for Black voices and stories.

In this vulnerable state, audiences are especially susceptible to embrace any mainstream offering, no matter how retrograde, formulaic, or detrimental, in order to quench their ostensibly insatiable representational thirst. This condition creates a precarious situation for Black film and television artists trapped in the inertia and exclusionary games of Hollywood's chronic racial tendencies. It is a cautionary tale that, in the end, reminds us of the horrid American reality that "once many plantations grew cotton; today, some grow movies [and TV shows]. But the imperatives remain much the same."[10] Sadly, though not surprisingly, the same "devalued images of African Americans can arise as the creations of ambitious Blacks themselves, squirming for a break, and perhaps success, in the same mainstream movie business."[11] The desert landscape of nuanced Black voices in Hollywood only intensifies audiences' thirst for Black stories that resonate with their embodied experiences. Therefore, deep critical scrutiny becomes essential for any Black-themed commercial media product created within the intricate dynamics of the politics of thirst. Any commercial media product that appropriates what is known in popular parlance as Black "dope-ness"—whether in fashion, vernacular language, music, cultural objects, aesthetics, or other distinctly Black practices—is an active conduit for Hollywood's commodification and co-optation, preserving the long and wrenching winter of the American dream/nightmare.

In his acceptance speech for the Spingarn Medal at the 2013 NAACP Image Awards ceremony, the venerable actor and activist Harry Belafonte delivered a stirring call to action, emphasizing a cultural imperative for Black stars who have amassed substantial wealth to leverage their influence to improve Black communities and collective solidarity. He declared, "Paul Robeson, he was the sparrow. He was an artist who made us understand the depth of that calling, when he said: 'Artists are the gatekeepers of truth. We are civilization's radical voice.' Never in the history of Black America has there ever been such a harvest of truly gifted and powerful artists as we witness today. Yet, our nation hungers for their radical song. Let us not sit back silently. Let us not be charged with patriotic treason."[12] Belafonte's impassioned address morally indicted contemporary Black artists and celebrities, urging them to shoulder the responsibility of upholding the mantle of Black excellence. This concept, Belafonte argued, was not simply an aspirational ideal but an inextricable facet of Black American heritage. Reflecting on a similar cultural imperative, W. E. B. Du Bois, in 1903, envisioned an enlightened vanguard of educated Black leadership, the fabled "Talented Tenth," who would guide and elevate the broader community. Nearly fifty years later, Du Bois revisited this concept, acknowledging the blind spots and limitations inherent in his original vision, writing, "I assumed that with knowledge, sacrifice would automatically follow. In my youth and idealism, I did not realize that selfishness is even more natural than sacrifice [and] it was quite possible that my plan of training a talented tenth might put in control and power, a group of selfish, self-indulgent, well-to-do men [and women] without any real care, or certainly no arousing care, as to what became of the mass of American Negroes."[13] Inside the crucible of late American capitalism, Du Bois's words continue to speak to the souls of Black folk with profound urgency. Many contemporary Black media moguls, executives, and cultural producers, despite occupying positions of power, have succumbed to the sunken place of adopting dominant views and the myths of rugged individualism. The Black Pack production cycle, in contrast, pillories that social logic with an ironic collage of culture that expresses a counternarrative to the abjection of Blackness and racial self-denigration. In our modern context, Black audiences bound up in the politics of thirst can ill afford to be hoodwinked, bamboozled, or seduced by the industry's hollow promises made on boulevards of broken dreams.

The Aftermath: Post–Black Pack Hollywood

As a collaborative comedy crew, the Black Pack mocked Hollywood's institutional power and its racial politics. Their production of humor reveals insight into the social interplay between Black and white America, providing viewers with an opportunity to witness America through a Black gaze. In doing so, they produced work using various modes of Black resistance humor—that is, humor that transforms righteous anger, critique, and playfulness into piercing social commentary using double-talk, double meanings, strategic reversals, and biting satire that display a surprising range of creative vision. The Black Pack's cultural productions made audible and visible the experiences, stories, fantasies, ambitions, rituals, and anxieties prevalent in many Black communities. In Black Pack narratives, Blackness often turns the table on power, inverting the poles of authority, and the joke is on the dominant culture. Decades after the Black Pack's formation in Los Angeles, their cultural impact endures. Mooney, Murphy, Wayans, Townsend, and Hall banded together not only as brothers but also as "brothers" in a Black vernacular sense, collaborating to bring a Black gaze into the mainstream spotlight. Individually, their diverse careers have borne the twists and turns of the labyrinthine industry with varying degrees of success and setbacks.

Among them, Eddie Murphy remains the Black Pack's most acclaimed and influential member. But his post–Black Pack career has been marked by a roller coaster of critical and commercial fluctuations. The screwball comedy *The Distinguished Gentleman* (1992) was widely panned, earning a moderate return with $46 million at the box office. His reprisal of Axel Foley in *Beverly Hills Cop III* (1994), despite lackluster reviews, grossed over $119 million. And his subsequent foray into horror-comedy in Wes Craven's *Vampire in Brooklyn* (1995) was a commercial disappointment, recouping only $19 million on a $14 million budget. The late 1990s saw a shift in Murphy's comedic persona, moving toward less rebellious and more family-friendly roles in such films as *The Nutty Professor* (1996) and *Dr. Doolittle* (1998). Both movies were substantial box office hits, grossing $274 million and $294 million, respectively, and spawning hit sequels *Nutty Professor 2: The Klumps* (2000) and *Dr. Doolittle 2* (2001). On television, he collaborated with Larry Wilmore to cocreate *The PJs* (1999–2001), an animated series set in a New York City housing project, with Murphy lending his voice to the protagonist "Thurgood." Murphy also delivered a memorable and hilarious performance opposite Martin Lawrence in *Life* (1999), which marked Murphy's final appearance in an R-rated film for two decades. His focus on family-friendly fare peaked with his voicing of "Donkey" in the *Shrek* franchise. In 2015, Murphy's contributions to American comedy were recognized as culturally significant when the Kennedy Center awarded him the prestigious Mark Twain Prize for American Humor.

In recent years, Murphy returned with a fourth installment of his franchise character Axel Foley in *Beverly Hills Cop: Axel F* (2024), debuting on the streaming giant Netflix. He also delivered a long-awaited return to Zamunda in *Coming 2 America* (2021), released on the streaming service Amazon Prime, a homecoming of sorts for the Black Pack. These films connect audiences to a heartwarming reunion with beloved characters, engaging the complexities of nostalgia in remaking time-honored classics. The humor in these sequels, often broad and familiar, feels comforting but ultimately uninspired. On the other hand, Murphy's striking performance in *Dolemite Is My Name* (2019) delves into the vibrant, overlooked history of Rudy Ray Moore, the pioneering comedian and cult icon behind the outrageous Blaxploitation character "Dolemite." The film brilliantly recaptures Murphy's hilarious and transgressive comedic energy. He channels Moore's flamboyant persona and relentless pursuit of artistic expression in the face of industrial limitations. *Dolemite Is My Name* is a celebration of hustle, ingenuity, and the entrepreneurial spirit of Black creators who carve out space for themselves within the hostile world of American cinema. Murphy also starred in Amazon Prime's *Candy Cane Lane* (2023) and partnered with Netflix on *You People* (2023) and the autobiographical documentary *EDDIE* (2025). His performance on the *SNL* fiftieth-anniversary special (2025) also provided several sidesplitting moments for the show.

Keenen Ivory Wayans has also sustained a presence in Hollywood, although he initially faced challenges finding success as an actor after his Black Pack heyday. His appearance opposite action star Steven Seagal in *The Glimmer Man* (1996) fell short, earning only $20 million against a hefty $45 million budget. Additionally, his stint hosting the late night talk series *The Keenen Ivory Wayans Show* (1997–1998) failed to recapture the energy or viewership once dominated by Arsenio Hall. Wayans's second attempt at the action genre, *Most Wanted* (1997), was also met with disappointment, earning a mere $11 million on a $25 million production budget. Nevertheless, Wayans found his stride behind the camera as a producer, screenwriter, and director, successfully translating his signature parodic voice, popularized in *I'm Gonna Git You Sucka* and *In Living Color*, into a string of hit films starring his younger brothers. He directed Shawn and Marlon Wayans in the breakout horror parody *Scary Movie* (2000) and its sequel *Scary Movie 2* (2001), which grossed $278 million and $141 million, respectively. Wayans later cowrote with and directed Shawn and Marlon in the whiteface drag film *White Chicks* (2004) and the farcical comedy *Little Man* (2006), both surpassing the $100 million mark at the box office. In 2012, Wayans came to terms with Fox to host and executive produce an *In Living Color* reboot. Initially planned as a series of comedy specials with the potential for a full series pickup, the reboot aimed to revitalize Fox's prime-time lineup. Although there were high hopes for the revival, creative differences derailed the efforts. Damon Wayans, a pivotal member of the original cast, parted ways with the project, causing other cast members to follow suit. Consequently, despite filming the pilot episode, the *In Living Color* reboot never made it to air. In 2014, Keenen was cast as a celebrity judge on the hit NBC reality TV program *Last Comic Standing*. He also cowrote the urban spoof *Dance Flick* (2009) and several episodes of the TBS sitcom *Last OG* (2018–2021), further solidifying his enduring presence in the entertainment industry.

Since his days as the upstart Renaissance man of the Black Pack, Robert Townsend's post–Black Pack trajectory reflects the complex realities of navigating Hollywood's treacherous terrain. He cocreated, starred in, and directed *The Parent 'Hood* (1995–1999), a family sitcom chronicling the lives of middle-class parents raising children in New York City. The show aired five seasons in the separate and unequal landscape of the WB network. Townsend's last major studio directing effort, *B.A.P.S.* (1997), starring future Oscar winner Halle Berry, was met with disappointment. The New Line Cinema production earned a lackluster $7.3 million against its $10 million budget. Townsend's subsequent career shift from auteur to journeyman director-for-hire connotes a broader industry trend away from diverse authorship. He helmed two notable made-for-television movies, NBC's *Little Richard* (2000), a rock 'n' roll biopic, and *Carmen: A Hip Hopera* (2001), which marked pop singer Beyoncé Knowles-Carter's acting debut. Produced by MTV, the film offered a hip-hop reimagining of the classic opera and the renowned Dorothy Dandridge musical *Carmen Jones* (1954).

In recent years, Townsend has appeared in a recurring role on the evocative FX drama *The Bear* (2022–) and has primarily directed independent films and episodic television programs for a variety of networks. In 2018, he directed *Making the Five Heartbeats*, an independent documentary exploring the behind-the-scenes details of his cult classic Black Pack musical. Townsend's career arc from a prophetic comedic voice to a journeyman director tragically underscores the industry's persistent stranglehold on the output of Black cultural expression. And still, the enduring value of his work exceeds unfulfilled aspirations. The most prophetic moment of Townsend's career, appropriately enough, emanates from *Hollywood Shuffle*. The film's casting office sequence remains starkly relevant and resonant. In the scene, Townsend's character is warned by an aspiring Black actor, "Don't sell out, brother. Don't be a butler or a slave." These words are hauntingly prescient regarding the current plight of Black performers, who continue to grapple with the industry's recycling of racial tropes and the burden of representation. Case in point, in 2013, twenty-six years after the release of *Hollywood Shuffle*, it should perhaps be unsurprising that the highest-grossing and most critically acclaimed Black films of the year were Lee Daniels's *The Butler* and Steve McQueen's *12 Years a Slave*. Call it tragic irony. While undeniably well crafted, such films reinscribe a catalog of Hollywood images of Blackness as one-dimensional, fixed in a tableau of historical suffering and pain, and frozen in a glacier of passivity, offering little room for critical resistance. *Hollywood Shuffle* stands as a timeless indictment. It exposes the unimaginable rigidity of the film industry that continues to operate in opposition to Black cinematic progress. Townsend's film is a prophetic reminder of the industry's shortcomings. It endures as a clarion call for more inclusive and nuanced voices of Black humanity within American cinema that, unfortunately, have remained unanswered.

After his reign as the king of late night, Arsenio Hall stepped away from the searing glare of the Hollywood spotlight, exhausted with the capricious nature of fame. He returned to television in 1997 with *Arsenio*, a sitcom costarring Vivica A. Fox. The ill-fated program was canceled after seven episodes. Hall quickly landed a supporting role in the police procedural *Martial Law* (1998–2000), playing the wisecracking sidekick to martial artist Sammo Hung. The series was a surprise hit for CBS, but Hung did not renew his contract after disputes with the network over the racialized depiction of his character. In 2015, Hall's unlikely victory on the fifth season of the reality TV game show *The Celebrity Apprentice* reignited interest in a reboot of his signature late night program. Eighteen years after its cancellation, *The Arsenio Hall Show* returned to late night, aiming to recapture the magic that enthralled a generation. John Nogawski, then president of CBS Television, explained his decision to greenlight the series: "We're going to relight lightning in a bottle. The generation that watched [Hall] when they were 18–34 is now 35–54, and no one is really satisfying them. Arsenio should appeal to those 35- to 54-year-olds that are right in the sweet spot of the demographic of those Tribune-owned CW stations."[14] The reboot aired with solid ratings, oozing with nostalgia. The premiere boasted a star-studded lineup ranging from the reclusive comic Chris Tucker to a rare televised stand-up performance by gadfly Paul Mooney and marquee names like Kanye West and Prince. The show's revival outdueled longtime industry veterans Jay Leno and David Letterman in the ratings for a brief, electrifying moment. Despite its initial surge, the program struggled to maintain momentum. While Hall continued to provide a platform for underrepresented artists, the power of the original show was elusive. As a middle-aged comedian, Hall was no longer a rebellious newcomer. His rough edges were sanded down by the conformity required to survive and advance in Hollywood. In an interview, Hall explains, "The white man didn't do nothing to me. I walked away, and now I'm back—and that's what the white man did. He allowed me to knock on the door 20 years later. . . . [But] there are too many cooks in the motherfucking Hollywood kitchen now. So much micromanagement you've got to fight even to get the teleprompter guy. And now they can tell you 15 minutes after a show's over if viewers have tuned out. . . . Man, it's a calculated, computerized demographers world out there . . . but I can only be Arsenio."[15] The second iteration of *The Arsenio Hall Show* was canceled after one season. Hall later returned to stand-up and interviewing pop cultural tastemakers on stage at the Netflix Is a Joke comedy festival.

For years, the volcanic humor of the Black Pack's venerable sage Paul Mooney remained a provocative force in comedy clubs nationwide. His no-holds-barred brand of Black resistance humor did not soften with age. He continued playing "whack-a-mole" on whiteness whenever he performed. After four decades in the industry, Mooney gained mainstream attention as a performer and writer on *Chappelle's Show* with sketches like "Ask a Black Dude" and "Mooney on Movies." When Chappelle abruptly walked away from the program in 2005, Mooney continued traveling extensively, performing stand-up with atomic wit and uncompromising commentary on race and society. He delivered a short turn as host of the reality TV court series *Judge Mooney* (2004) and a brilliant cameo in the horror-comedy *Meet the Blacks* (2016). Mooney also released several comedy specials, including *Jesus Is Black—So Was Cleopatra—Know Your History* (2007), *It's the End of the World* (2010), *The Godfather of Comedy* (2012), and his final stand-up film, *A Piece of My Mind: God Bless America* (2014), which was released on Netflix. Mooney's towering comedic genius and fearless approach to addressing taboo subjects made him a legendary figure in the comedy world. His impact on comedy and culture is immeasurable, touching countless lives with his humor and insight. Paul Mooney passed away on May 19, 2021, at age seventy-nine. He will be remembered as not just a humorist but as a fearless truth-teller, a Black Pack trailblazer, and an icon whose influence has indelibly shaped American comedy.

Into the Afro-Future and Beyond: The Enduring Legacy of Black Resistance Humor

Even after the release of their final production, the inspiration from the Black Pack's innovative comedic material echoes in the output of a new generation of modern disciples. These inheritors have also achieved mainstream recognition by adapting and evolving the dimensions of Black resistance humor with a blend of jokes and comedic styles that evince a willingness to confront the gargoyles of American racism and Hollywood power structures that continue to marginalize Black voices. Primary illustrations include the blistering social commentary of Wanda Sykes, Chris Rock, and Dave Chappelle; the scathing wit of Katt Williams, Eddie Griffin, and Amanda Seales; and the insightful ridicule of Larry Wilmore, Jessica Williams, Phoebe Robinson, W. Kamau Bell, Key & Peele, and the Lucas Brothers. Even the introspective musings of Jerrod Carmichael and Michal Che or the genre-blending humor of Donald Glover are a testament of Black resistance humor's enduring ability to serve as a wellspring of inspiration for new generations of emerging comedians.

Chris Rock, of course, appeared in three pivotal Black Pack productions: *I'm Gonna Git You Sucka*, *Boomerang*, and *In Living Color*. Following his tenure on *Saturday Night Live*, Rock's ascent to comedic prominence was propelled by his raw and unapologetic HBO special, *Bring the Pain* (1996). In the special, Rock stalks frenetically across the stage, tackling socially, culturally, and politically charged topics, sparing no one from his ire. He assertively uses racial reversal, a critical tool of Black resistance humor, to delve into the highly charged atmosphere surrounding the verdict in the O. J. Simpson murder trial. Rock defiantly proclaims,

> *People say the jury was so stupid. But if they were white people, they would have done the exact same shit. Because if that was Jerry Seinfeld charged with double murder and the only person that found the glove just happened to be in the Nation of Islam . . . Jerry would be a free man.*[16]

Rock's comedic material, particularly in *Bring the Pain*, as Terrence T. Tucker suggests, encapsulates "the best of hip-hop": "Underneath Rock's energetic, blunt tone is a finely tuned critique of America that centralizes working-class African American experience."[17] *Bring the Pain* garnered critical acclaim, clinching two Emmy Awards and cementing its status as one of the signature stand-up performances in comedy history. His HBO late night series *The Chris Rock Show* (1997–2000) further established him as a resistant Black voice, combining the stage presence of Eddie Murphy with the acerbic barbs of Paul Mooney. His ability to inspect America's neurotic racial maladies resulted in *Time* magazine declaring him "the funniest man in America" in 2001. Beyond numerous film roles, Rock also released more comedy specials, including *Bigger and Blacker* (1999), *Never Scared* (2004), *Kill the Messenger*

(2008), and *Tambourine* (2018). Rock later found himself in a double bind as the host of the eighty-eighth annual Academy Awards ceremony, a year with no Black performers nominated. Some activists called for Rock to decline his role as host and boycott the Oscars. He did not. This scenario, however, highlights the irrationality of the industry's racialized logic.

At the 2022 Academy Awards, in his role as presenter, Rock, onstage once more, was publicly assaulted by actor Will Smith. The moment generated significant controversy, with Smith slapping Rock in the face, presumably in response to the comic's joke about Jada Pinkett Smith's hairstyle. While some dismissed the incident as a momentary lapse in judgment, a closer examination reveals a complex undercurrent involving issues of patriarchal power and American masculinity. The appropriateness of Rock's joke, potentially insensitive to Jada Pinkett Smith's alopecia, remains debatable; however, Smith's violent reaction overshadowed the joke and the entire Oscars ceremony as a whole. Further complicating matters was Smith's profanity-laced outburst on a global public platform, given his decades-long pristine "good guy" persona, which compels considerations about the often-fraught interplay between mental health, masculinity, race, and image management within the Hollywood machine. The incident prompted public debates over humor, free speech, and the clash between artistic license and comedic freedom. Rock responded to the matter one year later in the first-ever live Netflix comedy special, *Chris Rock: Selective Outrage* (2023). Here, he evokes his trademark sermonic shout-speak comedic style:

> *Ya'll know what happened to me. Getting smacked by "Suge Smith." People asking, "Did it hurt?" It still hurts. I got "Summertime" ringing in my ears. . . . I rooted for Will Smith my whole life, I root for this motherfucker. And now, I watch "Emancipation" just to see him get whupped. Got me rooting for massa, okay. Hit 'em again, massa. Hit 'em again. You missed a spot, massa. . . . People say "Chris, how come you didn't do nothing back?" 'Cause I got parents. That's why. And you know what my parents taught me? Don't fight in front of white people.*[18]

Mic drop.

Comedians like Eddie Griffin and D. L. Hughley made a name for themselves as stand-up comics in the 1990s. Their comedic material has matured from primarily scatological to more nuanced politically Black readings of race, class, and American politics in the mainstream and on social media. The incisive comedy of Micah "Katt" Williams has ignited several controversies and still managed to create destabilizing moments of Black resistance humor in the public sphere. His provocative and cerebral stand-up specials include *Kattpacalypse* (2012), *Katt Williams: Priceless: Afterlife* (2014), *Katt Williams: Great America* (2018), and *World War III* (2022). In Williams's explosive 2024 interview with former NFL star Shannon Sharpe on the popular podcast *Club Shay Shay*, the mercurial comic publicly exposed Hollywood industry corruption and discredited well-known Black comics for joke-stealing and other behind-the-scenes chicanery. Williams's criticisms went viral on social media, triggering a maelstrom of speculation and unearthing the fractured nature of contemporary Black American comedy and dredging up age-old disputes over comedians pilfering jokes.

Dave Chappelle, another Black Pack acolyte, first gained attention on *Def Comedy Jam* in the '90s, which led to a supporting role in Eddie Murphy's *The Nutty Professor* and the lead in the stoner film *Half Baked* (1998). As Danielle Fuentes Morgan notes, Chappelle "emerged as perhaps an unexpected microcosm of the potentials of satire and its inherent drawbacks."[19] His sketch series on Comedy Central, *Chappelle's Show*, struck a resounding chord in popular culture. The program's oppositional humor drew inspiration from its comedic ancestors *In Living Color* and *The Richard Pryor Show*. Chappelle's humor modifies the Black Pack's stylistic elements with hip-hop sensibilities geared toward the millennial generation. *Chappelle's Show* flourished on a sophomoric tightrope, showcasing biting and at times subversive tendencies. However, the ambivalent engagement of racial stereotypes was the backbone of Chappelle's production of humor, which predictably propelled the show into stratospheric popularity. After two seasons on the air, DVD sales of *Chappelle's Show* shattered all-time records. He was crowned the "comic genius of America."[20] Still, in 2005, ostensibly exasperated by the psychic costs of Hollywood's racial cauldron of conformity, Chappelle abruptly walked off the show. His exit coincided with him declining a $50 million contract extension that sent ominous shockwaves reverberating through the industry. A year later, Chappelle's appearance on the *Oprah Winfrey Show* shed light on the complexities surrounding his decision: "I felt like [the show] got me in touch with my inner coon, they stirred him up. When we were doing that [sketch that ignited his departure] and that guy laughed, I felt like they got me."[21] This encounter speaks to Chappelle's complex psychic and social struggle with Du Boisian double consciousness, the burden of representation, and the institutional divide that overdetermines the careers of Black film and television artists in the Hollywood game. His decision to leave television for a decade reflects those enormous tensions.

Chappelle's reemergence came in November 2016, hosting *Saturday Night Live*. His opening monologue addressed the forty-fifth U.S. president's election and the anxieties many people of color felt following his victory. Chappelle quipped, "America has done it. We've actually elected an internet troll as our president"—a comedic jab that seemed to capture the national mood. The episode also featured a cameo appearance by Chris Rock in a sketch where he and Chappelle portrayed the lone Black attendees at a predominately white election night party for Democrats. Their sardonic performances incisively mocked and exposed the disconnect of white liberals seemingly blindsided by Donald Trump's win. After the Republican victory, one white guest remarks bewilderedly, "Oh my God, I think America is racist," to which Chappelle wryly retorts, "I remember my great-grandfather told me something like that. But you know, he was like, a slave or something." Chappelle's turn as host attacks the weight of history and the permanence of American racism, garnering *SNL* its highest ratings in years. While Chappelle's return was initially lauded, his subsequent work proved more controversial. His $60 million deal with Netflix yielded several stand-up specials that, while critically acclaimed (including several Grammy wins), incorporated routines criticized for sexist and transphobic rhetoric. This material betrays his established comedic persona as a social critic of myopic thinking, ultimately leading to, presumably, the reason behind Chappelle's shocking onstage attack at the Hollywood Bowl in 2022.

Amid the controversy, Chappelle delivered arguably his crowning stand-up performance in *Dave Chappelle: 8:46*, a Netflix special recorded in 2020. Filmed outdoors at the height of the COVID-19 pandemic, the special addressed the national outrage following the public murder of George Floyd, an unarmed Black man, by a white police officer in Minneapolis. Chappelle delivers a robust emotional response, echoing what bell hooks describes as a Black "killing rage."[22] He introspectively addressed the social unrest and rising social energies gripping the nation. In *8:46*, as Rick DesRochers suggests, "Chappelle works to confront racism by exposing its arbitrary and capricious nature, born of willful ignorance and ingrained hatred from America's resistance to dealing with this legacy of slavery and its complex relationship with immigration and colonization."[23] Chappelle's performance is visceral, raw, and cathartic. He transforms from a funny man to a comedic philosopher and a truth-speaking folk hero, signifying his most significant contribution to the legacy of Black resistance humor.[24]

Comedians David Alan Grier, Larry Wilmore, and the South African–born Trevor Noah have each, in some capacity, attempted to fill the "Black void"

Chappelle's departure left at Comedy Central. Grier, a frequent Black Pack collaborator and *In Living Color* standout, released his political lampoon *Chocolate News* in 2008 at the height of Obama election coverage. The program utilized a blend of satirical news segments and comedic sketches to tackle race and politics. It aired as a lead-in to the established series *The Daily Show with Jon Stewart* (1995–2015) and *The Colbert Report* (2005–2014). But Grier's show struggled to carve out an audience and was canceled after one season. Similarly, *The Nightly Show with Larry Wilmore* (2015–2016) and *The Daily Show with Trevor Noah* (2015–2022) showcased the respective comedians' oppositional viewpoints to address political and social issues. Wilmore and Noah employed Black resistance humor as a tool, dissecting current events through a critical lens. Another attempt to fill the Black gap at Comedy Central was Keegan Michael Key's and Jordan Peele's sketch series *Key & Peele* (2012–2015). Their humor, often cheeky and irreverent, satirized various topics from pop culture to Shakespeare. The duo's defining moment arrived at the 2015 White House Correspondents' Dinner, when Key, performing as his character "Luther"—known for hilariously interpreting President Obama's repressed anger—performed a live "anger translation" sketch with the president himself. This intertextual moment showcases the program's ability to push boundaries and capture the contemporary political comedic zeitgeist.

Jerrod Carmichael's HBO special *Rothaniel* (2023) and his sitcom *The Carmichael Show* (2015–2017) fearlessly delve into family dynamics and the evolving landscape of politics, race, and sexuality. Justin Simien's racial satire *Dear White People* (2014), set on the campus of a fictional predominately white university, excoriates American institutional racism in higher education. Meanwhile, Kenya Barris, creator of the Emmy-nominated sitcom *blackish* (2014–2022), delivers, arguably, his best work in the irreverent semiautobiographical Netflix series *#BlackAF* (2020), which uses racial satire to lampoon Black celebrity culture and the burden of representation in Hollywood. Barris's, Simien's, and Carmichael's sardonic energies expand on the provocative spirit of Black resistance humor in thought-provoking ways. On the other hand, *Sorry to Bother You* (2018), the scorching satire from rapper-activist-turned-writer-director Raymond "Boots" Riley, scrapes at the festering wounds of late-stage capitalism and racial commodification in his sci-fi absurdist debut feature. Riley crafts a dystopian tale where the line between humanity and capitalism blurs, exposing the grotesque underbelly of corporate exploitation as workers are literally transformed into equine beings—brutal symbols of unrelenting American greed. The film's satire echoes Marx's rejection of the capitalist machine and embraces the transformative potential of class solidarity, underlining the troubling consequences of placing profits over people. Likewise, Aaron McGruder's audacious animated sitcom *The Boondocks* (2005–2014) masterfully employs the parody and satire characteristic of Black Pack comedies, deconstructing white America's legacy of racial and social violence. The show's third season premiere offers a caustic denunciation of the media frenzy and misguided optimism surrounding President Obama's historic 2008 election, exposing the superficiality of perceived progress, as if Obama's win somehow represented the attainment of Black freedom in America. Scott Sanders's film *Black Dynamite* (2009) also mines and borrows from the Black Pack's legacy, an homage to *I'm Gonna Git You Sucka*. Sanders's film skillfully spoofs 1970s Blaxploitation-era tropes while embracing an action-oriented theme, ultimately paving the way for an unruly animated spin-off of the same name that aired from 2012 to 2015 on the cable network Adult Swim.

The comedic alchemy of Jessica Williams and Phoebe Robinson is unveiled in *2 Dope Queens* (2018–2019), a series of hour-long HBO specials adapted from their sensational podcast. Robinson's and Williams's humor pulses with a distinctly Black millennial heartbeat, a back and-forth riff on social justice filtered through the unapologetic lens of Black womanhood. Their confrontational comedic approach extends the influence of Black resistance humor in new and exciting ways, encompassing a wide range of topics, including race, sex, gender, the politics of Black hair, intersectionality, and the structures of patriarchal power. In their opening routine, Williams and Robinson craft a witheringly hilarious list of white people who should apologize to Black women for a multitude of transgressions:

WILLIAMS: Here's one, the white guy at the bar who's like, "I love chocolate."
And all of his fucking friends that do that too. That guy needs to apologize.

ROBINSON: I wanna say, white girls who are always like, "I wish I could tell someone to kiss my Black ass. That's so cool."

WILLIAMS: I got one . . . a white guy that should apologize . . . Maybe Thomas Jefferson.

ROBINSON: No maybe. Definitely . . . and also the people who are like "His lover Sally Hemings." Sally Hemings was not a lover.[25]

The *2 Dope Queens* make space for Black women to be heard and defy what Katelyn Hale Wood describes as the "physical and emotional loss of control in a culture that too often restricts, commodifies, or demonizes Black joy and embodied expression."[26] Robinson and Williams's production of humor synthesizes and adapts the comedic approaches of earlier figures like Moms Mabley and Paul Mooney. Likewise, the Black Pack's comedic incongruities also inform Robin Thede's *A Black Lady Sketch Show* (2019–2023), a program created, written, directed by, and starring Black women. This series refutes the notion that humor grounded in the subject position of Black womanhood forfeits commercial appeal. Thede's success exhibits the growing need for inclusive comedic voices in Hollywood and the potential for such perspectives to achieve mainstream recognition.

The FX network's Afrosurrealist antisitcom *Atlanta* (2016–2022) blazed a singular trail for millennial audiences, garnering acclaim for its inventiveness and satirical edge. The Donald Glover–led series featured an entirely Black writer's room and employed only directors of color. The subversive traditions of Black resistance humor heavily inform *Atlanta*'s hyperfocus on crafting disruptive comedic expressions rooted in playfulness, absurdism, and truth-telling through racial satirization. Glover's series operates on multiple levels. It lambastes the Black middle class, the hip-hop nightclub scene, and the trite racial conventions of rap music culture. One episode, directed by Glover, exemplifies the show's complexity, spinning a metatextual world where the protagonist "Paper Boi" (Brian Tyree Henry) finds himself a guest on a fictional talk show within the series. What unfolds is a cleverly interwoven satire of *The Charlie Rose Show*, the fallacy of a postracial America, and the persuasive tactics employed by corporate-owned media companies seeking to exploit a monolithic "Black" demographic. Glover somehow manages to use the series as a vehicle to deride pressing social issues like systemic racism, police violence against Black bodies, coparenting issues, and the politics of gender and racial identity. *Atlanta*'s humor, often dark and surrealist, serves as a pressure valve, a release for the racial anxieties simmering just beneath the nation's surface.

Within the cultural geography of contemporary Black cinema, three recent films exemplify the lasting influence of Black resistance humor and its constant reconfigurations: *American Fiction* (2023), *The Book of Clarence* (2023), and *They Cloned Tyrone* (2023). Each film, in varying ways, deploys subversive humor as a scalpel, dissecting the hostile racial climate that permeates society and exposing the seemingly invisible power structures that exploit and endanger Black life. Cord Jefferson's *American Fiction*, an adaptation of Percival Everett's novel *Erasure*, centers "Monk," a disillusioned Black writer compellingly portrayed by Jeffrey Wright. In a desperate act of frustration and protest, Monk pens a deliberately offensive novel under a pseudonym, weaponizing literary neominstrelsy to unmask the deeply ingrained racist ideologies that undergird the mainstream publishing industry. Chaos ensues when the book's unexpected commercial success forces Monk to grapple with a moral quandary of conscience and consequence. On the other hand, nestled at the crossroads of sacred and profane, director Jeymes Samuel's *The Book of Clarence* reimagines biblical lore through a Black gaze. Set in the year 33 CE in Jerusalem, the film follows Clarence, a street peddler portrayed by Lakeith Stanfield, as he concocts a scheme to exploit religious fervor for personal gain. The movie implements the tools of Black resistance humor through its satire, racial reversal, and social inversion, taking pointed jabs at organized religion, the oppressive nature of government hypocrisy, and celebrity worship. The film's stylistic cinematography and cleverly organized visual effects enhance the picture's energy and aesthetic allure.

By far the most piercing and intrepid of these contemporary films is *They Cloned Tyrone*, a thematically radical and creative film harnessing Black resistance humor into a hypnotic concoction—a captivating fusion of Afrofuturism, science fiction, satire, Afrosurrealism, and Black horror. Directed by Juel Taylor, this genre-bending picture, reminiscent of *Get Out* (2017), lays bare the absurdity and social precarity of Black life, shining a critical light on the insidious practices of scientific racism executed on Black bodies by the white medical establishment. *They Cloned Tyrone* is a relentless exercise in cinematic subversion, directly confronting tired racial tropes; its three protagonists are a drug dealer, a prostitute, and a pimp—emblematic of society's undesirables in a cruel underworld. Through dazzling and nuanced performances by John Boyega, Teyonah Parris, and Jamie Foxx, these characters are reimagined, sabotaging expectations to reveal a heroic trio, compelling audiences to reevaluate seemingly reprocessed racial caricatures. The three protagonists of this twisted tale raise chilling questions about social engineering, mind control, and physical autonomy after stumbling upon an insidious and clandestine deep-state operation designed to exploit Black communities and clone Black bodies. They uncover a nefarious process of chemical warfare across several spheres of their community—the infiltration of Black churches, liquor stores, beauty salons, rap music, nightclubs, and even fast-food chains, all a calculated effort to exert control over Black citizens and their labor. This terrifying scenario delivers an Afrofuturist denouncement of the persistent and shape-shifting nature of American enslavement, presenting a visually striking and unsettling portrayal of a dystopian reality where Black people are ensnared in the horrors of scientific materialism, an earthly manifestation of Dante's *Inferno* inside the nine circles of hell. The movie is a haunting reminder of slavery's enduring legacy, tracing a lineage of treacherous experimentation on Black bodies from historical atrocities like the Tuskegee experiment to unethical modern horrors like the stolen cells of Henrietta Lacks. Now the corrosive tentacles of systemic racism have taken on new forms; no longer are Blacks merely up against the terrors of the carceral state, police violence, limited access to capital, housing discrimination, and antiquated school systems but—*they cloning you now*, making room for a new breed of Enslaved people, just in time for the AI apocalypse.

American Fiction, *The Book of Clarence*, and *They Cloned Tyrone*, to varying degrees of success, combine the social and political edge of Black resistance humor with a willingness to push boundaries and challenge (and offend) corrupt authority in pursuit of a larger truth concerning Black liberation. The appeal and power of these cinematic provocations rest in their ability to evoke laughter amid discomfort, prompting audiences to confront the often hidden and treacherous ways in which the nation's searing racial temperature and the burdens of representation play out in the Black world. One can see how these films are heirs to the Black Pack's rebellious legacy, applying humor not as a soothing balm but as a nuclear detonator, forcing us to confront the uncomfortable racial quandary that lies just beneath the surface in our society. It is from this nightmare history that Black Americans are actively compelled not simply to awaken but to, at all costs—as they say in the politically Black vernacular expression—"stay woke," which is to occupy a heightened state of consciousness and vigilant awareness. Sadly, this resistant Black cultural idiom, which rose from the street corners of Black American communities as a mantra warning against the thalidomide fallacies of a postracial America, has been hijacked by the white corporate-owned conservative news media and truncated to simply one word, *woke*, reducing the resistant pro-Black slogan to a decidedly non-Black, negative connotation misused to describe a self-righteous left-wing political agenda, marking yet another iteration of white cultural (mis)appropriation of Blackness and its expressive elements.[27]

As we pensively gaze ahead into the Afro-Future, in this twilight of late America, the potential of Black film and television artists pivots on the axis of ownership, authorship, and creative freedom. For all intents and purposes, the future for Black media artists will be as illuminating or deceptive, as bright or bleak, as the awareness and visions birthed by its creators. If there is, in fact, a way forward outside of the decaying structures of Hollywood and late American capitalism, the possibility of progress rests in the independent media-making practices of inventive, politically Black, collectively minded artists, humorists, cultural producers, filmmakers, writers, critics, and executives. These new Black voices must engage in an ontological and epistemological shift, a movement toward decolonization. And much like the refreshing aroma of petrichor after late summer rain, the resistant spirit of the Black Pack lives on, inviting us to inhale deeply and reflect on our cultural memory, letting it guide us like a beacon light of hope to a redesigned, liberated sense of Black power in the poetic and political imaginary of the Afro-Future—proving, once and for all, that entertainment *can* have social relevancy and comedy can say—very *serious* things.

Appendix

The Complete List of Black Pack Productions

Film

Hollywood Shuffle (1987)
Directed by Robert Townsend; written by Robert Townsend and Keenen Ivory Wayans
Collaborators: Robert Townsend, Keenen Ivory Wayans, and Paul Mooney

Eddie Murphy: Raw (1987)
Directed by Robert Townsend; written by Eddie Murphy and Keenen Ivory Wayans
Collaborator: Eddie Murphy

Coming to America (1988)
Story by Eddie Murphy
Collaborators: Eddie Murphy and Arsenio Hall

I'm Gonna Git You Sucka (1988)
Directed and written by Keenen Ivory Wayans
Collaborator: Keenen Ivory Wayans

Harlem Nights (1989)
Directed and written by Eddie Murphy
Collaborators: Eddie Murphy, Arsenio Hall, and Richard Pryor
The Five Heartbeats (1991)
Directed by Robert Townsend; written by Robert Townsend and Keenen Ivory Wayans
Collaborators: Robert Townsend and Keenen Ivory Wayans
Boomerang (1992)
Story by Eddie Murphy
Collaborator: Eddie Murphy
Meteor Man (1993)
Directed and written by Robert Townsend
Collaborator: Robert Townsend
A Low Down Dirty Shame (1994)
Directed and written by Keenen Ivory Wayans
Collaborator: Keenen Ivory Wayans
Blankman (1994)
Collaborator: Arsenio Hall

Television

Uptown Comedy Express (HBO, 1987)
Written by Eddie Murphy, Robert Townsend, and Arsenio Hall
Collaborators: Eddie Murphy, Robert Townsend, and Arsenio Hall
Robert Townsend and His Partners in Crime (HBO, 1988–1991)
Directed by Robert Townsend; written by Robert Townsend and Keenen Ivory Wayans
Collaborators: Robert Townsend, Keenen Ivory Wayans, and Paul Mooney
The Arsenio Hall Show (1989–1994)
Written by Arsenio Hall
Collaborators: Arsenio Hall, Eddie Murphy, Keenen Ivory Wayans, Paul Mooney, and Robert Townsend
In Living Color (Fox, 1990–1994)
Written, created, and produced by Keenen Ivory Wayans
Collaborators: Keenen Ivory Wayans and Paul Mooney

The Royal Family (1991–1992)
  Collaborator: Eddie Murphy (Creator and Executive Producer)
Time Out: The Truth about HIV, AIDS, and You (1992)
  Written by Arsenio Hall
  Collaborator: Arsenio Hall
Townsend Television (Fox, 1993)
  Directed and written by Robert Townsend
  Collaborator: Robert Townsend

Music

Straight Up (1988)
  Music video released by Paula Abdul
  Collaborator: Arsenio Hall
So Happy (1989)
  Music album released by Eddie Murphy
Large and In Charge (1989)
  Music album released by Arsenio Hall under the name "Chunky A"
Dangerous (1992)
  Music album released by Michael Jackson
  "Remember the Time" music video featuring Eddie Murphy
Love's Alright (1993)
  Music album released by Eddie Murphy

Comedy Albums

Race (1993)
  Collaborator: Paul Mooney
Master Piece (1994)
  Collaborator: Paul Mooney

Acknowledgments

"Now unto Him that is able to do exceedingly abundantly above all that we ask or think, according to the power that worketh in us" (Ephesians 3:20). The development of this literary work has benefited from many enlightened conversations with colleagues and friends over many years. I'd like to acknowledge Nicole Solano and the entire editorial team at Rutgers University Press for believing in my vision and working to bring this project to the world in the manner that I imagined. This book is more than words on a page; it is a testament not just to my journey but to the embodiment of the lives, sacrifices, and legacies of so many who came before me. I stand on the shoulders of giants—Black artists, thinkers, scholars, family, and ancestors who blazed a trail for a young brother from Chicago to always reach higher, contribute, and serve. I am a product of many lives intertwined with mine, all unique threads in a vast tapestry. Each of us represents the miraculous result of a cosmic lottery—our very existence shaped by unfathomable odds. We're all the same, yet all so very different. I often contemplate the intricate web of events that had to unfold exactly as they did in order for us to exist—every person that had to meet, every birth, every loss, every challenge, every triumph, every lesson, every love that blossomed—all vital pieces of a masterful puzzle that led me here today.

Reflecting on this truth, I begin by thanking God for the many gifts, skills, talents, and abilities bestowed upon me. Thank you, Lord, for blessing my life, for being a lamp unto my feet and for guiding my path. To my ancestors (known and unknown), the countless souls who came before me and, despite the harshest conditions, survived and advanced, setting me on the road to success. To my paternal great-grandfather and great-grandmother, Ambus and Lucy Lee from Carthage, Arkansas, and my maternal great-grandfather and great-grandmother, John and Johnnie Mae from Tunica, Mississippi—who were all denied an opportunity for a formal education yet forged ahead, persevering through the brutal realities of the American South. To my paternal grandparents, Hermon and Erma, whose wisdom shaped my worldview. To my maternal grandfather, Herbert (who died before I was born), and my grandmother, Eula Mae, who left school after the fourth grade to work in the cotton fields of Mississippi before moving to the West Side of Chicago during the Great Migration—her home stored our family's extensive Black film and television videotape archive that molded my youthful imagination. To my mother, Gerome, you are the reason I succeed, the first in our family to graduate from college; you are my rock. Thank you for believing in me, for encouraging me to shine my light, and for buying those encyclopedias; they opened my mind to endless possibilities (and changed my life forever). To my father, Mickey, your electric bass solos in Granddaddy's church and blues riffs on your acoustic guitar in our living room provided a soundtrack to my childhood and are woven into the fabric of my consciousness.

To my intellectual ancestors: Dr. Martin Luther King Jr., Malcolm X, James Baldwin, Gwendolyn Brooks, Dr. W. E. B. Du Bois, Toni Morrison, Maya Angelou, Paul Robeson, and Fred Hampton—who have all inspired my spirit and fueled my journey. This book is my humble effort to contribute to the foundational legacy of cultural service and Black excellence that you have laid. I hope to one day inspire emerging generations as you have inspired me—from the hood to the Black church (and all points in between), from Black power to the ivory tower (and all points in between).

I desire to express appreciation to my high school teachers Bill Kirksey and Tim Sweeney, who nurtured my early potential; my mentors, Benjamin Starks, Belinda Starks, and Carl Boyd; my friend and first casting director, Sharon King; and my community college professors Melanie McQuitty and Sara Mortimer Boyd—thank you all for your guidance and encouragement; it made a world of difference. My heartfelt gratitude extends to the faculty and staff present during my time at the University of California, Los Angeles, School of Theater, Film, and Television, especially Teshome Gabriel, Cheri Smith, Billy Woodberry, Belinda Starkie, Bill McDonald, Allyson Field, Nick Browne, Fabian Wagmister, Vince Brook, and most notably, Denise Mann and John T. Caldwell. Your teachings profoundly impacted my development. Thank you for your early support and for seeing the value in my ideas and research in its infancy.

To the venerable faculty and staff present during my time in the Martin Scorsese Department of Cinema Studies at New York University, Tisch School of the Arts, including Mary Schmidt-Campbell, Anna McCarthy, Zhen Zhang, and Ella Shohat, thank you for nurturing my growth. I have such a deep sense of gratitude and appreciation for Ed Guerrero for stepping in and stepping up—your unwavering support, mentorship, advice, conversations, laughs, and critical insights have served as a powerful beacon. Thank you for your unshakable confidence in my abilities; your contribution far exceeded the call of duty, empowering me to seek a broad horizon. To Robert Stam, thank you for sharing your tremendous knowledge and introducing me to new ideas. Your early critiques of each chapter pointed me in the right direction and were instrumental to the development of this study and to shaping my thoughts. To Richard Allen, thank you for championing my work—your belief helped instill confidence in my abilities.

To my intellectual mentor, Herman Gray, thank you for being a role model of the highest order; your faith in me didn't just nurture my ideas—it helped me believe in them. To Bambi Haggins, thank you for going to bat for me—your writing showed me what was possible in the field and inspired my intellectual progress. Thank you to the faculty and staff present in the Film Studies Department during my time at University of North Carolina, Wilmington, especially Mariana Johnson (and John Jeremiah Sullivan), Aaron Cavazos, and Georg Koszulinski.

I certainly have much gratitude for all my esteemed colleagues at the San Francisco State University School of Cinema, particularly Aaron Michael Kerner, Daniel Bernardi, Johnny Symons, Mayuran Tiruchelvam, Laura Green, and Greta Snider—your leadership, encouragement, and support have meant so much to me. I would also like to acknowledge the many scholars, artists, and thinkers who have mentored and inspired me along the way, including Haki R. Madhubuti, Orron Kenyatta, Theaster Gates, Mukhtar K. Ali, Anna Everett, Beretta E. Smith-Shomade, Terri Francis, Zeinabu irene Davis, Celine Parreñas Shimizu, Nicole Fleetwood, Jacqueline Najuma Stewart, Christine Acham, Christopher H. Smith, Samantha N. Sheppard, Racquel J. Gates, La'Tonya Reese Miles, Jennifer DeVere Brody, Robin D. G. Kelley, Elaine Brown, Ericka Huggins, Kathleen Cleaver, Haile Gerima, Charles Burnett, Darnell Hunt, Stephen Duncombe, Jawanza Kunjufu, bell hooks, Cornel West, and Angela Y. Davis—your collective brilliance has sharpened my thinking and expanded my vision of the possible. And, of course, to the inspiring and dynamic artists that compose the Black Pack (my objects of study in this book): Paul Mooney, Eddie Murphy, Keenen Ivory Wayans, Robert Townsend, and Arsenio Hall. This work would not exist without your dazzling and courageous creative labor. Thank you for your contributions. I hope this book makes you proud. This work is also dedicated to the loving memory of my best friend, the brilliant Nelsan Ellis. I learned so much from you; thank you for always believing in me and supporting me. I miss you every day.

And a special thank you to *mon homme principal* King Artel Great, *papa l'a fait*. To everyone mentioned here—I am indeed grateful.

And, finally, to myself—a young brother from the West Side and South Side of Chicago—for the vision, strength, courage, discipline, wisdom, and focus to chart my own path. The sea refuses no river, and thus, I flow with, and feel comforted by, the ever-evolving currents of *wu wei*.

Notes

Introduction

1 Tim Brooks, *Lost Sounds: Blacks and the Birth of the Record Industry, 1890–1919* (Urbana: University of Illinois Press, 2004), 172–175.
2 Gayle Buckhalter, "Eddie Murphy and the Black Pack," *Los Angeles Times*, February 28, 1988.
3 Gerri Hirshey, "The Black Pack," *Vanity Fair*, July 1988, 60.
4 Hirshey, 118.
5 Additional members of the Rat Pack included Peter Lawford and Joey Bishop; Brat Pack members also included Emilio Estevez, Judd Nelson, Demi Moore, Andrew McCarthy, and Anthony Michael Hall.
6 "Bubble Hill" is the nickname of Eddie Murphy's luxurious East Coast mansion. The word *bubble* was slang for "party."
7 Hirshey, "Black Pack," 60.
8 Hortense J. Spillers, "Mama's Baby, Papa's Maybe: An American Grammar Book," in *Black, White, and in Color: Essays on American Literature and Culture* (Chicago: University of Chicago Press, 2003), 207.
9 *Saturday Night Live*, season 10, episode 9 "White like Me," directed by Andy Breckman, aired December 15, 1984, on NBC.
10 For a detailed discussion of these issues, see Ta-Nehisi Coates, "Case for Reparations," *The Atlantic*, June 15, 2014.
11 The political and artistic framework of Black resistance humor detailed in this book is utilized to designate humor developed and performed by people of African descent born in America, and it should not be confused with the literary tradition of black comedy or dark comedy.
12 Ella Shoat and Robert Stam, *Race in Translation: Culture Wars around the Postcolonial Atlantic* (New York: New York University Press, 2012), 14.
13 Christina Sharpe, *In the Wake: On Blackness and Being* (Durham, N.C.: Duke University Press, 2016), 15.

14 Mel Watkins, *On the Real Side: A History of African American Comedy*, 2nd ed. (Chicago: Chicago Review Press, 1999), 52.
15 Darryl J. Littleton, *Black Comedians on Black Comedy: How African-Americans Taught Us to Laugh* (New York: Applause Theatre & Cinema Books, 2008), 7.
16 Daniel Fuentes Morgan, *Laughing to Keep from Dying: African American Satire in the Twenty-First Century* (Urbana: University of Illinois Press, 2020), 12.
17 Watkins, *On the Real Side*, 66.
18 Berndt Ostendorf, *Black Literature in White America* (Totowa: Barnes and Noble Books, 1982), 37.
19 Glenda Carpio, *Laughing Fit to Kill: Black Humor in the Fictions of Slavery* (New York: Oxford University Press, 2008), 16.
20 Carpio, *Laughing*, 16.
21 Peter Randolph, *From Slave Cabin to Pulpit: The Autobiography of Rev. Peter Randolph* (Boston: James H. Earle, 1893), 204.
22 Yuval Taylor and Jake Austen, *Darkest America: Black Minstrelsy from Slavery to Hip-Hop* (New York: W. W. Norton, 2012), 3.
23 For a full discussion of "hidden transcripts," see James C. Scott, *Domination and the Arts of Resistance: Hidden Transcripts* (New Haven: Yale University Press, 1990).
24 Jesse A. Shipp and Alex Rogers, *Abyssinia* (stage play), scene 2, 1905.
25 Geneva Smitherman, *Talkin and Testifyin: The Language of Black America* (Boston: Houghton Mifflin, 1977), 252.
26 David Krasner, *Resistance, Parody, and Double Consciousness in African American Theatre, 1895–1910* (New York: St. Martin's Press, 1997), 106.
27 Krasner, 10.
28 Ed Guerrero, "Bamboozled: In the Mirror of Abjection," in *Contemporary Black American Cinema: Race, Gender and Sexuality at the Movies*, ed. Mia Mask (New York: Routledge, 2012), 123.
29 Langston Hughes, "Week by Week: Heads, Hair and Dreams," *Chicago Defender*, January 21, 1961 (national edition), 10.
30 Terrence T. Tucker, *Furiously Funny: Comic Rage from Ralph Ellison to Chris Rock* (Gainesville: University Press of Florida, 2020), 20.
31 Watkins, *On the Real Side*, 392.
32 Racquel Gates, "Subverting Hollywood from the Inside Out: Melvin Van Peebles's *Watermelon Man*," *Film Quarterly* 68, no. 1 (Fall 2014): 9–21.
33 Redd Foxx and Norma Miller, *The Redd Foxx Encyclopedia of Black Humor* (Los Angeles: Ward Ritchie Press, 1977), 95.
34 Dick Gregory, stand-up comedy performance, recorded live at the Hungry I Club in San Francisco, California, segment aired on the program *Walk in My Shoes* on September 19, 1961, on ABC.
35 Norman Mailer, "The White Negro," *Dissent Magazine*, Fall 1957.
36 bell hooks, *Reel to Real: Race, Class, and Sex at the Movies* (New York: Routledge, 1996), 84.
37 bell hooks, *We Real Cool: Black Men and Masculinity* (New York: Routledge, 2003), xiii.
38 Brandon J. Manning, *Played Out: The Race Man in 21st Century Satire* (New Brunswick: Rutgers University Press, 2022), 3.
39 There have been several high-profile police killings of unarmed Black citizens that have recently plagued this country including cases like George Floyd, Rayshard Brooks, Freddie Gray, Oscar Grant, Eric Garner, Tamir Rice, Laquan McDonald,

Walter Scott, Alton Sterling, Philando Castile, Breonna Taylor, Sandra Bland, and Atatiana Jefferson.

40 For a full discussion of "the Black gaze," see Tina M. Campt, *A Black Gaze: Artists Changing How We See* (Cambridge, Mass.: MIT Press, 2021).

41 Hirshey, "Black Pack," 61.

42 K. A. Neuendorf, Paul D. Skalski, Leo Jeffres, and David Atkin, "Senses of Humor, Media Use, and Opinions about the Treatment of Marginalized Groups," *International Journal of Intercultural Relations* 42 (September 2014): 3–5.

43 Mikhail Bakhtin, *Rabelais and His World* (Bloomington: Indiana University Press, 1984).

44 Robert Stam with Richard Porton and Leo Goldsmith, *Keywords in Subversive Film/Media Aesthetics* (Oxford: Wiley Blackwell, 2015), 69–70.

45 Henry Louis Gates Jr., *The Signifying Monkey: A Theory of African-American Literary Criticism* (New York: Oxford University Press, 1988).

46 William J. Harris, ed., *The LeRoi Jones/Amiri Baraka Reader* (New York: Basic Books, 2000).

47 Houston A. Baker Jr., *Modernism and the Harlem Renaissance* (Chicago: University of Chicago Press, 1987).

48 Stuart Hall, "What Is This 'Black' in Black Popular Culture?," in *Black in Popular Culture*, ed. Gina Dent (New York: New Press, 1992), 28.

49 Timothy Havens, *Black Television Travels: African American Media around the Globe* (New York: New York University Press, 2013), 81.

50 Ellis Cashmore, *Celebrity Culture*, 1st ed. (New York: Routledge, 2006), 131.

51 Cashmore, 131.

52 Richard Dyer, *Heavenly Bodies: Film Stars and Society*, 2nd ed. (New York: Routledge, 2004), 64.

53 Wesley Morris, "The Videos That Rocked America. The Song That Knows Our Rage," *New York Times*, June 3, 2020.

Chapter 1 Planet Provocative

1 James Baldwin, *The Last Interview and Other Conversations* (New York: Melville House, 2014), 7.

2 Paul Mooney, *Black Is the New White* (New York: Gallery Books, 2010), 114.

3 Mooney, 114.

4 Mooney, 101–103.

5 Daniel Fuentes Morgan, *Laughing to Keep from Dying: African American Satire in the Twenty-First Century* (Urbana: University of Illinois Press, 2020), 9.

6 Mooney, *Black*, 15.

7 For more insights into the history of the "Family Viewing Hour," see Willard D. Rowland, *The Politics of TV Violence: Policy Uses of Communication Research* (Beverly Hills: Sage, 1983).

8 In the twenty-first century, Cosby has become a disgraced and controversial public figure following his conviction for sexual assault. He served several years in prison before his conviction was overturned, and he was subsequently released.

9 Excerpt from Dick Gregory's first television appearance, recorded live at the Hungry I Club in San Francisco, California, segment aired on *Walk in My Shoes* on September 19, 1961, on ABC.

10 Richard Pryor, *Pryor Convictions, and Other Life Sentences* (New York: Pantheon Books, 1995), 72.

11 Bambi Haggins, *Laughing Mad: The Black Comic Persona in Post-soul America* (New Brunswick: Rutgers University Press, 2007), 50.
12 Joy Hamann, "Las Vegas," *Hollywood Reporter*, October 11, 1967.
13 Dennis Hunt, "Black Comedy and the Pryor Commitment," *Los Angeles Times*, April 11, 1974, 92.
14 David Felton, "This Can't Be Happening to Me," *Rolling Stone*, October 10, 1974, 41.
15 Pryor, *Pryor Convictions*, 93.
16 Terrence T. Tucker, *Furiously Funny: Comic Rage from Ralph Ellison to Chris Rock* (Gainesville: University Press of Florida, 2018), 2.
17 Glenda R. Carpio, *Laughing Fit to Kill: Black Humor in the Fictions of Slavery* (New York: Oxford University Press, 2008), 7.
18 Mooney, *Black*, 115.
19 Mooney, 16.
20 Mooney, 18.
21 Richard Dyer, *White* (New York: Routledge, 1997), 1–2.
22 Mooney, *Black*, 21–23.
23 James C. Scott, *Domination and the Arts of Resistance: Hidden Transcripts* (New Haven: Yale University Press, 1990), 20.
24 Lisa Kennedy, "The Black Familiar," *Village Voice*, October 16, 1990.
25 Fuentes Morgan, *Laughing*, 1.
26 James Baldwin, "The Negro in American Culture; No. 3; the Negro Writer in America; Part 2," American Archive of Public Broadcasting, 1961, accessed April 20, 2022, https://americanarchive.org/catalog/cpb-aacip-526-rr1pg1jw0s.
27 Mooney, *Black*, 106.
28 Mooney, 30.
29 Mooney, 101–102.
30 Robin D. G. Kelley, "Into the Fire: 1970 to the Present," in *To Make Our World Anew: The History of African Americans from 1880*, ed. Robin D. G. Kelley and Earl Lewis (New York: Oxford University Press, 2008), 575.
31 Tucker, *Furiously Funny*, 2.
32 Fuentes Morgan, *Laughing*, 5.
33 Fuentes Morgan, 5.
34 Mooney, *Black*, 141.
35 Mooney, 130.
36 Scott Saul, *Becoming Richard Pryor* (New York: HarperCollins, 2014), 181–182, 483.
37 Mooney, *Black*, 127–133.
38 For a full discussion of *Sanford and Son*, see Adrien Sebro's *Scratchin' and Survivin': Hustle Economics and the Black Sitcoms of Tandem Productions* (New Brunswick: Rutgers University Press, 2023).
39 Robert Stam, "From Hybridity to the Aesthetics of Garbage," *Social Identities: Journal for the Study of Race, Nation, and Culture* 3, no. 2 (1997), 277.
40 Mooney, *Black*, 144.
41 Mooney, 145.
42 James H. Cone, *Malcolm and Martin and America: A Dream or a Nightmare* (New York: Orbis, 1991), 309.
43 Mooney, *Black*, 145.
44 Mooney, 145.
45 *Wattstax*, directed by Mel Stuart (1973; Los Angeles, CA: Columbia Pictures, theatrical, February 4, 1973).

46 Mooney, *Black*, 9.
47 Scott Ethier, "In Ellington's Shadow: The Life of Billy Strayhorn," *Humanities* 27, no. 6 (November/December 2006), 15–19.
48 For an augmented version of this argument, see Meghan Sutherland, *The Flip Wilson Show* (Detroit: Wayne State University Press, 2008).
49 Donald Bogle, *Prime Time Blues: African Americans on Network Television* (New York: Farrar, Straus & Giroux, 2001), 181.
50 Sutherland, *Flip Wilson Show*, xvii.
51 "Television: Struggling to Leave the Cellar," *Time*, May 14, 1979.
52 William Boddy, *Fifties Television: The Industry and Its Critics* (Urbana: University of Illinois Press, 1990), 103–104.
53 "Television."
54 "Television."
55 Mooney, *Black*, 159–161.
56 Mooney, 163.
57 Christine Acham, *Revolution Televised: Prime Time and the Struggle for Black Power* (Minneapolis: University of Minnesota Press, 2005), 152.
58 "Show Business: A New Black Superstar," *Time*, August 22, 1977, 66–67.
59 Richard Pryor, Oscars Ceremony, ABC, March 28, 1977.
60 David S. Silverman, *You Can't Air That: Four Cases of Controversy and Censorship in American Television Programming* (Syracuse: Syracuse University Press, 2007), 93.
61 Louie Robinson, "Richard Pryor Talks . . . about Love, Life, Humor, Marriage—and What Happened to His Television Show," *Ebony*, January 1978, 116.
62 John J. O'Connor, "TV: Pryor's Art Is Strong Stuff—Soap Weak," *New York Times*, September 13, 1977, 62.
63 Silverman, *You Can't Air That*, 93.
64 *The Richard Pryor Show*, season 1, episode 1, "40th President," written by David Banks, Jeffrey Barron, Booker Bradshaw, Paul Mooney, and Richard Pryor, aired September 13, 1977, on NBC.
65 Haggins, *Laughing Mad*, 215.
66 Elizabeth Alexander, *The Black Interior* (Minneapolis: Graywolf Press, 2004), x.
67 *The Richard Pryor Show*, season 1, episode 2, "Egypt 1909," written by David Banks, Jeffrey Barron, Booker Bradshaw, Paul Mooney, and Richard Pryor, aired September 20, 1977, on NBC.
68 Mel Watkins, *On the Real Side: A History of African American Comedy* (Chicago: Lawrence Hill, 1999), 81.
69 Robinson, "Richard Pryor Talks," 117.
70 "Richard Pryor: Live in Concert (1979)," IMDb, accessed February 28, 2023, https://www.imdb.com/title/tt0079807/.
71 Mooney, *Black*, 214.
72 Mooney, 214.
73 Mooney, 215.
74 Mooney, 1.
75 Mooney, 2.
76 Darryl J. Littleton, *Black Comedians on Black Comedy: How African-Americans Taught Us to Laugh* (New York: Applause Theatre & Cinema Books, 2008), 315.
77 "Paul Mooney Performance Bio," Caroline's on Broadway, accessed October 28, 2013, http://www.carolines.com/paul-mooney-bio/.

78 *In Living Color*, season 1, episode 9, "Introducing . . . Homey D. Clown," written by Keenen Ivory Wayans, Franklyn Ajaye, Kim Bass, and Paul Mooney, aired June 17, 1990, on Fox.
79 Mooney, *Black*, 217.
80 Mooney, 223.
81 Mooney, 105–106.
82 Fuentes Morgan, *Laughing*, 2.
83 Ed Guerrero, "Bamboozled: In the Mirror of Abjection," in *Contemporary Black American Cinema: Race, Gender and Sexuality at the Movies*, ed. Mia Mask (New York: Routledge, 2012), 120.
84 Mooney, *Black*, 236.
85 Mooney, 237–238.
86 Fuentes Morgan, *Laughing*, 2.
87 Mooney, 256–257.
88 Paul Laurence Dunbar, *The Collected Poetry of Paul Laurence Dunbar*, ed. Joanne M. Braxton (Charlottesville: University of Virginia Press, 1993), 81.
89 Mooney, *Black*, 92.

Chapter 2 Black Star Power

1 Ralph Ellison, *The Collected Essays of Ralph Ellison*, ed. John F. Callahan (New York: Modern Library, 1995), 104–130.
2 Ed Guerrero, *Framing Blackness: The African American Image in Film* (Philadelphia: Temple University Press, 1993), 128.
3 "Eddie Murphy," The Numbers, accessed February 28, 2015, https://www.the-numbers.com/person/700401-Eddie-Murphy.
4 Tina M. Campt, *A Black Gaze: Artists Changing How We See* (Cambridge, Mass.: MIT Press, 2021), 8.
5 Rat Pack members also included Peter Lawford and Joey Bishop.
6 Brat Pack members also included Judd Nelson, Demi Moore, Andrew McCarthy, and Anthony Michael Hall.
7 See David Krasner, *Resistance, Parody, and Double Consciousness in African American Theatre, 1895–1910* (New York: St. Martin's Press, 1997).
8 For a more expansive discussion on the notion of "film Blackness," see Michael Boyce Gillespie's *Film Blackness: American Cinema and the Idea of Black Film* (Durham, N.C.: Duke University Press, 2016).
9 Daniel Fuentes Morgan, *Laughing to Keep from Dying: African American Satire in the Twenty-First Century* (Urbana: University of Illinois Press, 2020), 4.
10 Fuentes Morgan, *Laughing*, 21.
11 For an in-depth analysis, see Jacques Rancière, *The Politics of Aesthetics* (London: Bloomsbury, 2013).
12 Tom Shales and James Andrew Miller, *Live from New York: An Uncensored History of "Saturday Night Live," as Told by Its Stars, Writers and Guests* (repr., New York: Back Bay Books, 2003).
13 Stephen Steinberg, "The Liberal Retreat from Race during the Post-Civil Rights Era," in *The House That Race Built: Black Americans, U.S. Terrain*, ed. Wahneema Lubiano (New York: Vintage Books, 1997), 22.
14 Robert Dallek, *Ronald Reagan: The Politics of Symbolism* (Cambridge, Mass.: Harvard University Press, 1999), 33.

15 Glenda R. Carpio, *Laughing Fit to Kill: Black Humor in the Fictions of Slavery* (New York: Oxford University Press, 2008), 4.
16 Robin D. G. Kelley, "Into the Fire: 1970 to the Present," in *To Make Our World Anew: The History of African Americans from 1880*, ed. Robin D. G. Kelley and Earl Lewis (New York: Oxford University Press, 2008), 575.
17 Christina Sharpe, *In the Wake: On Blackness and Being* (Durham, N.C.: Duke University Press, 2016), 15.
18 Carpio, *Laughing*, 4.
19 Richard Campbell and Jimmie Reeves, *Cracked Coverage: Television News, Reaganism and the Journalistic Crusade against Cocaine Use* (Durham, N.C.: Duke University Press, 1994).
20 For a detailed analysis, see Michelle Alexander's *The New Jim Crow: Mass Incarceration in the Age of Colorblindness* (New York: New Press, 2010).
21 Saidiya Hartman, *Lose Your Mother: A Journey along the Atlantic Slave Route* (New York: Farrar, Straus & Giroux, 2007), 39–40.
22 Quoted in Frank Sanello, *Eddie Murphy: The Life and Times of a Comic on the Edge* (New York: Birch Lane Press, 1997), 193.
23 Spike Lee, "Eddie!," *Spin Magazine*, October 1990, 36.
24 Edward W. Said, *Culture and Imperialism* (New York: Alfred A. Knopf, 1994), 210.
25 "Eddie Murphy: Raw (1987)," Box Office Mojo, accessed February 28, 2024, https://www.boxofficemojo.com/title/tt0092948.
26 Bambi Haggins, *Laughing Mad: The Black Comic Persona in Post-soul America* (New Brunswick: Rutgers University Press, 2007), 72.
27 "Eddie Murphy Mellows Out: Eddie Murphy Reigns as 'Black Pack' Leader," *Orlando Sentinel*, July 1, 1988.
28 "Eddie Murphy."
29 Sanello, *Eddie Murphy*, 148.
30 Racquel J. Gates, *Double Negative: The Black Image and Popular Culture* (Durham, N.C.: Duke University Press, 2018), 70–71.
31 Ada Gay Griffin, "Seizing the Moving Image," in *Black Popular Culture*, ed. M. Wallace and G. Dent (Seattle: Bay Press, 1992), 231.
32 Fredric Jameson, "Reification and Utopia in Mass Culture," *Social Text*, no. 1 (Winter 1979): 130–148.
33 Kathy Huffhines, "The Black Pack Leader Eddie Murphy Has Given His Group a Name," *Associated Press*, July 15, 1988.
34 James C. Scott, *Weapons of the Weak: Everyday Forms of Peasant Resistance* (New Haven: Yale University Press, 1985).
35 Houston A. Baker Jr., *Modernism and the Harlem Renaissance* (Chicago: University of Chicago Press, 1987).
36 Gates, *Double Negative*, 37.
37 Mark Dery, "Black to the Future," in *Flame Wars: The Discourse of Cyberculture* (Durham, N.C.: Duke University Press, 1994).
38 "Coming to America (1988)," Box Office Mojo, accessed February 28, 2015, https://www.boxofficemojo.com/title/tt0094898/?ref_=bo_se_r_1.
39 Fuentes Morgan, *Laughing*, 3.
40 Walter Leavy, "Eddie Murphy, Richard Pryor, Redd Foxx: Three Generations of Black Comedy," *Ebony*, January 1990, 103.
41 Sanello, *Eddie Murphy*, 173.

42 For a more detailed analysis, see Houston Baker, *Blues, Ideology, and Afro-American Literature: A Vernacular Theory* (Chicago: University of Chicago Press, 1984).
43 Michael Wilmington, "Movie Review: Eddie Murphy's 'Harlem Nights': Slick, Slack," *Los Angeles Times*, November 17, 1989.
44 Gene Siskel, "Film Review: Harlem Nights," *Chicago Tribune*, November 17, 1989.
45 Kwame Ture and Charles V. Hamilton, *Black Power: The Politics of Liberation* (New York: Vintage Books, 1992), 3.
46 Eddie Murphy, Oscar Ceremony, ABC, April 11, 1988.
47 "Harlem Nights (1989)," The Numbers, accessed February 28, 2015, https://www.the-numbers.com/movie/Harlem-Nights#tab=summary.
48 Fuentes Morgan, *Laughing*, 9.
49 "Another 48 Hrs. (1991)," The Numbers, accessed February 28, 2015, https://www.the-numbers.com/movie/Another-48-Hrs#tab=summary.
50 J. Hammer and A. Murr, "The Fall of Frank Mancuso," *Newsweek Magazine*, May 5, 1991, 66.
51 Sanello, *Eddie Murphy*, 190.
52 Fuentes Morgan, *Laughing*, 3.
53 B. L. Fredrickson and T. Roberts, "Objectification Theory," *Psychology of Women Quarterly* 21 (1997): 173–206.
54 I'd like to give a special shout-out here to my students at Spelman College, whose lively classroom discussions about *Boomerang* helped contribute to the expansion of my insights on the conflicts among Marcus, Jacqueline, and Angela.
55 bell hooks, *Killing Rage: Ending Racism* (New York: Henry Holt, 1995), 96.
56 Although Grier and Lawrence and Damon Wayans are not official Black Pack members, they each offer value to comedic social discourse as adjacent contributors in multiple Black Pack productions.
57 Kenneth Turan, "Film Review: 'Boomerang': Eddie Murphy's Romantic Fling," *Los Angeles Times*, July 1, 1992.
58 Turan.
59 Harry Allen, "Telling Time: On Spike Lee and the 'Reality' of *Clockers*," *Village Voice*, October 3, 1995, 84.
60 "Boomerang (1992)," Box Office Mojo, accessed February 28, 2015, https://www.boxofficemojo.com/title/tt0103859/?ref_=bo_se_r_1.
61 Gates, *Double Negative*, 40.
62 Gates, 38.
63 I define *cultural prestidigitation* as the method by which a marginalized artist, cultural worker, or image-maker utilizes the mechanisms of the dominant system to make that system work to their advantage in advancing a counterhegemonic sensibility, largely without notice.
64 Fuentes Morgan, *Laughing*, 7.

Chapter 3 The Mothership

1 This quote from Billy Wilder is widely referenced and has become a part of the American cultural lexicon, predominantly attributed to Wilder rather than being traced to a specific interview, book, or article.
2 Rebecca Krefting, *All Joking Aside: American Humor and Its Discontents* (Baltimore: Johns Hopkins University Press, 2014), 18.

3 See Nelson George, *Post-soul Nation: The Explosive, Contradictory, Triumphant, and Tragic 1980s as Experienced by African Americans (Previously Known as Blacks and before That Negroes)* (New York: Viking Press, 2004).

4 James Snead, *White Screens, Black Images: Hollywood from the Dark Side*, ed. Colin MacCabe and Cornel West (New York: Routledge, 1994), 107.

5 In his critique of capitalism, Herbert Marcuse combined the analyses of Marx and Freud, theorizing two concepts of repression: basic and surplus. For Marcuse, "basic repression" refers to a modification of instincts that is necessary for the perpetuation of human survival, while "surplus repression" refers to the restrictions necessitated by social domination. See Herbert Marcuse, *Eros and Civilization: A Philosophical Inquiry into Freud* (Boston: Beacon Press, 1966), 35.

6 For nearly two decades, *The Jeffersons* would hold the distinction of being the longest-running sitcom in TV history. However, in the postnetwork era, it would relinquish this record to TBS's syndication breakthrough, the etiolated *Tyler Perry's House of Payne*, which aired a mind-numbing 264 episodes in only eight seasons, surpassing *The Jeffersons*' 253 episodes in eleven seasons.

7 George, *Post-soul Nation*, ix.

8 Esther Fein, "Robert Townsend Has Fun at Hollywood's Expense," *New York Times*, April 19, 1987, H-18.

9 Fein, H-18.

10 See Donald Bogle, *Toms, Coons, Mulattoes, Mammies, and Bucks: An Interpretive History of Blacks in American Films* (New York: Viking Press, 2016).

11 For a detailed analysis of "black pain," see Deborah Walker King, *African Americans and the Culture of Pain* (Charlottesville: University of Virginia Press, 2008).

12 Krefting, *All Joking Aside*, 17.

13 Fein, "Robert Townsend," H-18.

14 "She's Gotta Have It (1986)," Box Office Mojo, accessed March 4, 2023, https://www.boxofficemojo.com/title/tt0091939/?ref_=bo_se_r_1.

15 Erich Leon Harris, *African American Screenwriters Now* (Los Angeles: Silman-James Press, 1996), 138.

16 Richard Harrington, "Having Fun with Hollywood," *Washington Post*, March 24, 1987, C1.

17 Harrington, C1.

18 Kathy O'Malley, "Nothing's Black and White for Comic Turned Director," *Chicago Tribune*, June 10, 1987, D3.

19 Brandon J. Manning, *Played Out: The Race Man in 21st Century Satire* (New Brunswick: Rutgers University Press, 2022), 6.

20 Manning, 6.

21 Robert Sklar, *Movie Made America: A Cultural History of American Movies* (New York: Vintage Books, 1994), 148–153.

22 Fein, "Robert Townsend," H-18.

23 "Hollywood Shuffle (1987)," Box Office Mojo, accessed March 4, 2023, https://www.boxofficemojo.com/title/tt0093200/?ref_=bo_se_r_1.

24 Darryl Dickson-Carr, *African American Satire: The Sacredly Profane Novel* (Columbia: University of Missouri Press, 2001), 3.

25 Frederick Wasser, *Veni, Vidi, Video: The Hollywood Empire and the VCR* (Austin: University of Texas Press), 76.

26 Wasser, 80.

27 Staffan Burenstam Linder, *The Harried Leisure Class* (New York: Columbia University Press, 1970).
28 Paul B. Lindstrom, "Home Video: The Consumer Report," in *The VCR Age: Home Video and Mass Consumption*, ed. Mark R. Levy (Newbury Park: Sage, 1989), 46–47.
29 Wasser, *Veni, Vidi, Video*, 155.
30 HBO launched in 1972; however, in 1975 the network paid a hefty sum to access Satcom 1, RCA's new communication satellite. See Wasser, 82.
31 Bambi Haggins and Amanda Lotz, "Overview: At Home on the Cutting Edge," in *The Essential HBO Reader*, ed. Gary R. Edgerton and Jeffrey P. Jones (Lexington: University Press of Kentucky, 2008), 153.
32 James Poniewozik, "How HBO Does Diversity (and Doesn't)," *Time*, October 4, 2005.
33 Haggins and Lotz, "Overview," 156.
34 Haggins and Lotz, 156.
35 Wayne Federman, *The History of Stand Up: From Mark Twain to Dave Chappelle* (Beverly Hills: Independent Artists Media, 2021), 86.
36 Krefting, *All Joking Aside*, 18.
37 Robert Stam, *Subversive Pleasures: Bakhtin, Cultural Criticism, and Film* (Baltimore: Johns Hopkins University Press, 1992), 95.
38 Krefting, *All Joking Aside*, 18.
39 Clarence Waldron, "Robert Townsend's 'Five Heartbeats': A Story of '60s Soul Groups," *Jet*, April 1, 1991, 24.
40 Wilson Morales, "The Five Heartbeats 20th Anniversary: Exclusive: 20 Years Later, Robert Townsend, Michael Wright, and Leon Talk 'The Five Heartbeats,'" Blackfilm.com, March 29, 2011, accessed March 8, 2023, https://www.blackfilm.com/read/the-five-hearbeats-20th-anniversary/.
41 Jeffrey Wells, "A Look inside Hollywood and the Movies: SUPER MEN: 'Blankman,' Meet 'Meteor Man,'" *Los Angeles Times*, May 2, 1993.
42 Artel Great, "Black Cinema Matters," *New Republic*, September 11, 2020.
43 Ed Guerrero, "The Spectacle of Black Violence as Cinema," in *Cinematic Sociology: Social Life in Film*, ed. Jean-Anne Sutherland and Kathryn M. Feltey (Thousand Oaks: Sage, 2009), 70.
44 Gregory Braxton, "As Robert Townsend Sees It: He's Fighting Stereotypes with 'Meteor Man' and New TV Show," *Los Angeles Times*, August 3, 1993.
45 *Blankman* was a film adaptation based on Damon Wayans's popular character on the sketch comedy series *In Living Color* (1990–1994). Both *Meteor Man* and *Blankman* were major financial flops.
46 Artel Great, "Bury Me in the Ocean: *Marvel's Black Panther* and the Politics of Performative Wokeness," in *Black Cinema & Visual Culture: Art and Politics in the 21st Century*, ed. Artel Great and Ed Guerrero (London: Routledge, 2023), 43.
47 Tina M. Campt, *A Black Gaze: Artists Changing How We See* (Cambridge, Mass.: MIT Press, 2021), 7.
48 Manning, *Played Out*, 3.
49 Clyde Taylor suggests that the role of the Black independent filmmaker as Renaissance man speaks to deeper systemic issues of access and lack of capital. He argues that the "economic explanation is used to excuse a kind of Third World Renaissance man syndrome. In repressed environments, those who have acquired any literacies are forced to act as pan-literates, functioning as physicians, poets, and political leaders all at once." See Clyde Taylor, "The Paradox of Black Independent Cinema," *Black Film Review* 4, no. 4 (Fall 1988): 2.

50 Ed Guerrero, "Black Stars in Exile: Paul Robeson, O. J. Simpson, and Othello," in *Paul Robeson: Artist and Citizen*, ed. Jeffery C. Stewart (New Brunswick: Rutgers University Press, 1998), 275.

51 Townsend's *Meteor Man* superhero was made into a comic book spin-off of the same name. Marvel Comics released a six-issue *Meteor Man* limited series in August 1993.

Chapter 4 The Hipness Litmus

1 Douglas T. Miller and Marion Nowak, *The Fifties: The Way We Really Were* (New York: Doubleday and Company, 1977), 361–362.

2 Ben Bagdikian, *The New Media Monopoly* (Boston: Beacon Press, 2004), 50.

3 John T. Caldwell, *Televisuality: Style, Crisis, and Authority in American Television* (New Brunswick: Rutgers University Press, 2007), 352–353.

4 Toni Morrison, *Playing in the Dark: Whiteness in the Literary Imagination* (New York: Vintage Books, 1992).

5 Christine Acham, *Revolution Televised: Prime Time and the Struggle for Black Power* (Minneapolis: University of Minnesota Press, 2004), 19–20.

6 Robin R. Means Coleman, *African American Viewers and the Black Situation Comedy: Situating Racial Humor* (New York: Garland, 1998), 68.

7 Joan Rivers, "Can I Talk? I Am Mad and Sad and Feel Attacked—So Here Is the Truth about Why I Left Tonight," *People*, May 26, 1986.

8 Itabari Njeri, "Fresh Talk: 'We Be Havin' a Ball,' Says Arsenio Hall. But Can the Talk Show Host's Hip New Style Succeed on Late-Night?," *Los Angeles Times Magazine*, April 16, 1989.

9 Njeri.

10 Njeri.

11 Mel Watkins, *On the Real Side: A History of African American Comedy* (Chicago: Lawrence Hill, 1999), 20.

12 Arsenio Hall, 16th Annual People's Choice Award, Post-win Press Conference, CBS, March 11, 1990.

13 James Brown, "The Payback," vinyl, on *The Payback*, Polydor, 1974.

14 Tricia Rose, *Black Noise: Rap Music and Black Culture in Contemporary America* (Hanover, Conn.: Wesleyan University Press, 1994), 21.

15 Njeri, "Fresh Talk."

16 Njeri.

17 Erik Hedegaard, "Arsenio Hall," *Rolling Stone*, October 24, 2013, 18.

18 Njeri, "Fresh Talk."

19 W. E. B. Du Bois famously wrote of "double consciousness," while in the 1960s, Ralph Ellison echoed Wright's idea of "double vision" in *Shadow and Act*.

20 Richard Wright, *The Outsider* (New York: HarperCollins, 1953), 47.

21 Jean-Paul Sartre, *Nausea*, trans. Lloyd Alexander (New York: New Directions, 1964).

22 Njeri, "Fresh Talk."

23 Zoe Haylock, "Arsenio Hall on Hosting His Talk Show during the L.A. Riots: 'I Was Twitter,'" *Vulture*, February 16, 2021.

24 Njeri, "Fresh Talk."

25 Njeri.

26 Njeri.

27 Timothy Greenfield-Sanders and Elvis Mitchell, *The Black List* (New York: Atria Books, 2008).

28 Adrien Sebro, *Scratchin' and Survivin': Hustle Economics and the Black Sitcoms of Tandem Productions* (New Brunswick: Rutgers University Press, 2023), 121–122.
29 Ed Guerrero, *Framing Blackness: The African American Image in Film* (Philadelphia: Temple University Press, 1993), 207.
30 Bambi Haggins, *Laughing Mad: The Black Comic Persona in Post-soul America* (New Brunswick: Rutgers University Press, 2007), 108.
31 Ellis Cashmore, *The Black Culture Industry* (New York: Routledge, 1997), 2.
32 Brandon J. Manning, *Played Out: The Race Man in 21st Century Satire* (New Brunswick: Rutgers University Press, 2022), 6.
33 Norma Miriam Schulman, "Laughing across the Color Barriers: In Living Color," *Gender, Race and Class in Media: A Text Reader*, ed. Gail Dines and Jean M. Humez (Thousand Oaks: Sage, 1995), 2.
34 Schulman, 22.
35 Daniel M. Kimmel, *The Fourth Network: How Fox Broke the Rules and Reinvented Television* (Chicago: Ivan R. Dee, 2004), 91.
36 Herman Gray, *Watching Race: Television and the Struggle for Blackness* (Minneapolis: University of Minnesota Press, 1995), 138.
37 Donald Bogle, *Prime Time Blues: African Americans on Network Television* (New York: Farrar, Straus & Giroux, 2001), 366.
38 Haggins, *Laughing Mad*, 209.
39 Kristal Brent Zook, *Color by Fox: The Fox Network and the Revolution in Black Television* (New York: Oxford University Press, 1999), 105.
40 Herman S. Gray, *Cultural Moves: African Americans and the Politics of Representation*, 1st ed. (Los Angeles: University of California Press, 2005), 123.
41 Watkins, *On the Real Side*, 454.
42 Kimmel, *Fourth Network*, 118.
43 Kimmel, 118.
44 Quoted in Zook, *Color by Fox*, 105.
45 Zook, 3. The Black American population currently accounts for 14.4 percent of the total U.S. population.
46 Gray, *Watching Race*, 144.
47 See Stuart Hall, "Encoding/Decoding," in *Culture, Media, Language*, ed. Stuart Hall, Dorothy Hobson, Andrew Lowe, and Paul Willis (London: Hutchinson, 1980), 134.
48 Robert Stam, *Subversive Pleasures: Bakhtin, Cultural Criticism, and Film* (Baltimore: Johns Hopkins University Press, 1992), 219.
49 Ella Shohat and Robert Stam, *Unthinking Eurocentrism: Multiculturalism and the Media* (New York: Routledge, 2013), 210.
50 David Peisner, "*In Living Color* at Super Bowl: How It Birthed the Modern Half-Time Spectacle," *Rolling Stone*, February 18, 2018, accessed April 4, 2024, https://www.rollingstone.com/culture/culture-features/super-bowl-half-time-in-living-color-wayans-122887/.
51 Ericka N. Goodman-Hughey, "Super Bowl Half Time Show Never the Same after Jennifer Lopez and *In Living Color*," ESPN, January 30, 2020, accessed April 14, 2024, https://www.espn.com/espn/story/_/id/28592073/super-bowl-half-show-never-same-jennifer-lopez-living-color.
52 Peisner, "*In Living Color*."
53 Goodman-Hughey, "Super Bowl."
54 Kimmel, *Fourth Network*, 135.
55 Suzanna Danuta Walters, *All the Rage: The Story of Gay Visibility in America* (Chicago: University of Chicago Press, 2001), 118.

56 Kimmel, *Fourth Network*, 138.
57 Franz Fanon, *Black Skin, White Masks: Experiences of a Black Man in a White World*, trans. Charles Lam Markmann (New York: Grove Press, 1967), 88.
58 Havens, *Black Television Travels: African American Media around the Globe* (New York: New York University Press, 2013), 13.
59 "A Low Down Dirty Shame (1994)," Box Office Mojo, accessed March 21, 2024, https://www.boxofficemojo.com/title/tt0110399/?ref_=bo_se_r_2.
60 *The Arsenio Hall Show*, season 6, episode 105, written by J. Anthony Brown, Davey DiGiorgio, and Arsenio Hall, aired February 25, 1994, on Paramount Television.
61 Paul Mooney in *Mo' Funny: Black Comedy in America*, written and directed by Yvonne Smith, HBO Films, 1993.
62 *Oprah's Next Chapter*, Arsenio Hall interview, airdate October 20, 2013, OWN.

Coda

1 James Baldwin, *The Devil Finds Work* (New York: Random House, 1976), 59.
2 Baldwin, 59.
3 Ellis Cashmore, *The Black Culture Industry* (New York: Routledge, 1997), 1.
4 Ed Guerrero, "The Spectacle of Black Violence as Cinema," in *Cinematic Sociology: Social Life in Film*, ed. Jean-Anne Sutherland and Kathryn M. Feltey (Thousand Oaks: Sage, 2009), 93.
5 Kristal Brent Zook, *Color by Fox: The Fox Network and the Revolution in Black Television* (New York: Oxford University Press, 1999), 101.
6 Rebecca Krefting, *All Joking Aside: American Humor and Its Discontents* (Baltimore: Johns Hopkins University Press, 2014), 72.
7 Yuval Taylor and Jake Austen, *Darkest America: Black Minstrelsy from Slavery to Hip-Hop* (New York: W. W. Norton, 2012), 187–188.
8 Artel Great, "Bring the Payne: The Erasure of the Black Sitcom and the Emergence of *Tyler Perry's House of Payne*," in *From Madea to Media Mogul*, ed. TreaAndrea M. Russworm, Samantha N. Sheppard, and Karen M. Bowdre (Jackson: University of Mississippi Press, 2016), 168.
9 Great, 168.
10 Ed Guerrero, *Framing Blackness: The African American Image in Film* (Philadelphia: Temple University Press, 1993), 9.
11 Ed Guerrero, "Bamboozled: In the Mirror of Abjection," in *Contemporary Black American Cinema: Race, Gender and Sexuality at the Movies*, ed. Mia Mask (New York: Routledge, 2012), 109.
12 *The 44th NAACP Image Awards*, written by T. Faye Griffin and Jon Macks, aired February 1, 2013, on Fox.
13 W. E. B. Du Bois, *The W. E. B. Du Bois Reader*, ed. David Levering Lewis (New York: Henry Holt, 1995), 348.
14 Paige Albiniak, "Ricki, Arsenio Hope to Party like It's 1993," *Broadcasting & Cable*, July 23, 2012, 36.
15 Erik Hedegaard, "Arsenio Hall," *Rolling Stone*, October 24, 2013, 18, 20.
16 *Chris Rock: Bring the Pain*, written by Chris Rock, aired June 1, 1996, on HBO.
17 Terrence T. Tucker, *Furiously Funny: Comic Rage from Ralph Ellison to Chris Rock* (Gainesville: University Press of Florida, 2018), 243.
18 *Chris Rock: Selective Outrage*, written by Chris Rock, aired March 4, 2023, on Netflix.

19 Danielle Fuentes Morgan, *Laughing to Keep from Dying: African American Satire in the Twenty-First Century* (Urbana: University of Illinois Press, 2020), 151.
20 Kevin Powell, "Heaven, Hell and Dave Chappelle," *Esquire*, April 29, 2006.
21 *The Oprah Winfrey Show*, season 21, episode 68, aired February 3, 2006, in syndication.
22 See bell hooks, *Killing Rage: Ending Racism* (New York: Henry Holt, 1995).
23 Rick DesRochers, *The Comic Offense: From Vaudeville to Contemporary Comedy* (London: Bloomsbury Academic, 2014), 122.
24 Artel Great, "Too Hot for TV: Black Sketch Comedy and the Politics of Crossing-Over," *Black Camera: An International Film Journal* 13, no. 2 (Spring 2022): 171.
25 *2 Dope Queens*, season 1, episode 1, written by Phoebe Robinson and Jessica Williams, aired February 2, 2018, on HBO.
26 Katelyn Hale Wood, *Cracking Up: Black Feminist Comedy in the Twentieth and Twenty-First Century United States* (Iowa City: University of Iowa Press, 2021), 5.
27 See also Artel Great, "Bury Me in the Ocean: *Marvel's Black Panther* and the Politics of Performative Wokeness," in *Black Cinema & Visual Culture: Art and Politics in the 21st Century*, ed. Artel Great and Ed Guerrero (London: Routledge, 2023), 38.

Index

Page numbers in italics refer to figures.

About the Author

ARTEL GREAT is the George and Judy Marcus Endowed Chair in African American Cinema Studies and assistant professor of film and media at the San Francisco State University, School of Cinema. He is also an Independent Spirit Award–nominated filmmaker and coeditor of *Black Cinema & Visual Culture: Art and Politics in the 21st Century.*